# FOLKESTONE

## From Old Photographs

ALAN F. TAYLOR

AMBERLEY

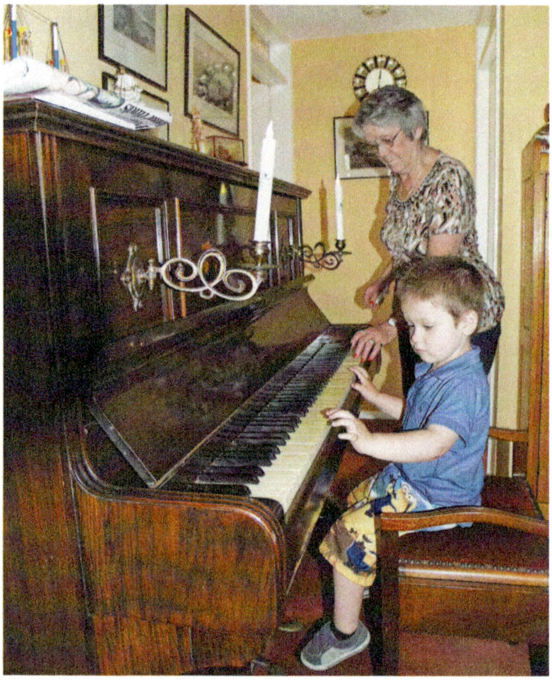

*I dedicate this book to my wife and my only grandchild, Eoin.*

First published 2017

Amberley Publishing
The Hill, Stroud
Gloucestershire, GL5 4EP

www.amberley-books.com



British Library Cataloguing in Publication Data.

A catalogue record for this book is available from the British Library.

ISBN 978 1 4456 7604 3 (print)
ISBN 978 1 4456 7605 0 (ebook)

Origination by Amberley Publishing.
Printed in the UK.

# Introduction

In 1564, there were 125 houses in Folkestone with a population of between 600 and 700. At that time, the place was a fairly small fishing village. At the close of the eighteenth century the number of houses had increased to 450 and the population had risen to around 2,000 inhabitants. By 1841 the population was 4,413.

The coming of the railway in 1843 with a service from London to Folkestone, the South Eastern Railway's takeover of Folkestone Harbour and its investment in cross-Channel travel and the opening of a service from Folkestone to Boulogne were the three most important factors that changed Folkestone from a small fishing village to a fashionable resort and a busy cross-Channel port.

The town expanded dramatically and by 1881 the population had reached 18,822.

Large hotels were being built to accommodate the wealthy. A theatre, bathing establishment and a pleasure pier were all built before the turn of the century, and by this time the population had risen to 29,900.

Six new Anglican churches had been consecrated, as well as a Roman Catholic and Nonconformist church.

Fashionable Folkestone came to an end with the advent of the First World War. With an enormous influx of refugees arriving and the use of the Harbour as a prime military embarkation point, the town was forced to rapidly adjust, with the population at this time being 34,163. After the First World War, Folkestone realised that if it was to survive as a holiday resort it would have to attract working-class families, not just the wealthy. Thus, Floral Folkestone was born, and small hotels and boarding houses prospered.

The Second World War saw the town become an armed camp as 35,000 people were evacuated.

In the late 1940s and early 1950s Folkestone had to re-establish itself again as a resort. In the last fifty-five years it developed a considerable amount of light industry, had grown as a residential and trading centre, and had enjoyed an expanding market for the retired. The building of the M20 and the Channel Tunnel have meant that Folkestone has undergone several major changes, and now, in the dawning years of a new millennium, Folkestone is equipped with a high-speed rail link to London with travel times of less than an hour. With the philanthropic investment of Roger de Haan, it is undergoing another change of guise as the town seeks to reinvent itself as a hub for arts and high culture, and the population is around 43,000.

Most of the photographs used in this book have not been published before. Some of the images dating from around 1900 are unique because they came from two family photograph albums that I was fortunate to purchase a few years ago. The dates quoted in the captions are from Pike's, Parsons' and Kelly's Folkestone Street Directories, so may not be accurate by one or two years either way.

Alan F. Taylor, 2017

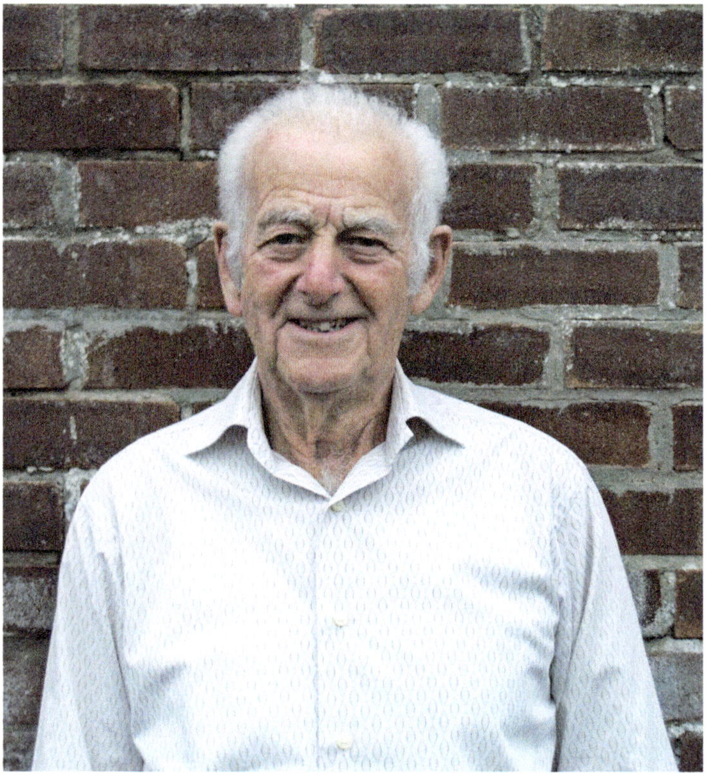

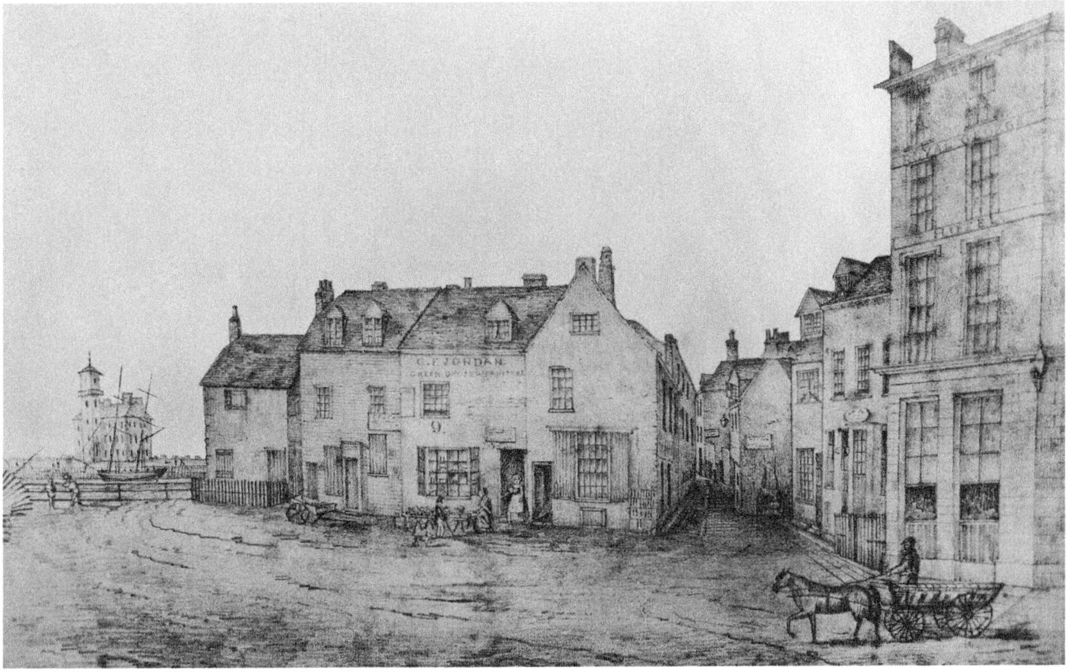


This drawing dates between 1845 and 1858. On the extreme right is the Royal George Hotel and on the extreme left is the South Eastern Railways Company's offices and harbour masters residence.

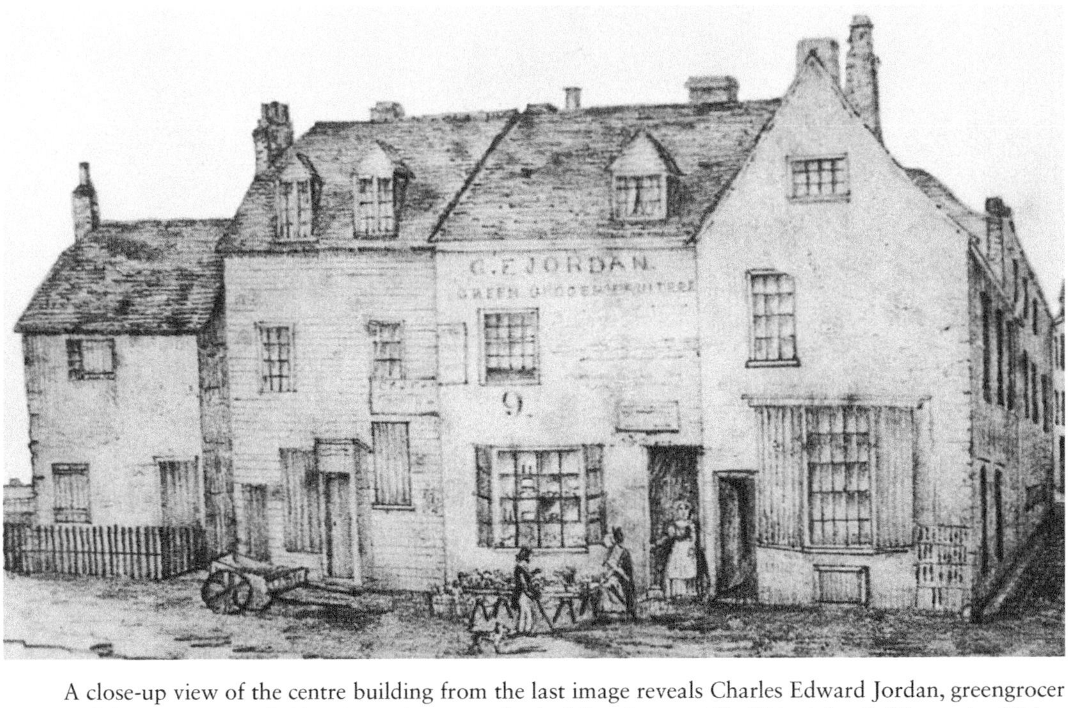


A close-up view of the centre building from the last image reveals Charles Edward Jordan, greengrocer and fruiterers, Kingsbridge Street. In 1915 the building became 'Ye Olde Arke Café', run by Walter Banks, and then finally the Ark Café, which was demolished in 1987.

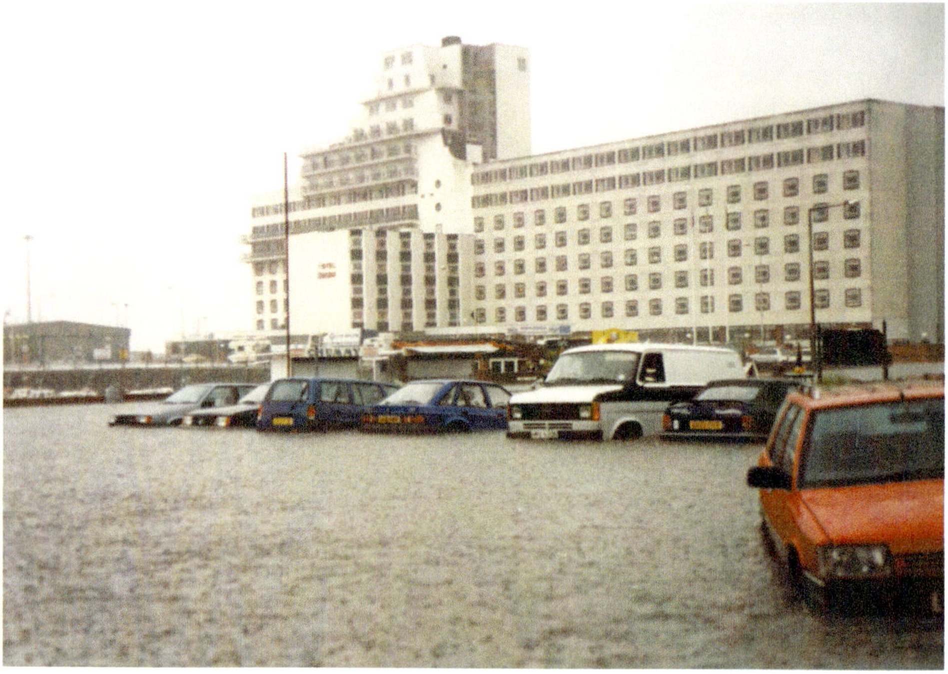

Flooding at Beach Street car park (now the site of the fountain) after heavy rain on 12 August 1996. The Pent wall behind the whelk barrow was knocked down to allow the water to run into the harbour.

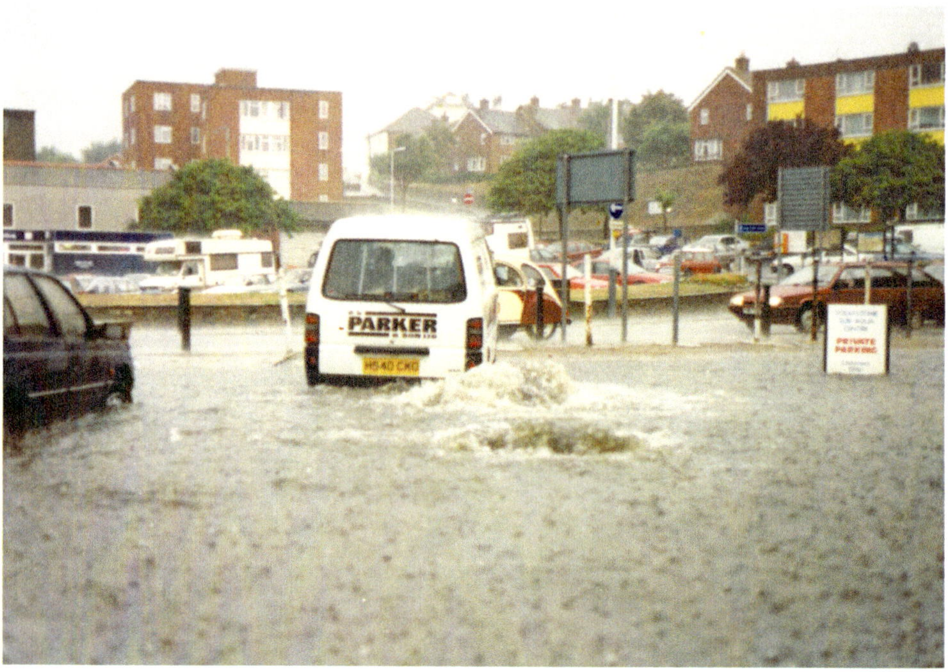


Flooding in Beach Street after torrents of rain on 12 August 1996. Note the water coming up through the manhole!

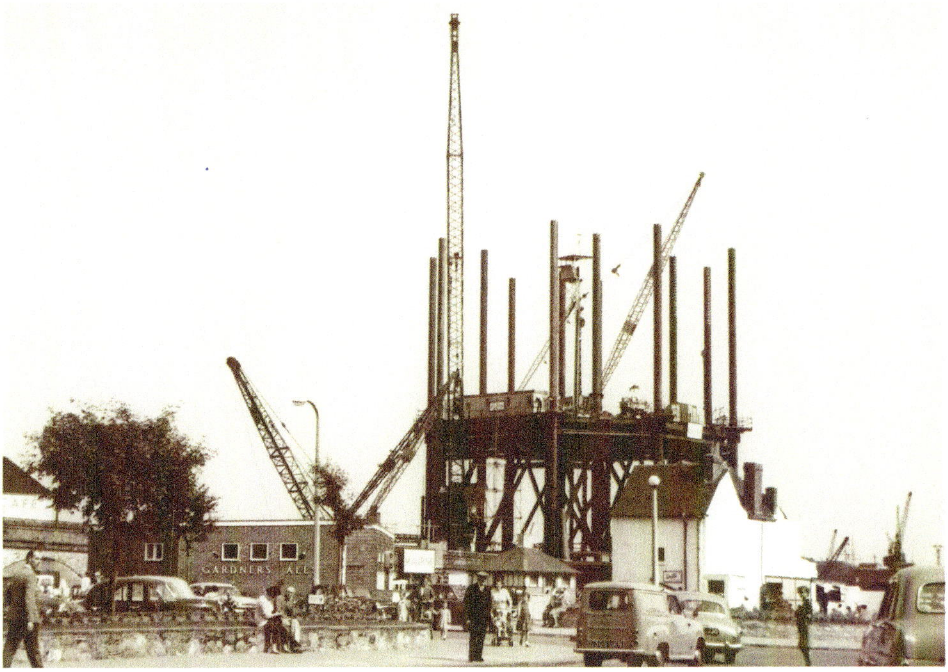

The massive structure towering over the Ark Café is a cooling tower that was built for Dungeness in 1961. When completed it was floated down to Dungeness on tanks.

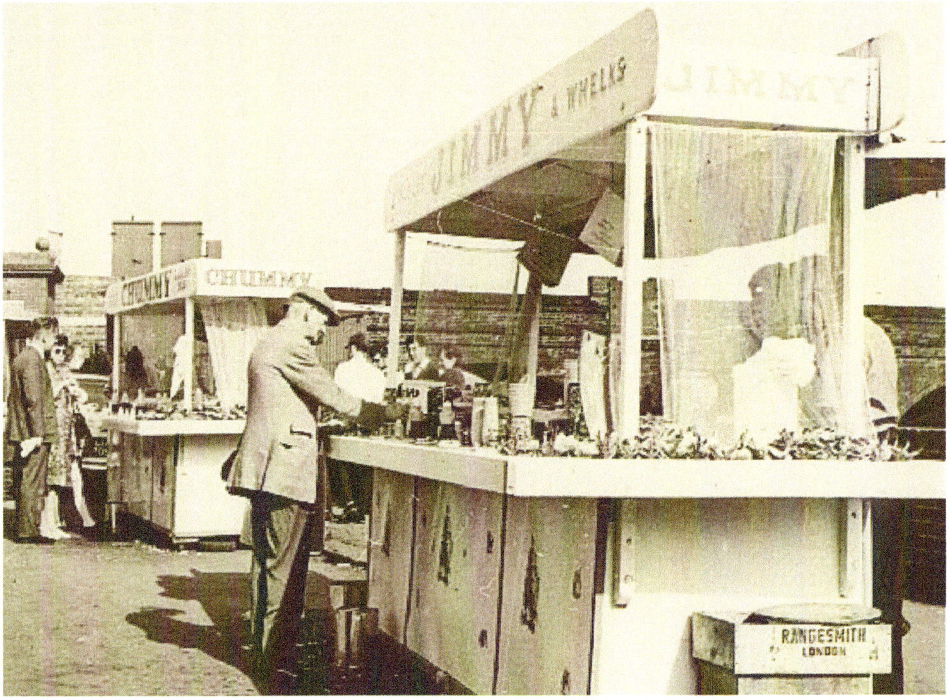


Two whelk barrows on the Pent wall. In the foreground is Jimmy's, which was owned by Alfie Waller, followed by Chummy's, which was formerly owned by Lucy Ward (née Lucy Waller).

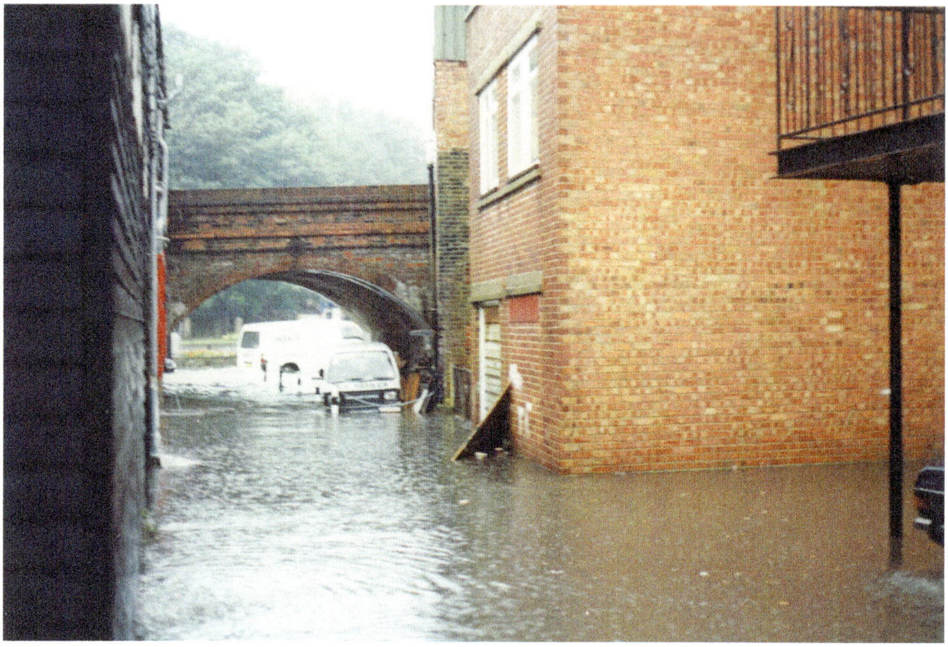

Flooding on the Stade, formerly Back Street, after torrential rain on 12 August 1996. On the left-hand side can be seen the back of the Shell shop, while on the right, against the railway branch line, is the blacksmith's workshop, formerly owned by the Ovenden family.

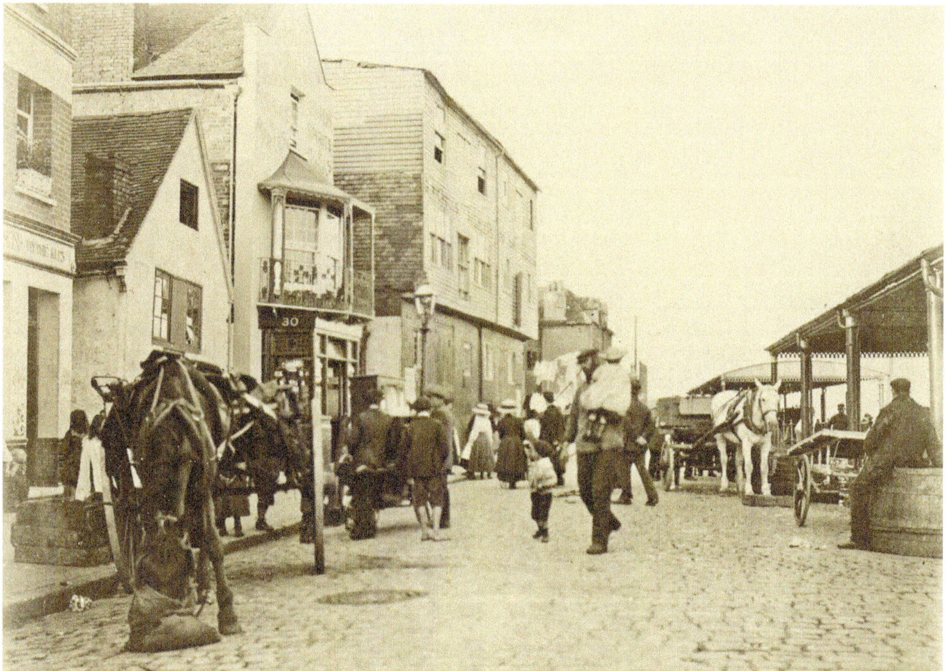

A busy scene looking east along the Stade. On the left-hand side, the building with the balcony is the Jubilee Inn, followed by E. Nicholls, sailmaker. On the right are fish sheds two and three.

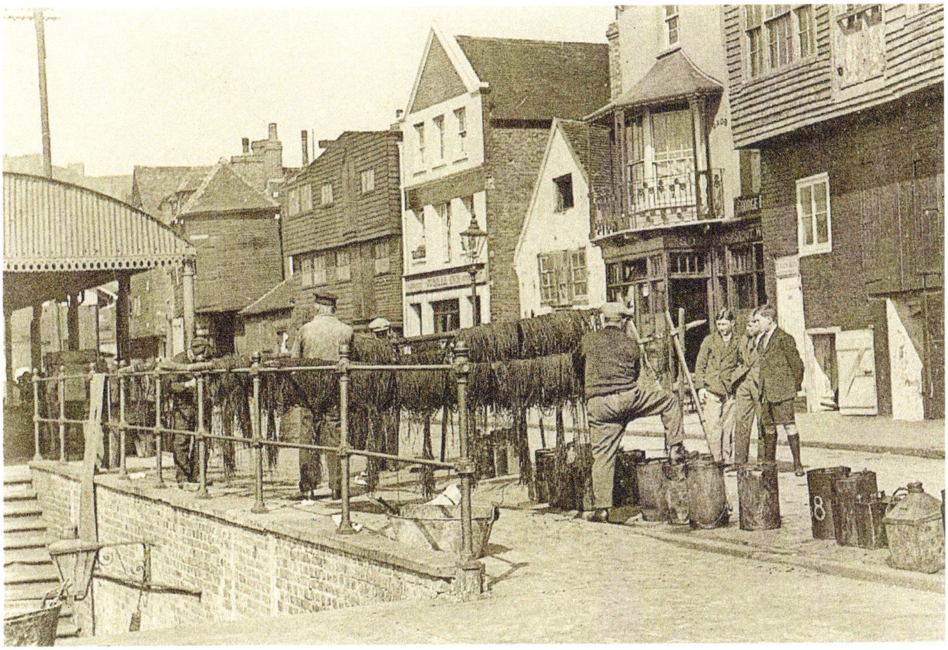

This is a similar view to the last one, but looking the opposite way. On the left can be seen steps that led to a tunnel under the Stade to a wooden landing, fish shed number two, fishermen working on their long-lines, E. Nicholls, Jubilee Inn, Oddfellows Arms and Arthur Goddard (fish wholesaler and fish curer).

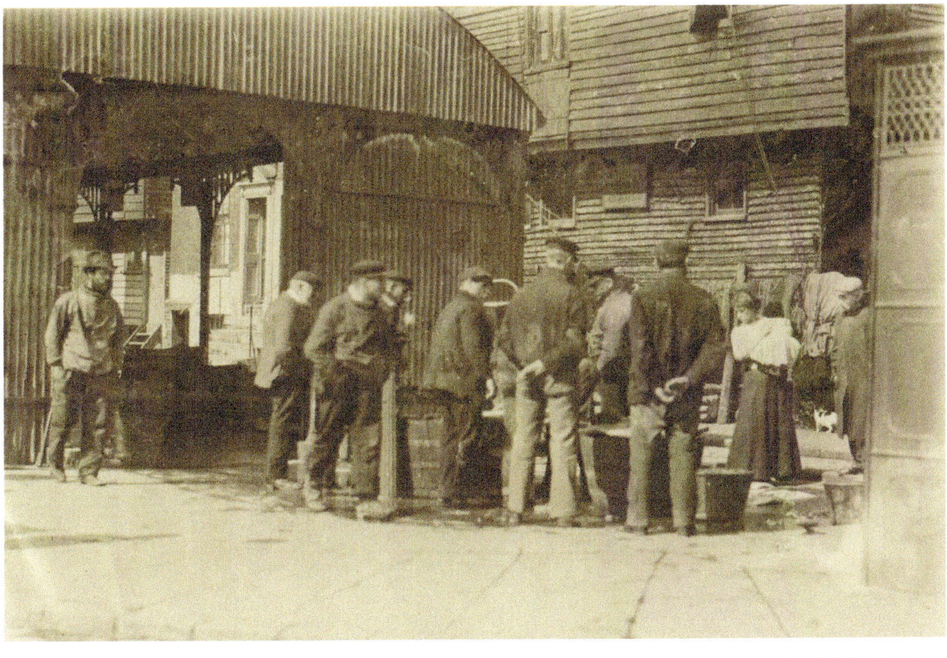

These fishermen seen here by the side of fish shed number one are viewing a catch of fish that has just been landed, *c.* 1900. On the right-hand side one can see the end of the gents' toilet known as a pisser – standing only!

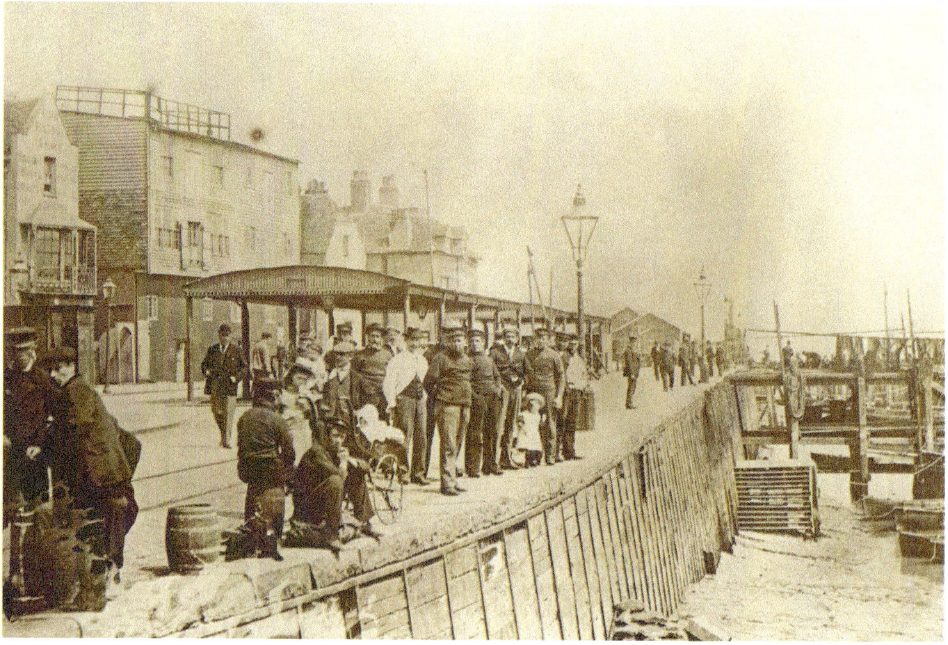

A view looking east along the Stade in around 1900; on the left-hand side can be seen fish sheds numbers two and three, while on the right is the landing mentioned on page 9, followed by the fishermen's jetty.

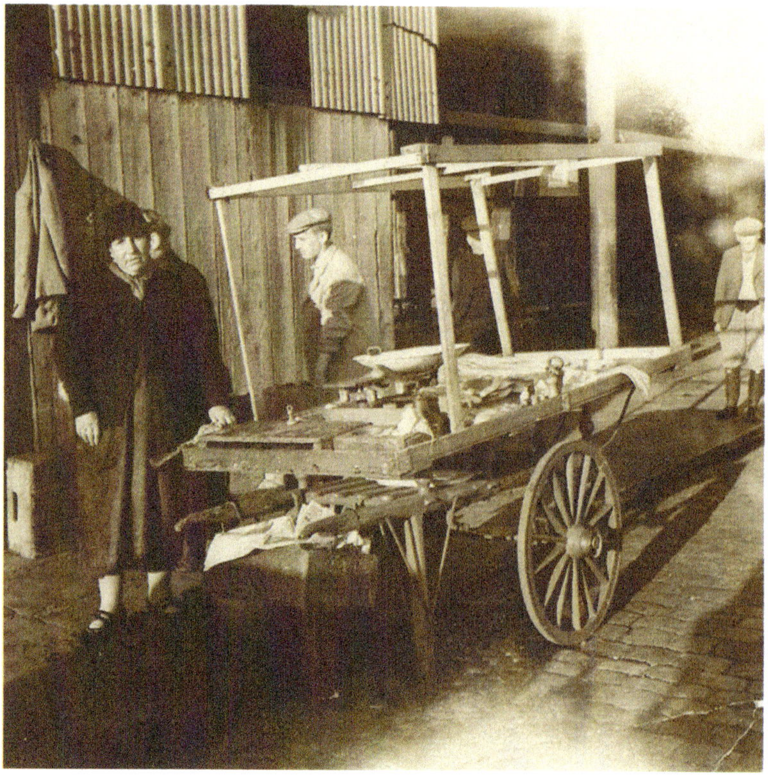

Old Lottie Waller standing by her fish barrow at the left-hand end of fish shed number one (now Folkestone Trawlers fish shop). The man behind Lottie's barrow is her son-in-law, Joe Johnson, who was also a fish retailer; he had a shop at No. 22 Cheriton Road.

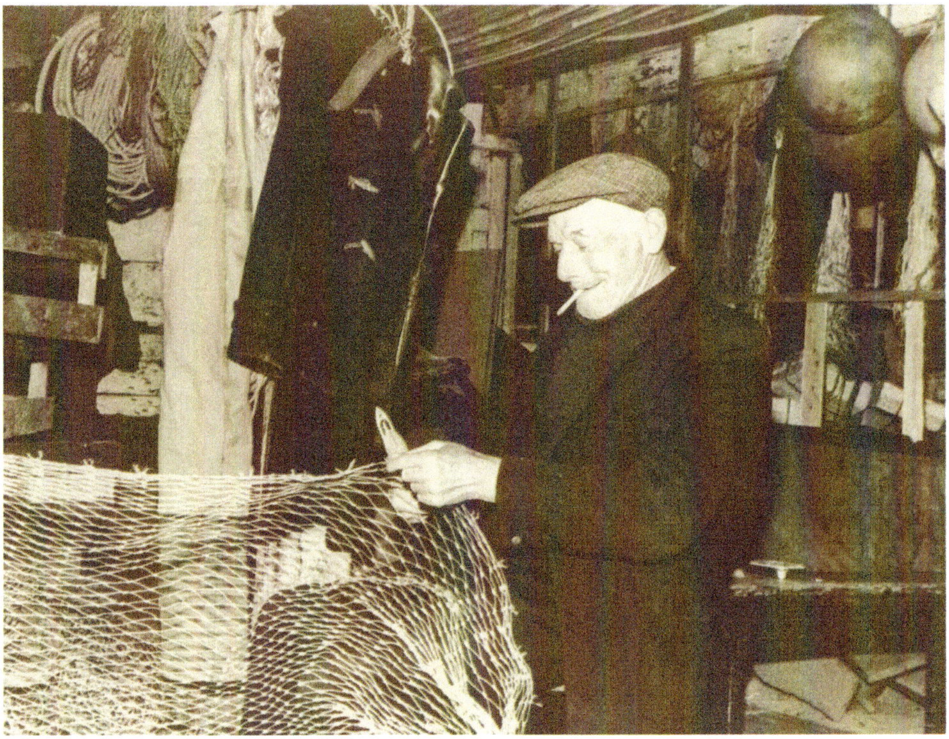

Retired fisherman David 'Lobby' Spearpoint (1901–80) is seen here in my store making trawl nets. When I was fishing in the 1960s, Dave helped me bait my long-lines, among other jobs.

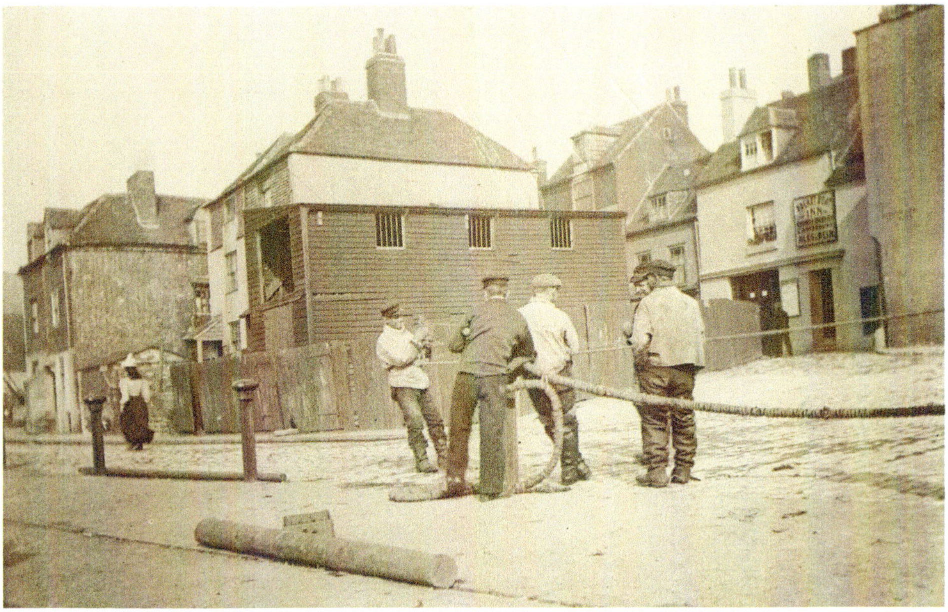

These fishermen seen here on the Stade are making a ground rope for a trawl net. The weatherboard building behind them became the workshop of Frank Warman, shipwright, while the white building behind it is the Packet Boat Inn, Radnor Street.

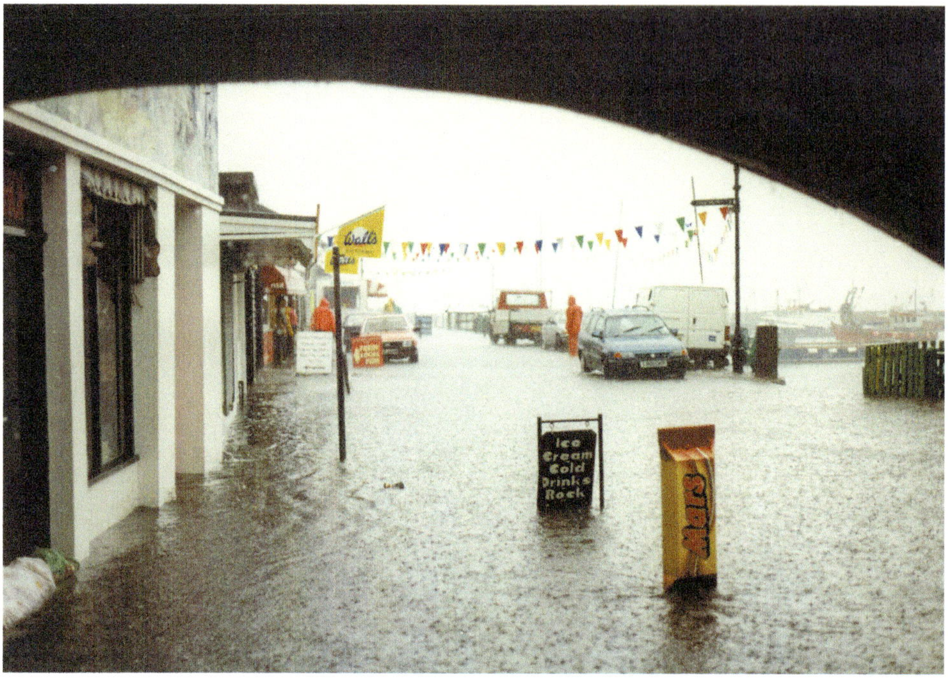


After torrential rain on 12 August 1996, the Stade flooded. On the left-hand side is the Shell shop, followed by two kiosks and Folkestone Trawlers fish shop, which had the water come in the back door and run out the front door.

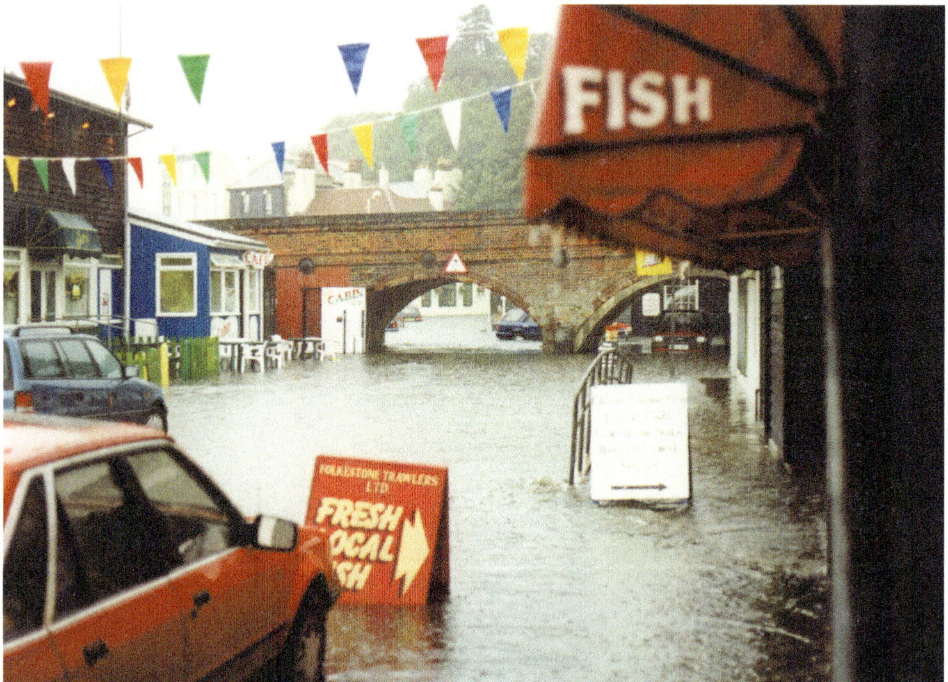


More flooding scenes on the Stade, looking towards the branch railway line.

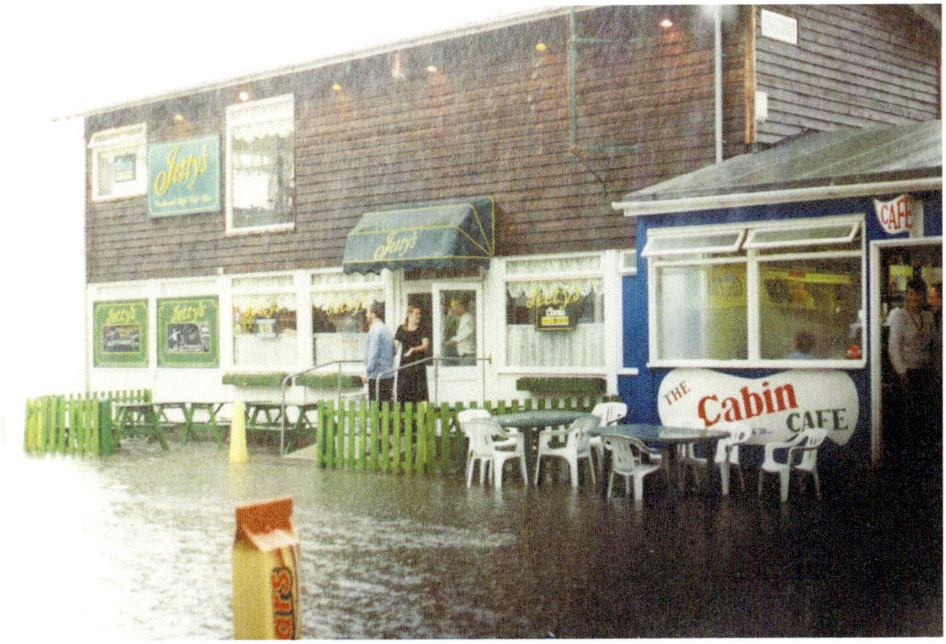


The staff of Jetty's bar and The Cabin Café are seen here looking rather anxious; they are probably hoping the water doesn't rise too high and flood their premises.

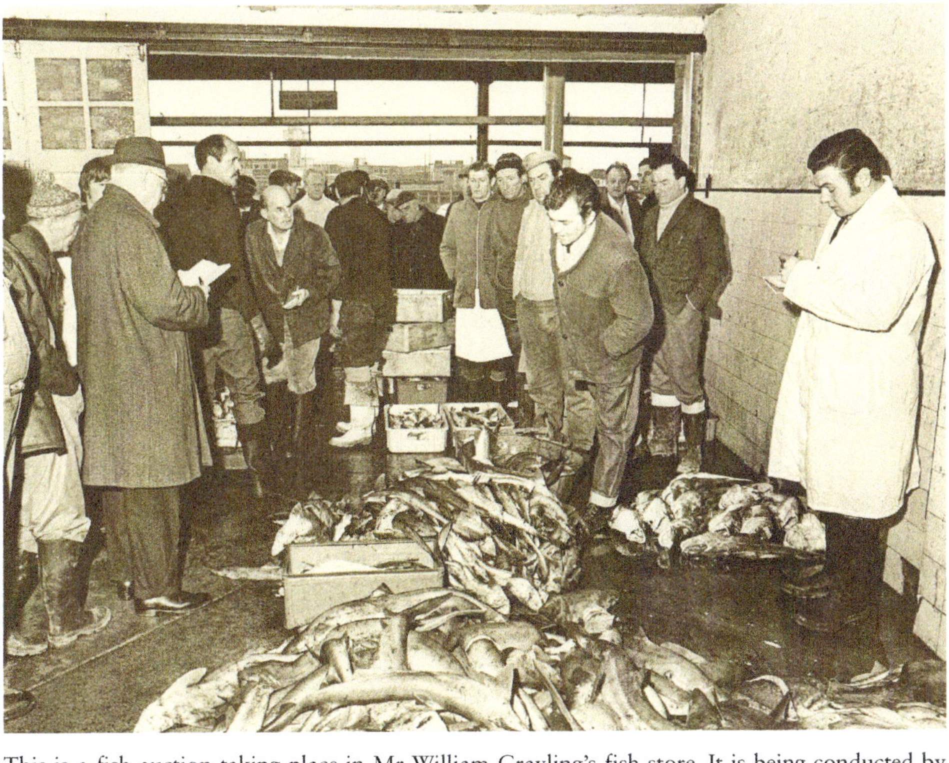

This is a fish auction taking place in Mr William Grayling's fish store. It is being conducted by Roland Gammon who is taking over the business, September 1971.

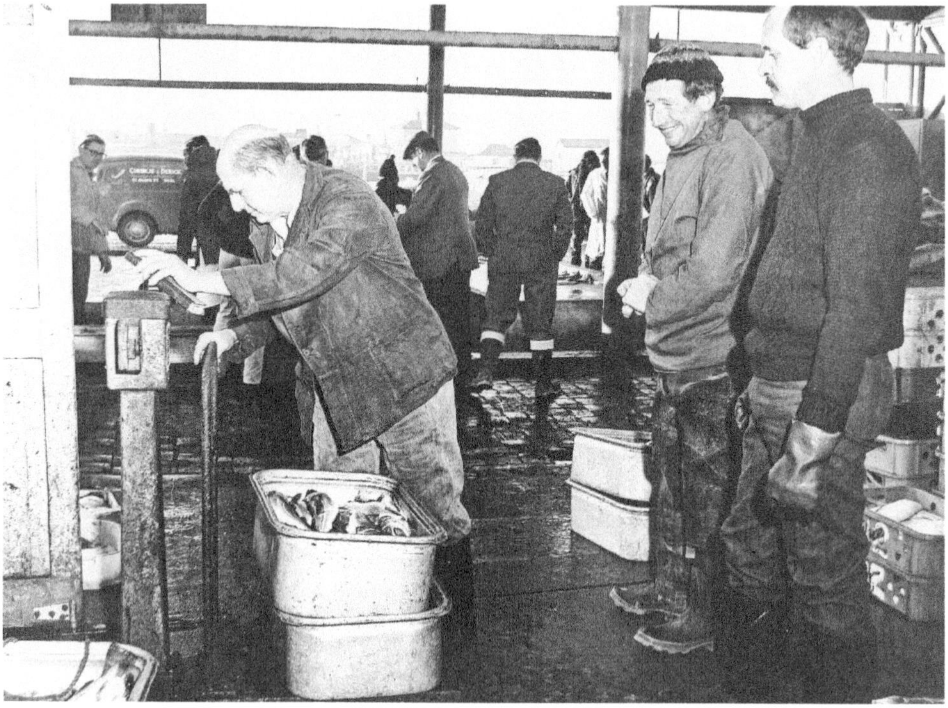

One of William Grayling's employees, Steve 'Skinny' Spearpoint, is seen here weighing a catch of fish, while Bill Harrison and David Anslow, also an employee, look on.

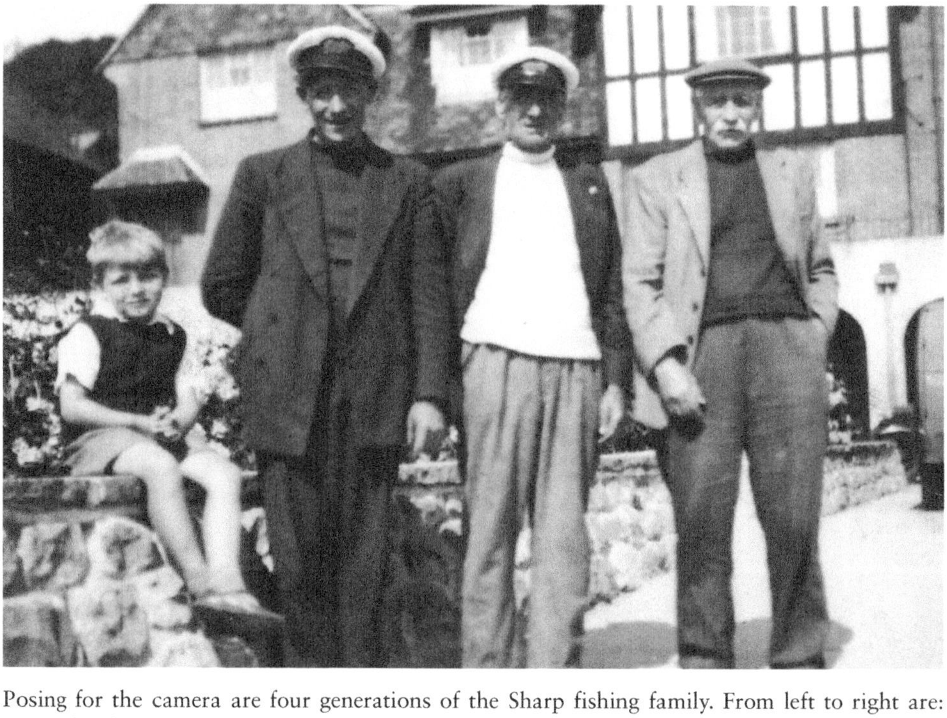

Posing for the camera are four generations of the Sharp fishing family. From left to right are: Harry, his father Harry Douglas, Harry James and Harry Henry 'Gare'.

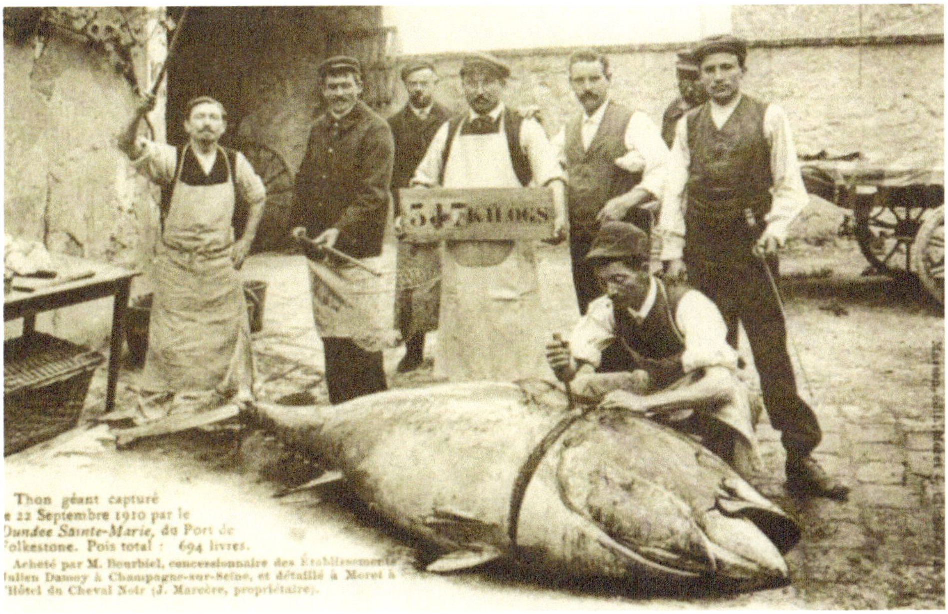


This giant tunny was caught on 22 September 1910 by the fishing boat *Dundee Sainte-Marie* from the port of Folkestone. It weighed 694 lbs (347 Kilograms). It was brought by M. Bourbiel, employed by the wholesalers Julien Damoy at Champagne-on-Seine and retailed to Moret at Black Hotel (proprietor J. Marcere).

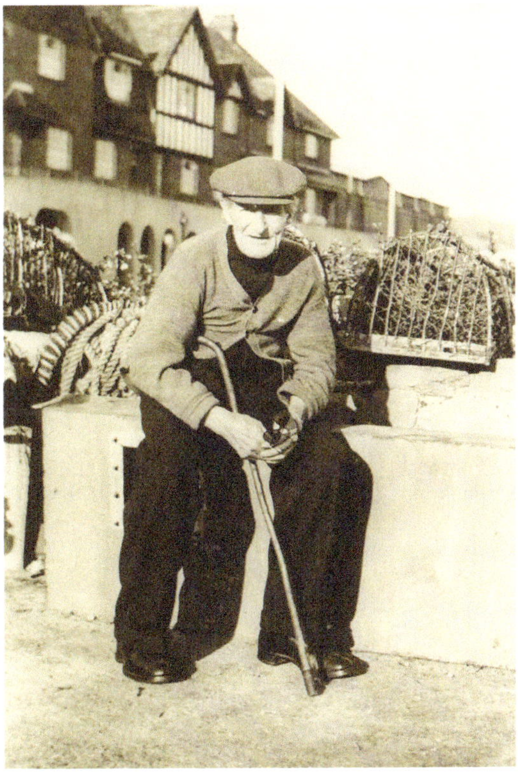

Fisherman Richard Brice (1877–1955) came from one of the oldest fishing families in Folkestone. He fished for fifty-four years, starting at the age of thirteen. His first boat was *The Telegram*, owned by Edmund Major, but he later fished in his father's boat, the *Florence Nightingale*, of which he became owner. His last boat was the *Golden Sunset* FE79, which became his son's. He married Sara Ann Reed, who was born and brought up in the Warren.

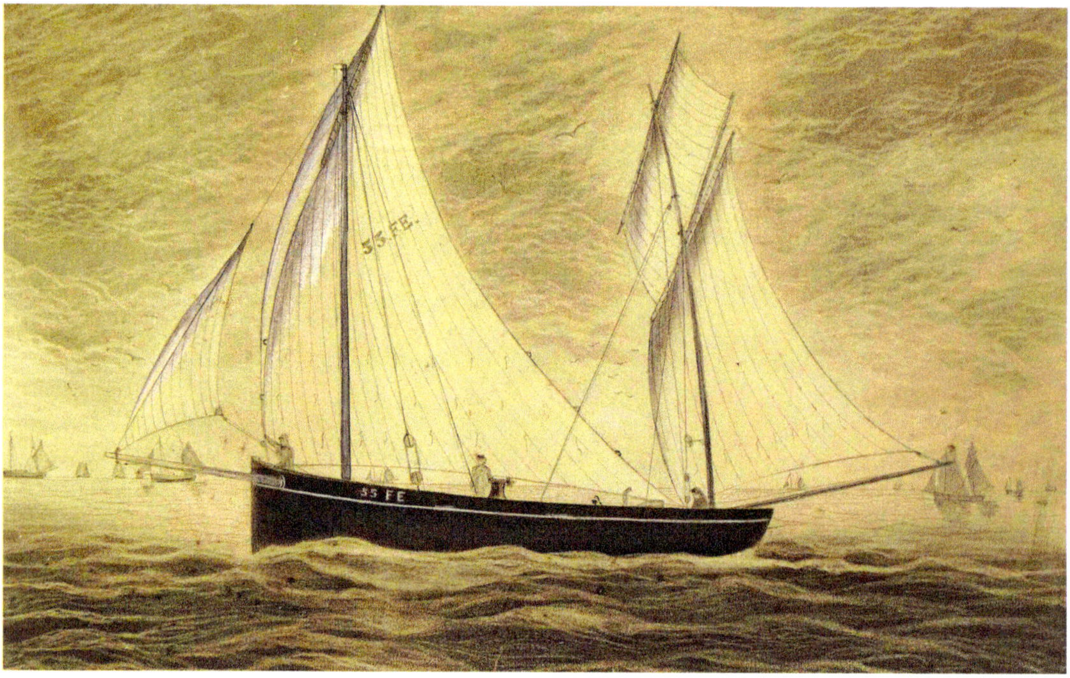


This is a drawing of the fishing lugger *Florence Nightingale* FE55. She was registered at Folkestone on 13 December 1923 and was broken up on 5 July 1933.

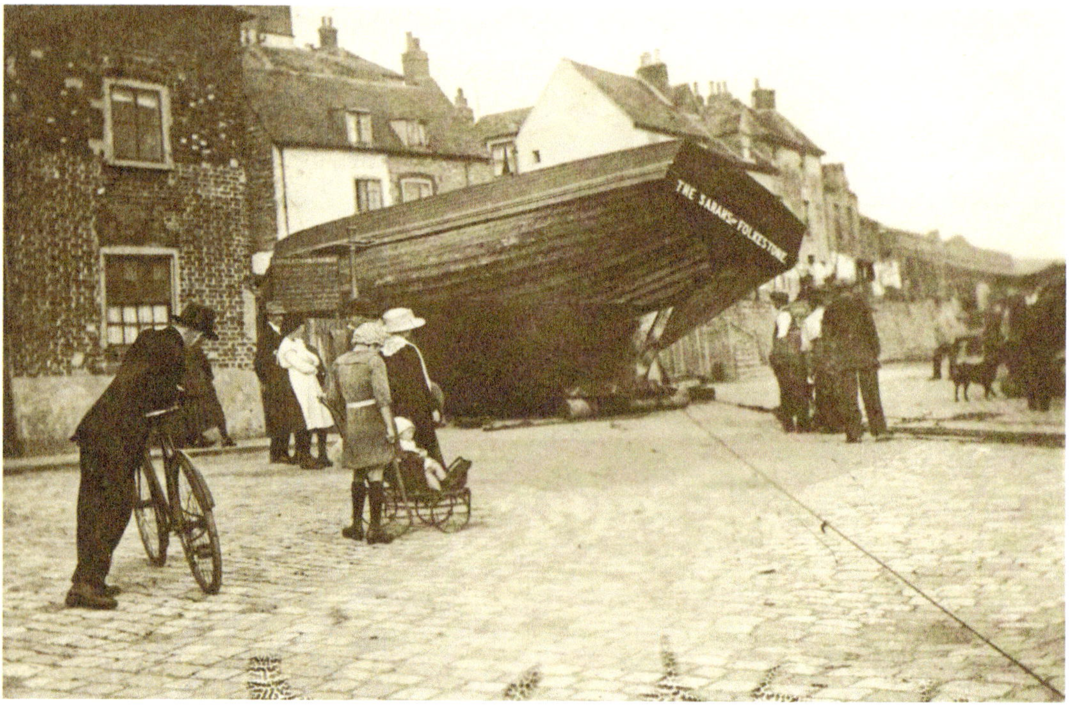


*The Sarahs* FE71, nicknamed 'Ugly Duckling', 1920. *The Sarahs* was built here on the Stade by Tom Saunders. She is seen here being pulled out to the edge of the quay ready to launch.

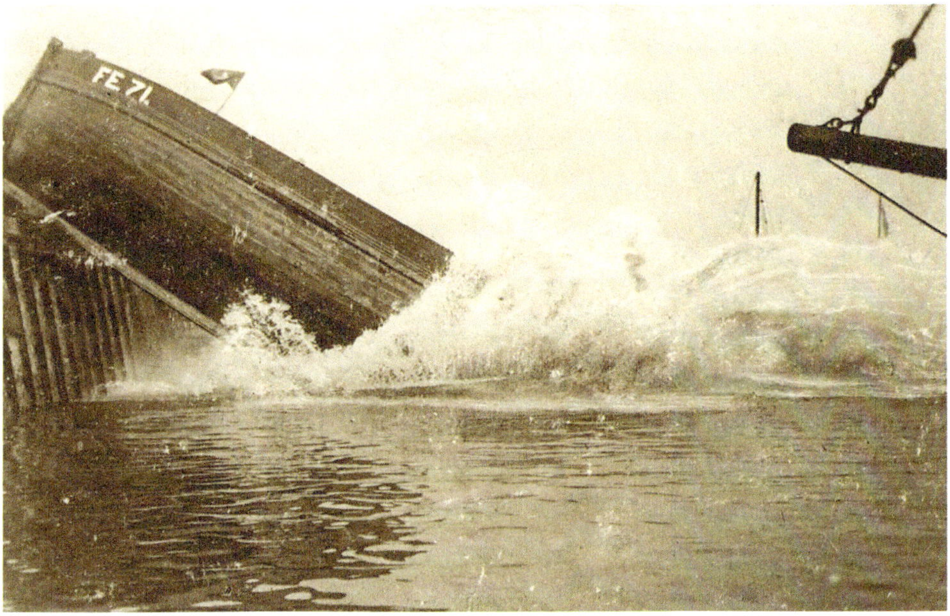


*The Sarahs* being launched at high tide, which was around noon. My late father, Fred Taylor, actually witnessed the launching; he was in the same class as Roland 'Fergy' Noble who told them the boat was going to be launched and my father, with other children, went to see this spectacular event!

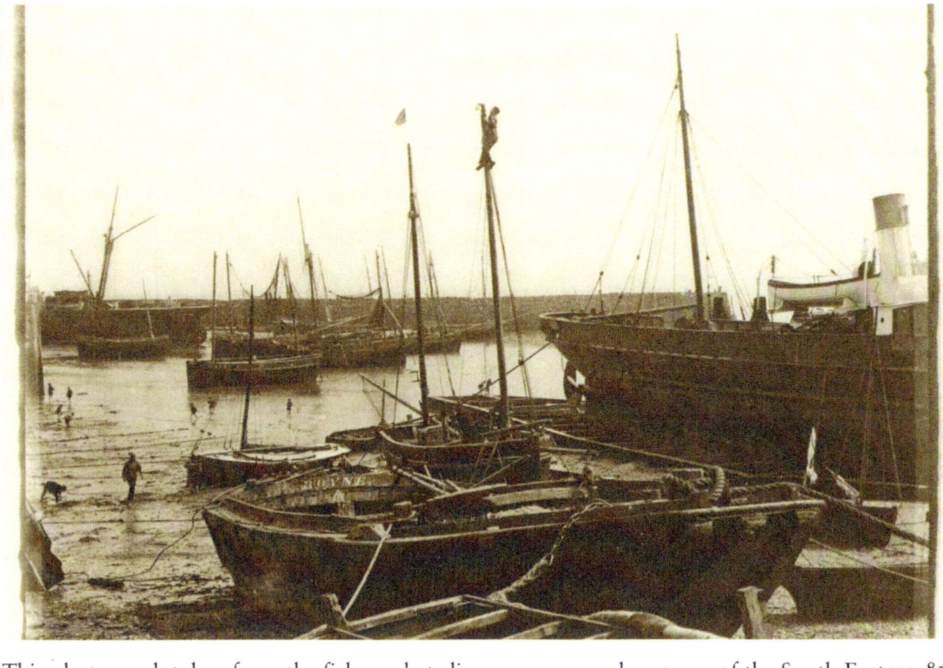

This photograph taken from the fish market slipway, *c.* 1900, shows one of the South Eastern & Chatham Railway Company's cargo ships on the grid-iron for maintenance. Note the fisher boy at the top of the mast; he is possibly threading a rope through the truck (a circular wooden cap fitted to the top of a mast with one or two small sheaves).

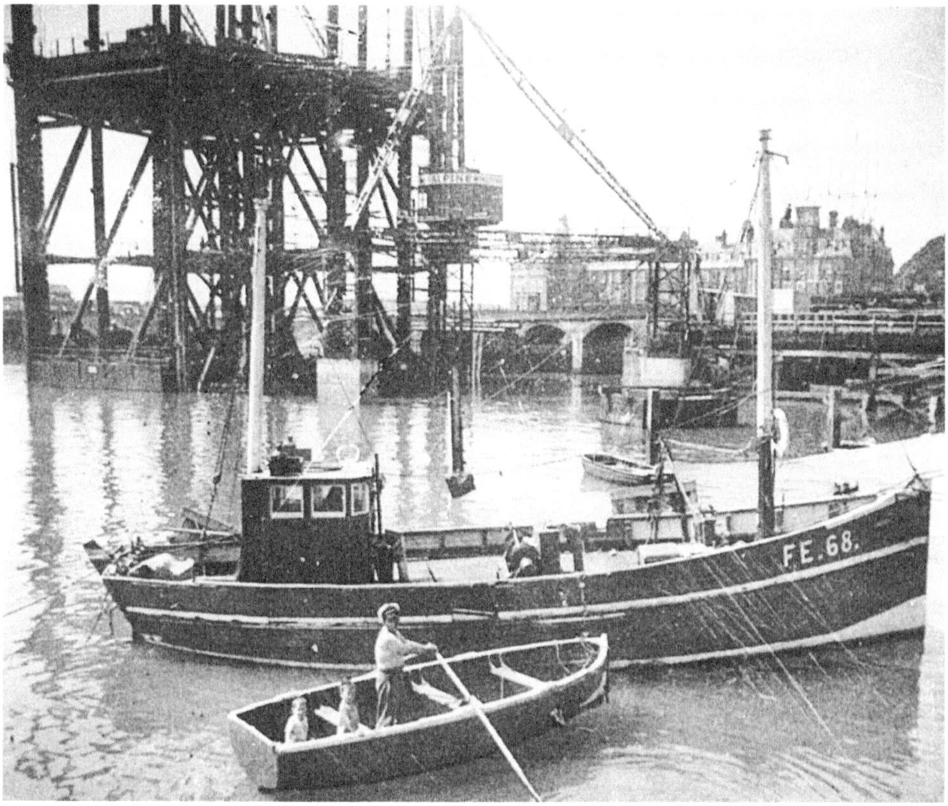


Harry 'Tom Pepper' Featherbe with his two sons David and Pierre are about to board the fishing vessel *Invicta* FE68. Note the structure in the background dominating the skyline; it is the cooling tower being built for Dungeness Power station.

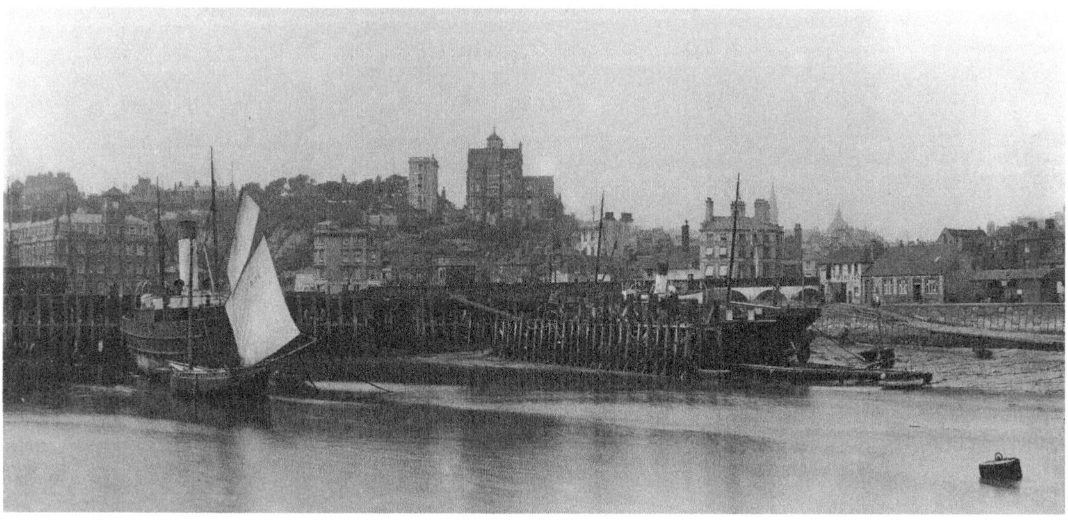

On the left, the fishing lugger has a square rigged mission sail set and a mission topsail, which would only be set in very light winds. On the right, one of the South Eastern & Chatham Railway Company's cargo ships is moored alongside the jetty, known as the *Hawk*.

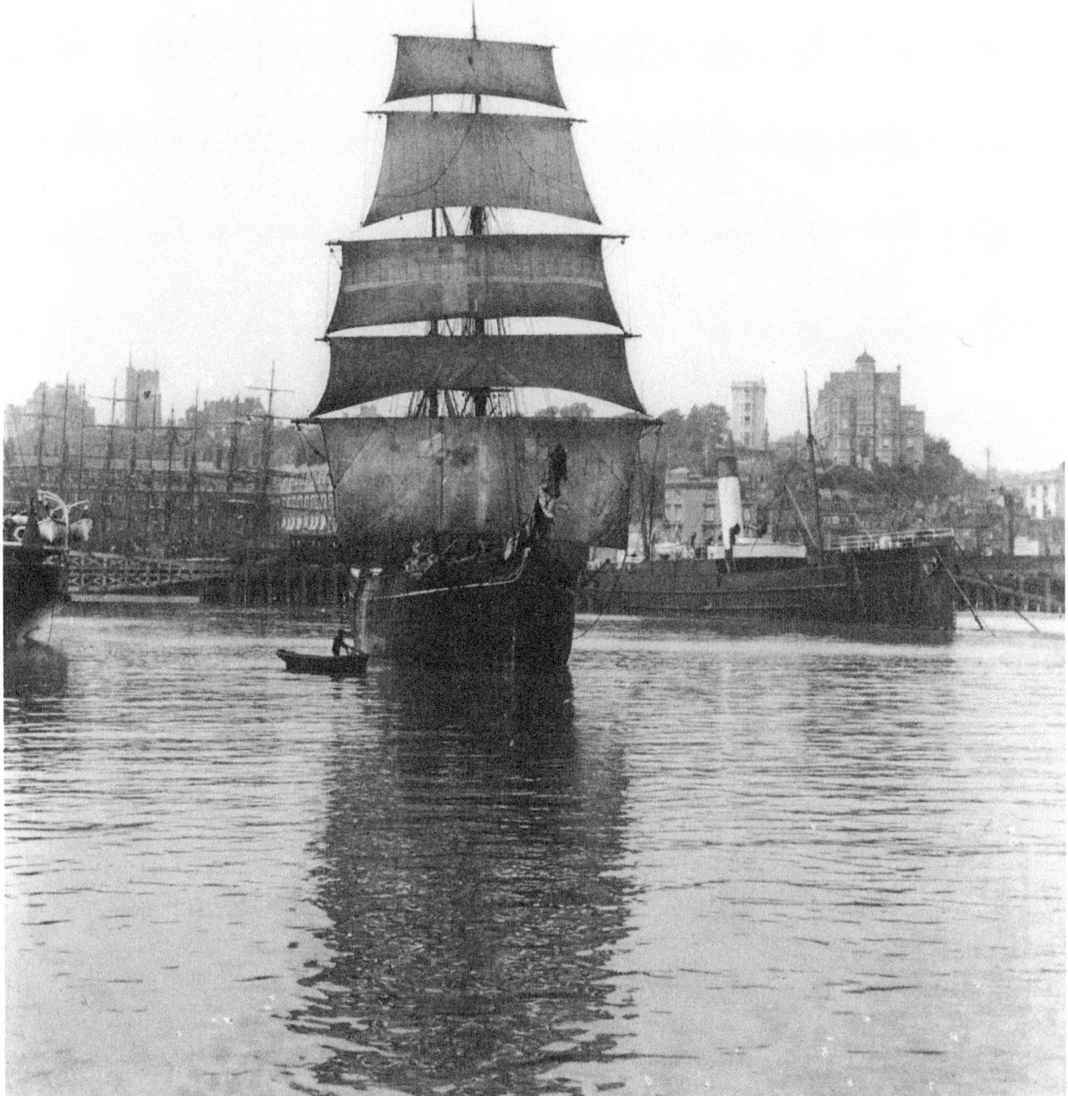

The brigantine *Cypress* seen here leaving Folkestone fully rigged. She was registered at Sunderland in 1860 and Folkestone in 1888, at which time the owner was Richard Godden Saunders. The vessel was sold to the French in 1909.

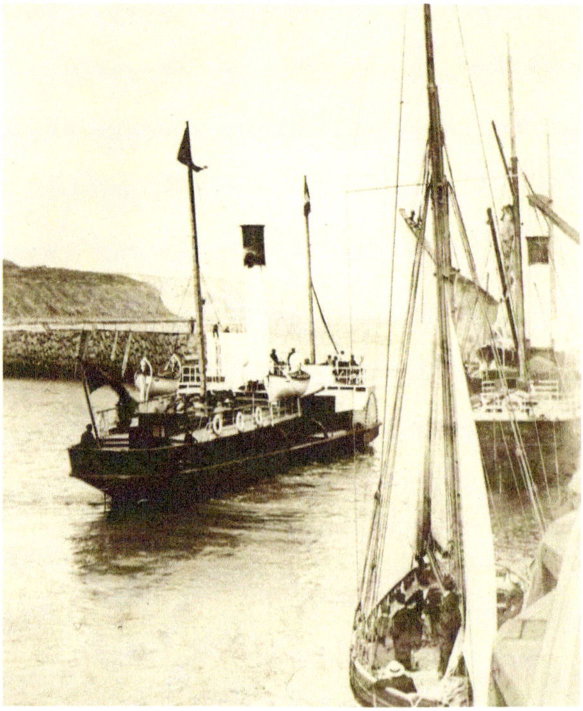

The paddle steamer *Myleta* leaving the South Quay; she is one of the South Eastern Railway Company's excursion steamers, which operated short non-landing excursions either to St Margaret's Bay or to Dungeness. She was in service at Folkestone from 1891 to 1909.

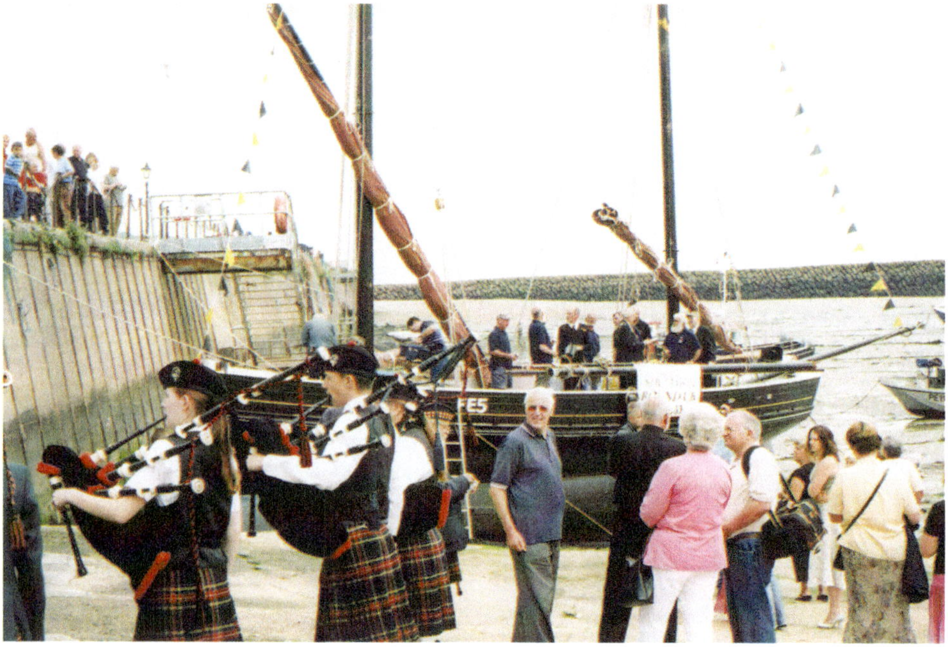


The fishing vessel *Happy Return* FE5, built at Kitto's yard, Porthleven, was decommissioned from fishing in 1998. She was obtained by Mount's Bay Lugger Association, who restored her to a sailing lugger. She returned to Folkestone from Penzance for her 100th anniversary, arriving on 26 July 2005. She was greeted by the Pipe Band and Mayor George Bunting after sailing from Penzance to Folkestone leg for Sailathon and the Fisherman's mission, raising £10,000.

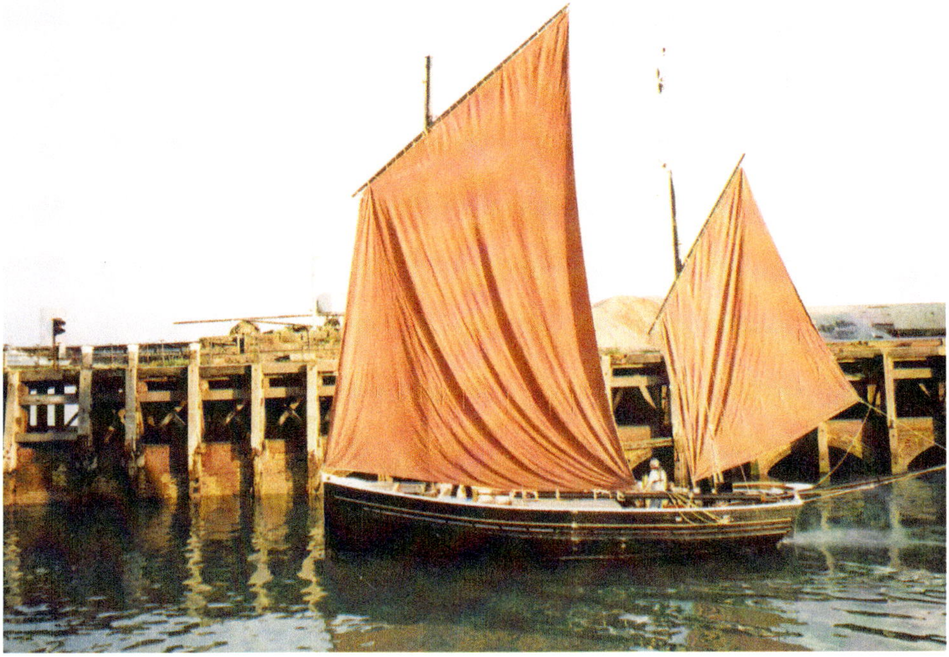

The *Happy Return* FE5 leaving Folkestone on her return trip to Penzance at 19.30 hours on 28 July 2005.

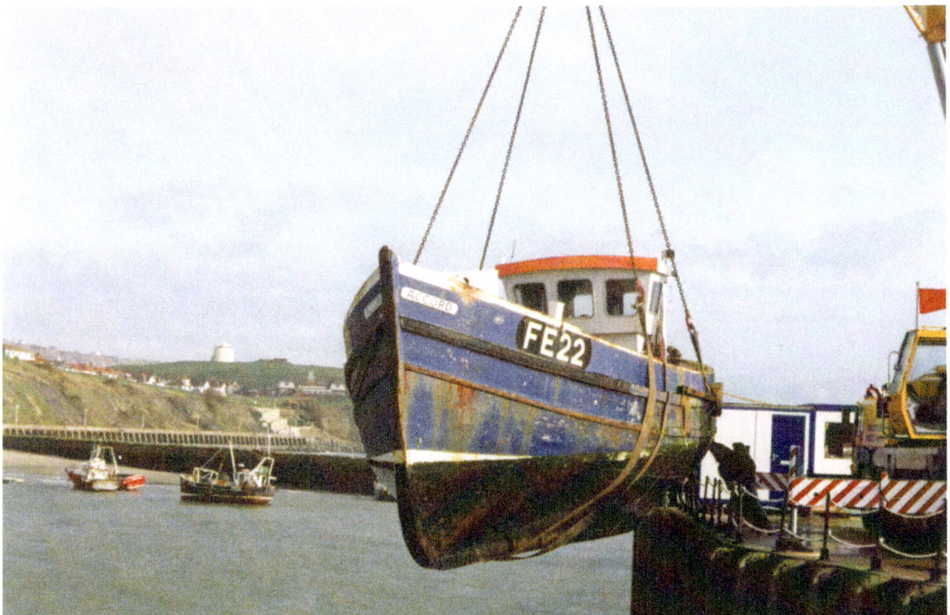


The trawler *Accord* FE22 was built at Whitby in 1958. She came to Folkestone in 1964, the owner being the late Bert Reed. She was decommissioned on 5 January 1998 and is seen here being craned out of the water to be taken to the Rotunda Amusement Park for an added attraction, where she remained until 6 March 2007 when she was cut-up for scrap.

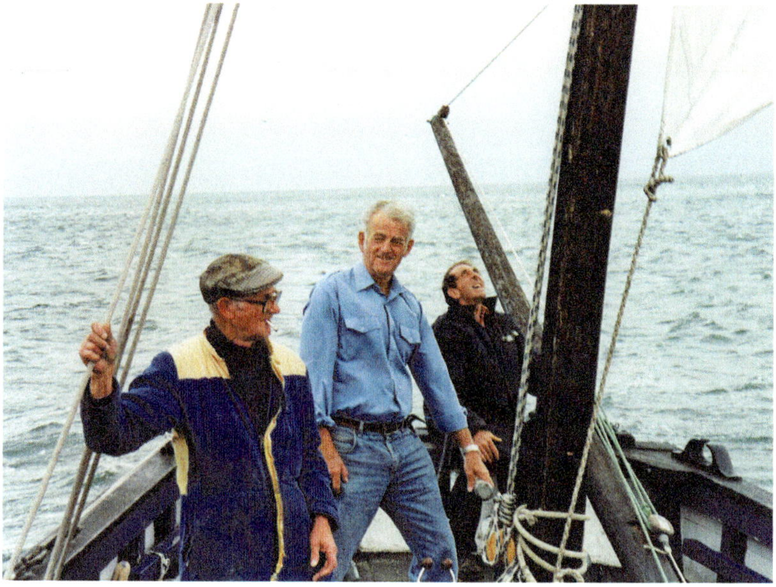

The fishing lugger *Three Brothers* FE93 was built at Mevagissey, Cornwall, in 1901 for William May, who left her in his will to his sons Bert and Harry. She was deregistered in 1996 and at a later date acquired by shipwright Barry Hobbs, who restored her to a sailing lugger. Out sailing off Folkestone 13 August 1996 is the late fisherman Charlie Petts with myself at the helm and Barry Hobbs.

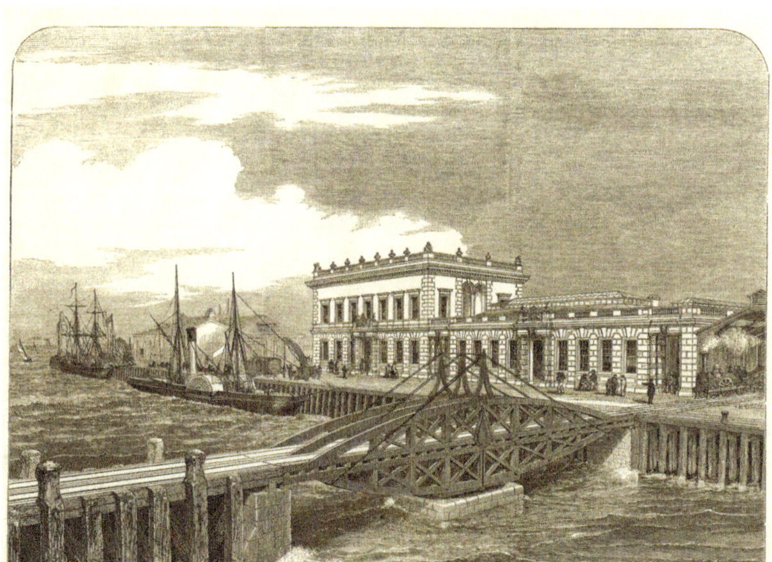


An engraving from the Building News dated 14 January 1859; a view taken from the Inner Harbour shows the New Custom House designed by architect James Murray and constructed by Messrs Lucas Brothers for the South Eastern Railway Company. Work started in 1854 and the building opened in 1859. The railway station (right) was built by Mr Hill of Whitechapel, 1850, and the swing bridge was opened on 1 January 1849.

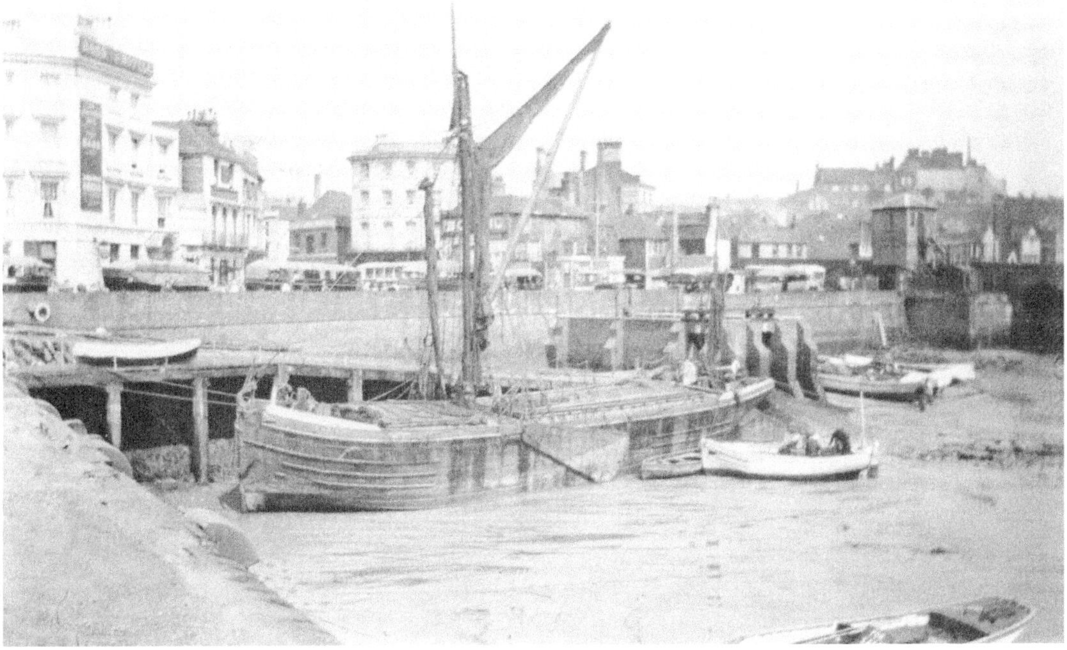

Moored alongside the inner harbour slipway is the Spritsail barge *Vampire* in 1925. She is 79 tons, built at Sittingbourne in 1898, registered (108361) at London, E3, and owned by E. J. & W. Goldsmith of London.

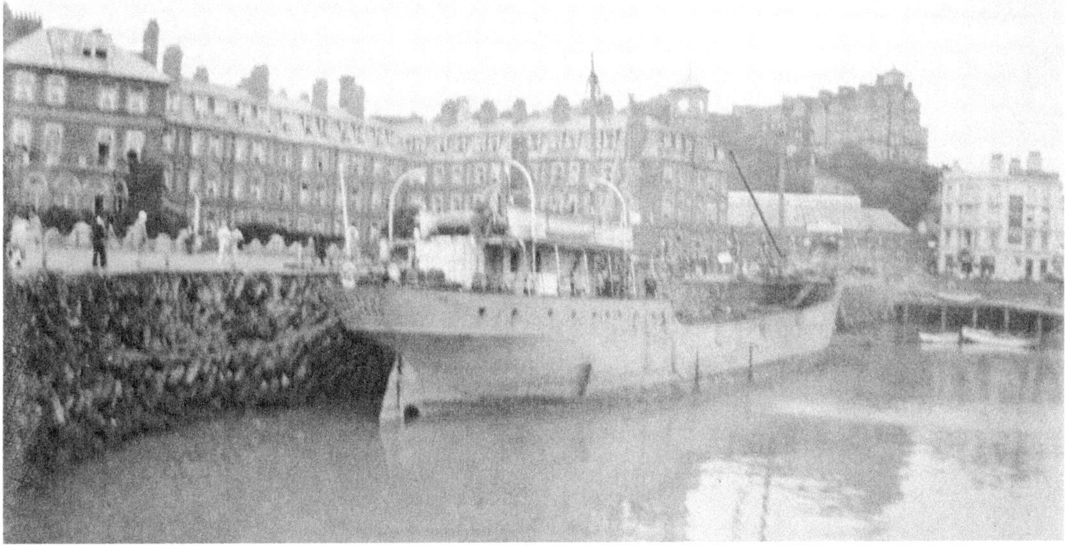

The cargo ship *Aarsten* from Tonsberg, Norway, is unloading her cargo of ice in August 1925 in the inner harbour. She is possibly one of the first ships that took over from the sail ships.

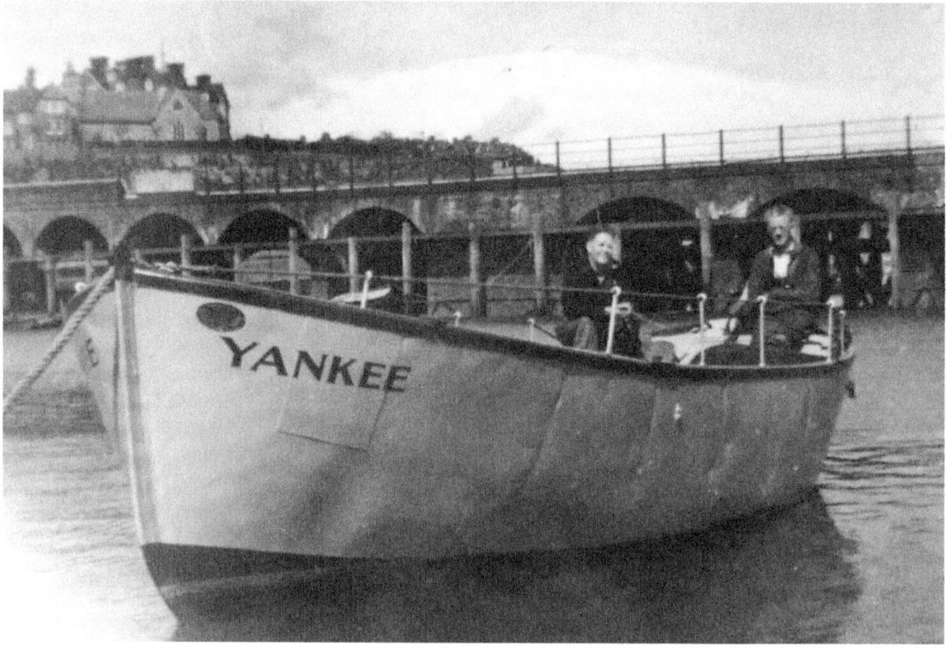


This motor lifeboat was purchased by my father and Bert Prior in 1946. She came off the USS *North Eastern Victory*, a 7,612-ton cargo ship that ran aground on the Goodwin Sands on 24 December 1946. They converted it into a pleasure boat carrying twelve paying passengers. My father and Bert put a crew in her who ran her for the summer of 1947, after which she was sold as a going concern.

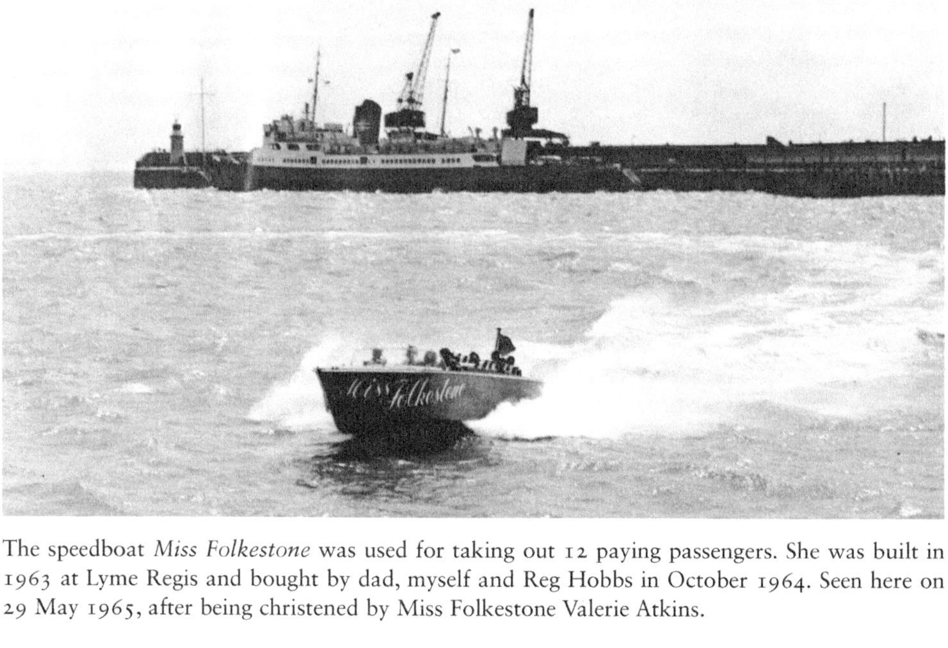

The speedboat *Miss Folkestone* was used for taking out 12 paying passengers. She was built in 1963 at Lyme Regis and bought by dad, myself and Reg Hobbs in October 1964. Seen here on 29 May 1965, after being christened by Miss Folkestone Valerie Atkins.

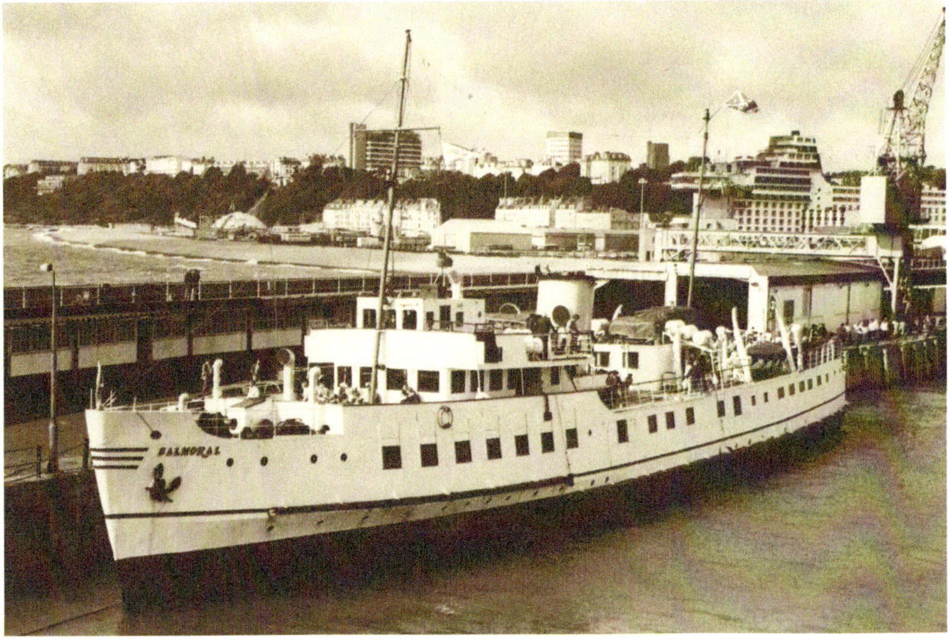


The excursion ship MV *Balmoral* entered service in 1949. She was built to replace the paddle steamer PS *Balmoral*, which was built in 1900. Seen here at Folkestone on 23 September 1987.

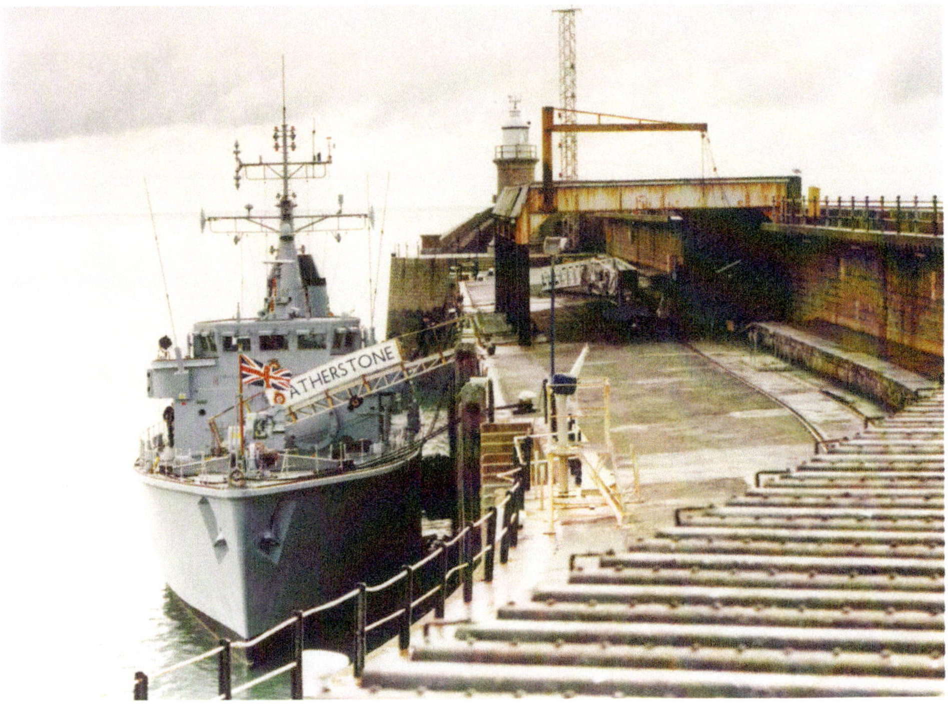


HMS *Atherstone* is a Hunt-class mine countermeasures vessel, launched on 1 March 1986. She is moored in number one berth Folkestone Harbour on a visit for the Shepway Festival, 1 September 1995.

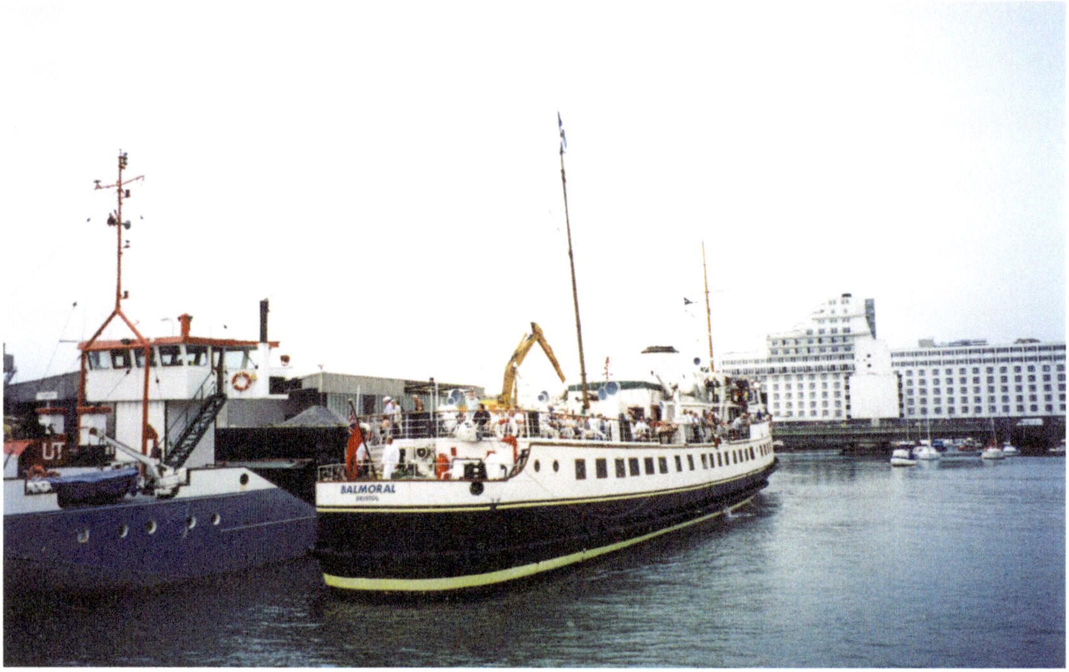


The excursion ship *MV Balmoral*, going astern passing the bulk carrier *Union Pluto*, which is moored on the South Quay. She is on a trip round the coast and up the Thames to Tower Bridge on 27 June 2003. It was her last visit to Folkestone due to the poor condition of the harbour.

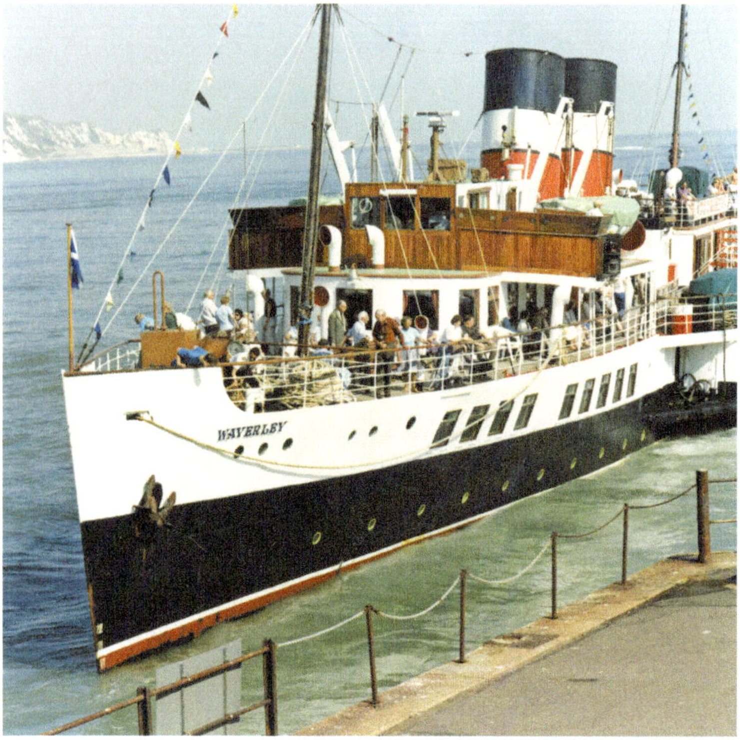


The excursion Paddle Streamer *PS Waverly* visiting for the Shepway Festival in September 1991. On the last day of the festival (Saturday) she did an evening trip to Dover and back, after which she laid off The Leas to watch the fireworks.

Mercedes Gleitze, a twenty-one-year-old typist, first visited Folkestone in the summer of 1922. She had just taken part in the *Daily Sketch* prize competition to swim the English Channel (starting from Dover), but lack of training forced her to abandon the swim after 3½ hours when her shoulder muscles gave out. Her ambition was to become a professional open-water swimmer – a unique occupation for a woman in those days – and she planned to use the English Channel crossing as a platform to start her chosen career. Over the following five years she made Folkestone her training headquarters, and on 7 October 1927, on her eighth attempt, she became the first British woman (and third woman) to succeed, swimming from Cap Gris-Nez to St Margaret's Bay in 15 hours 15 minutes.

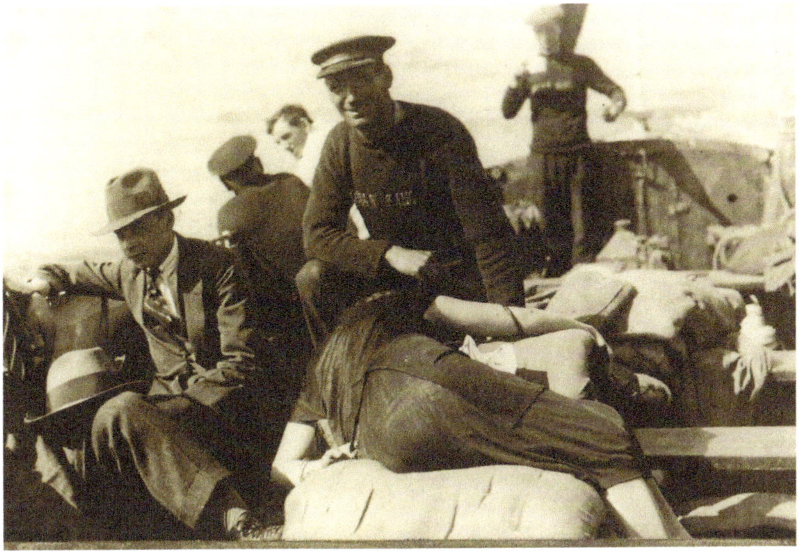

Harry Sharp, pilot, and Mercedes resting before her swim; news photographer Stanley Devon is also present (wearing the trilby hat).

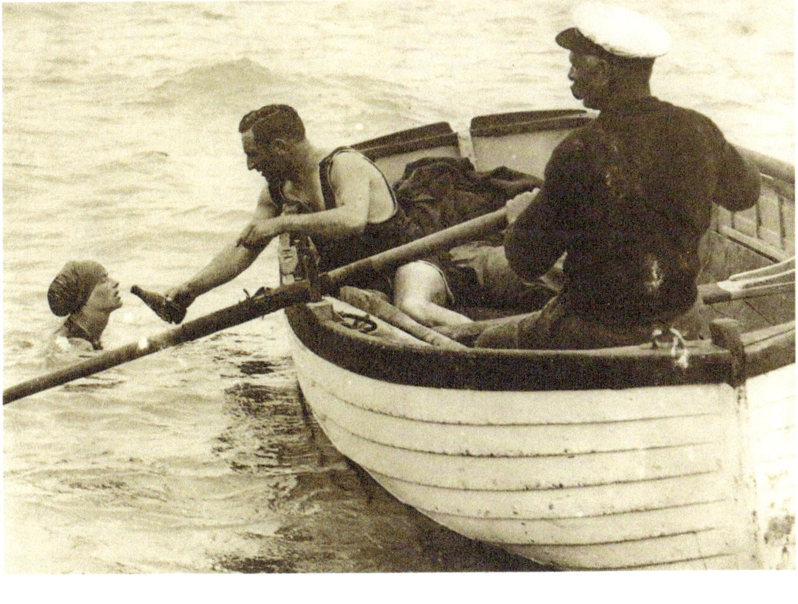

Mercedes is seen here in water drinking Ovaltine.

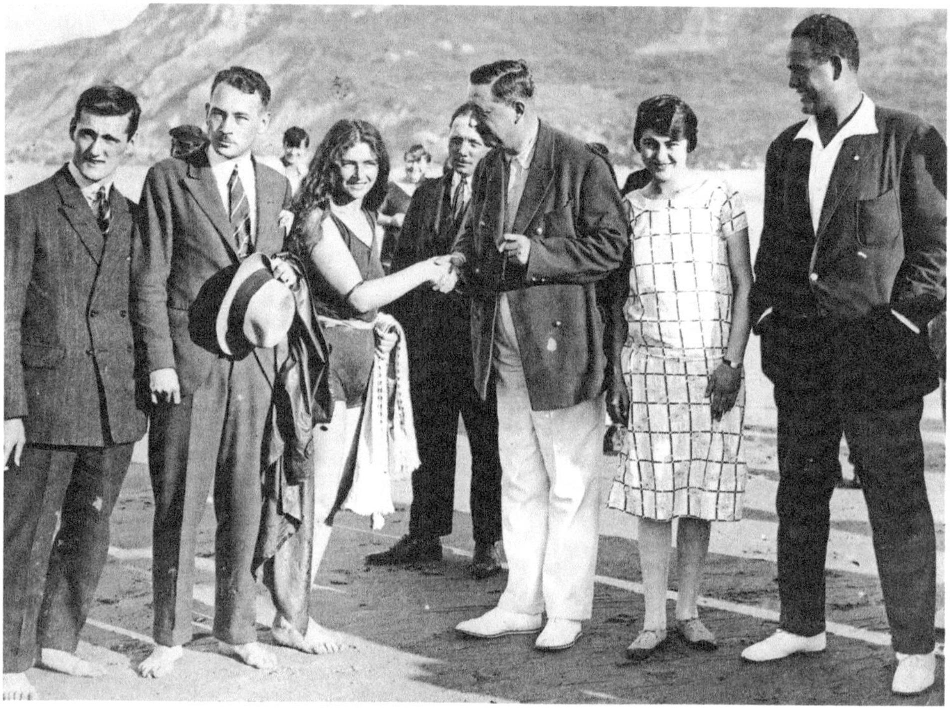

Mercedes shaking hands with the Mayor of Calais, M. Leon Vincent. The man on the right is Ishak Helmy, an Egyptian Channel swimmer.

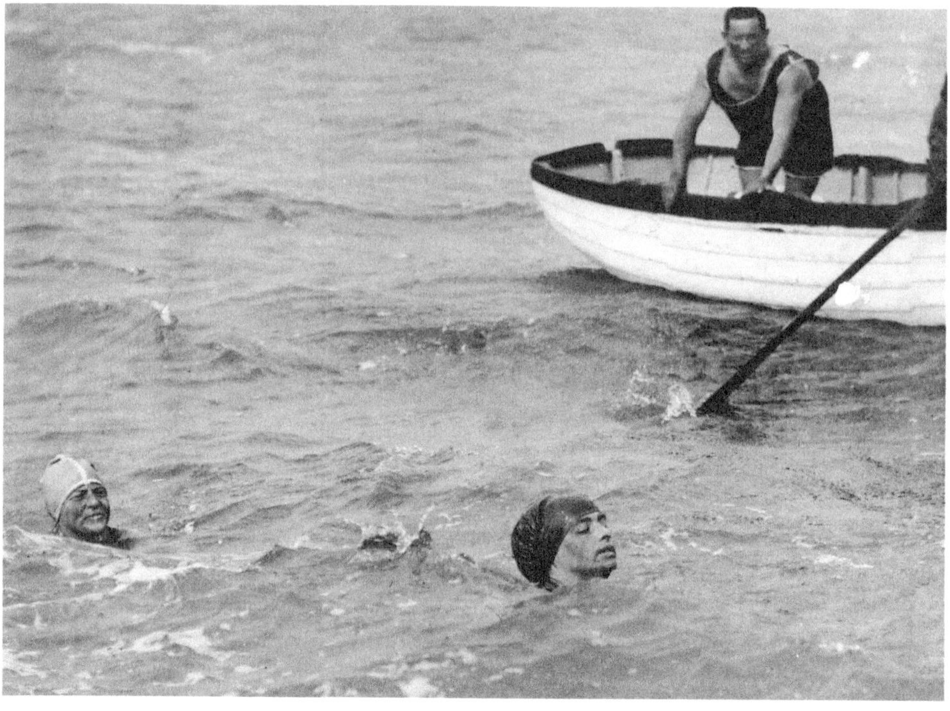

Mercedes is seen here in the black bathing hat.

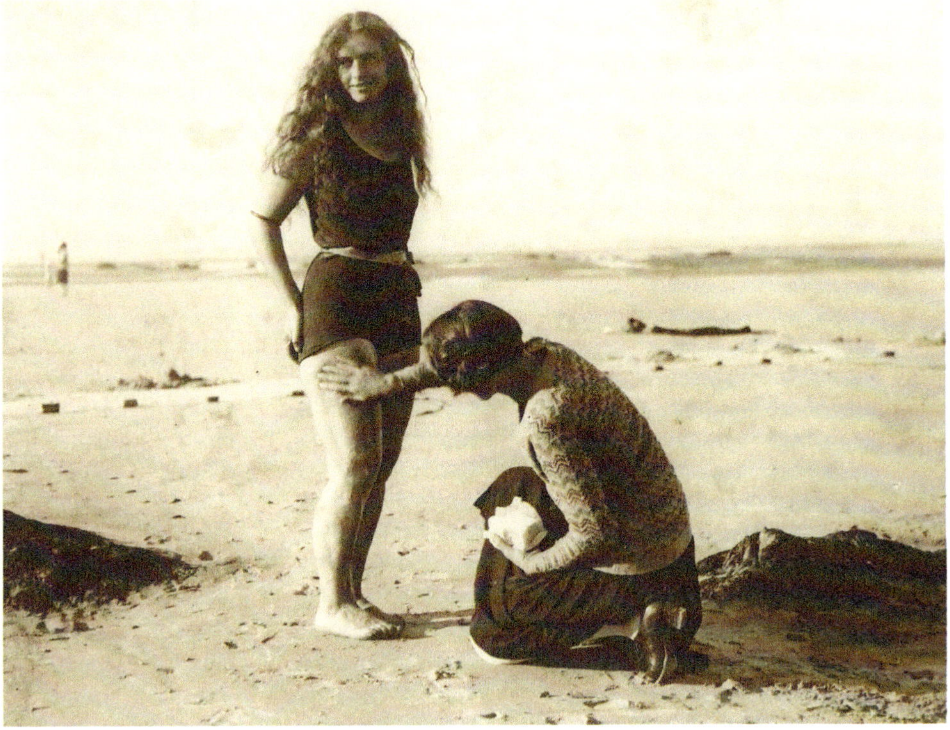

Mercedes seen here with her sister Doloranda, who is applying the grease.

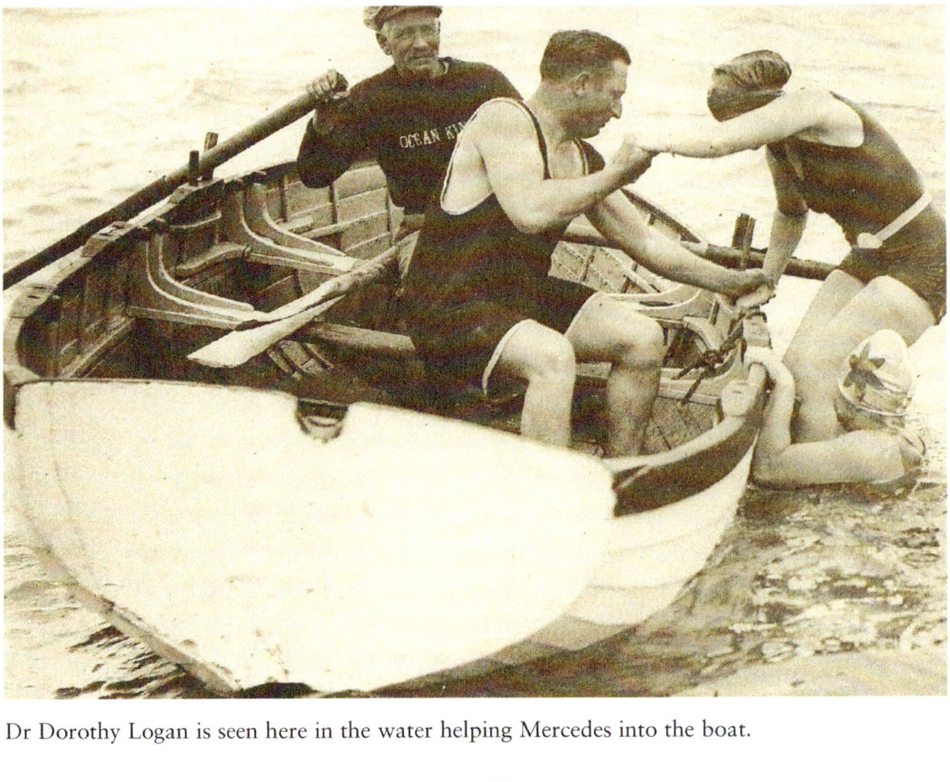

Dr Dorothy Logan is seen here in the water helping Mercedes into the boat.

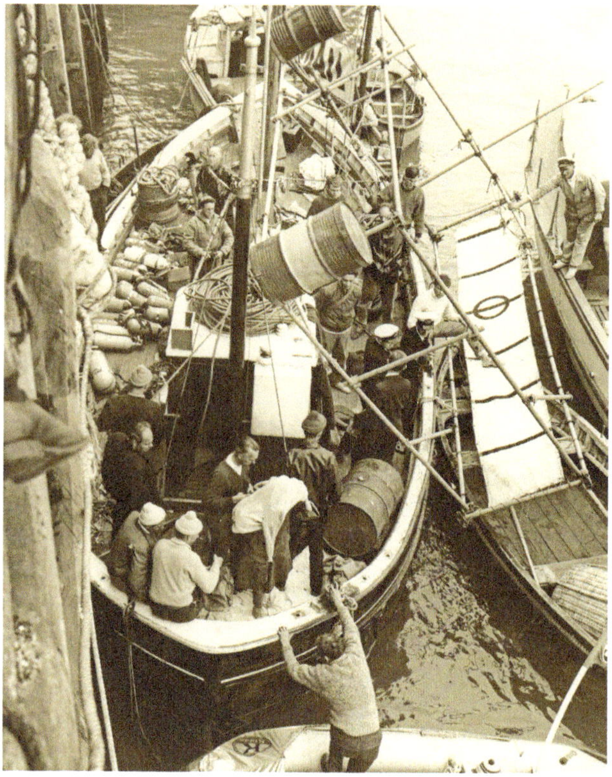

Jane Baldasare, the American underwater swimmer, is pictured (foreground on board the fishing boat *Fair Chance*) on her return to Folkestone harbour after abandoning her attempt to swim the Channel underwater, 17 August 1960.

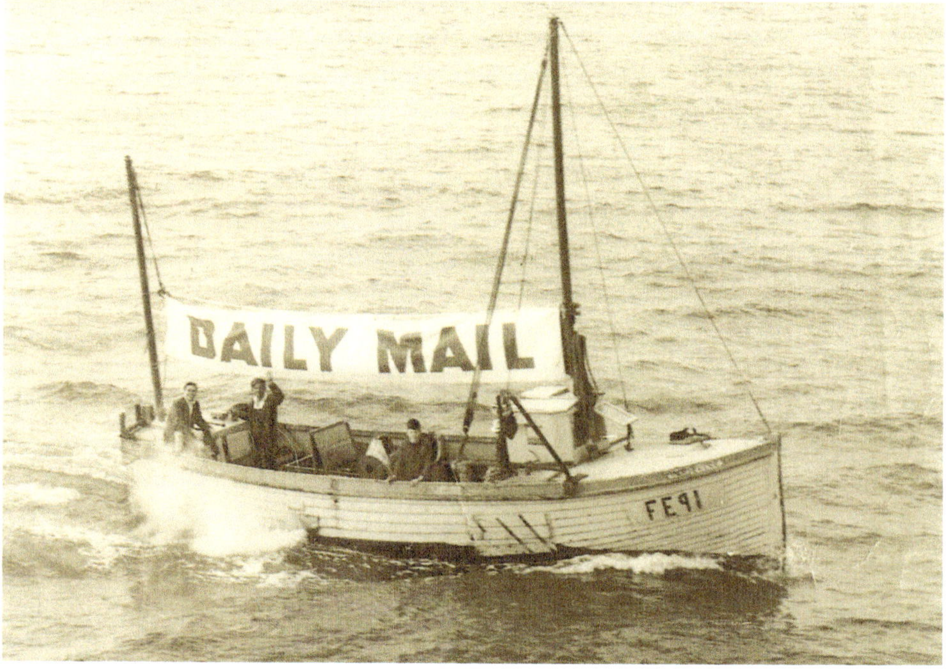


Jane Baldasare's swim was sponsored by the *Daily Mail*. FE91 was one of the official boats. She was owned by Harry Featherbe, who is on the helm.

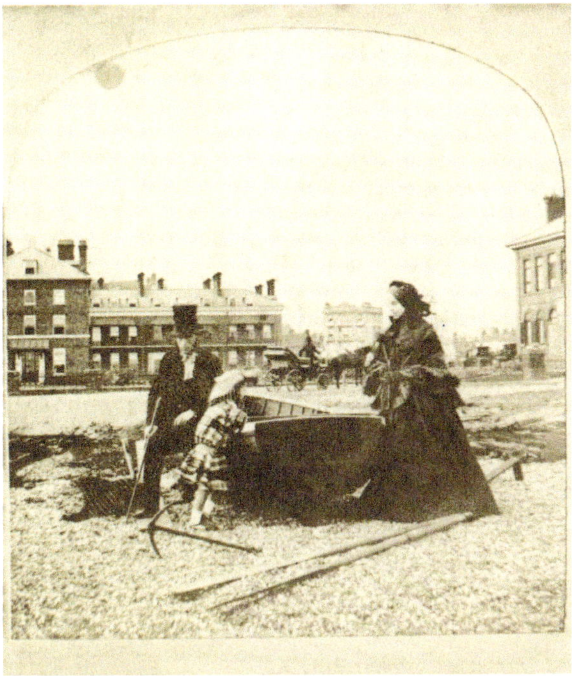

On the left can be seen the Pavilion Hotel, London and Paris Hotel, and the part of the South Eastern Railway's harbour master's office and residence *c.* 1860. Note the gentleman in his stovepipe hat and little girl, both in their elegant Victorian attire.

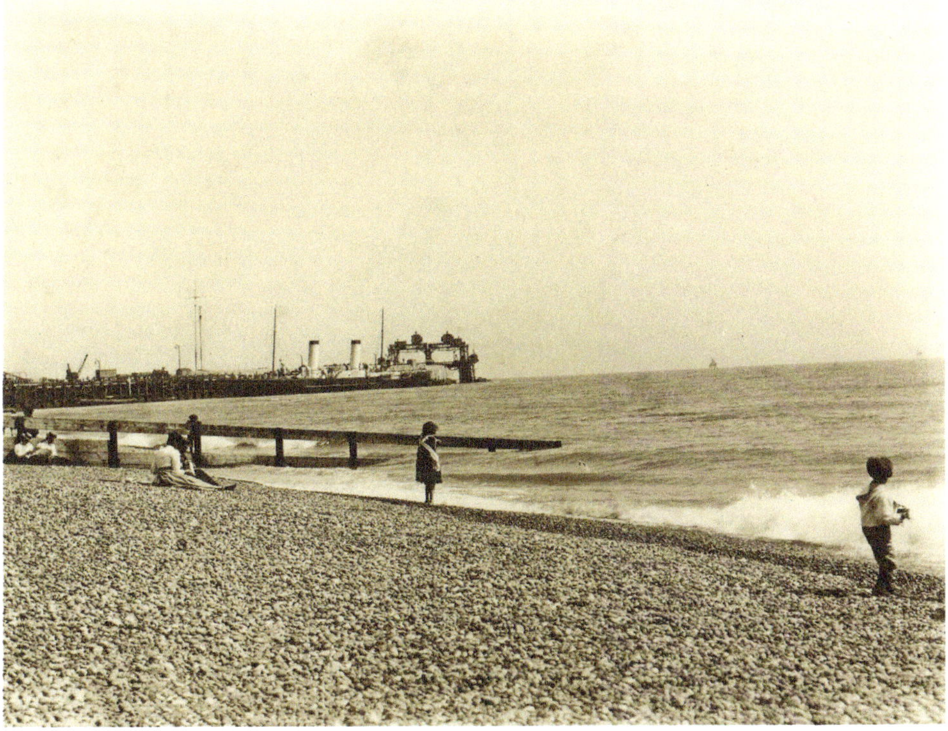

The west side of the pier showing the pier extend under construction *c.* 1900 to become the pier we know today. The paddle steamer is either the *PS Victoria*, which was built in 1886, or the *Empress*, built 1887.

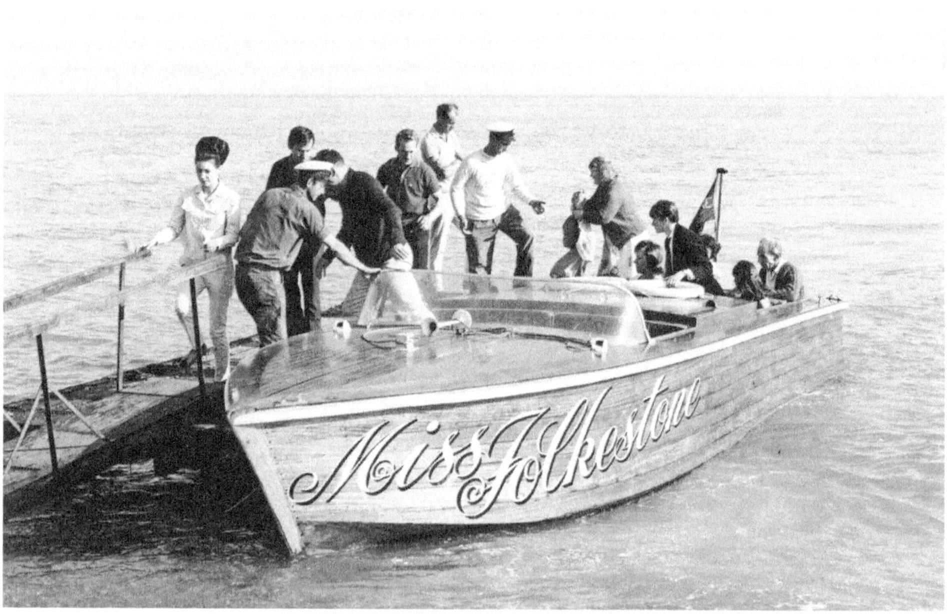


When the tide was out in the inner harbour we operated from the beach, taking out our passengers using this landing stage. I am at the front of the boat unloading passengers while Jimmy Dean is aft in the summer of 1965.

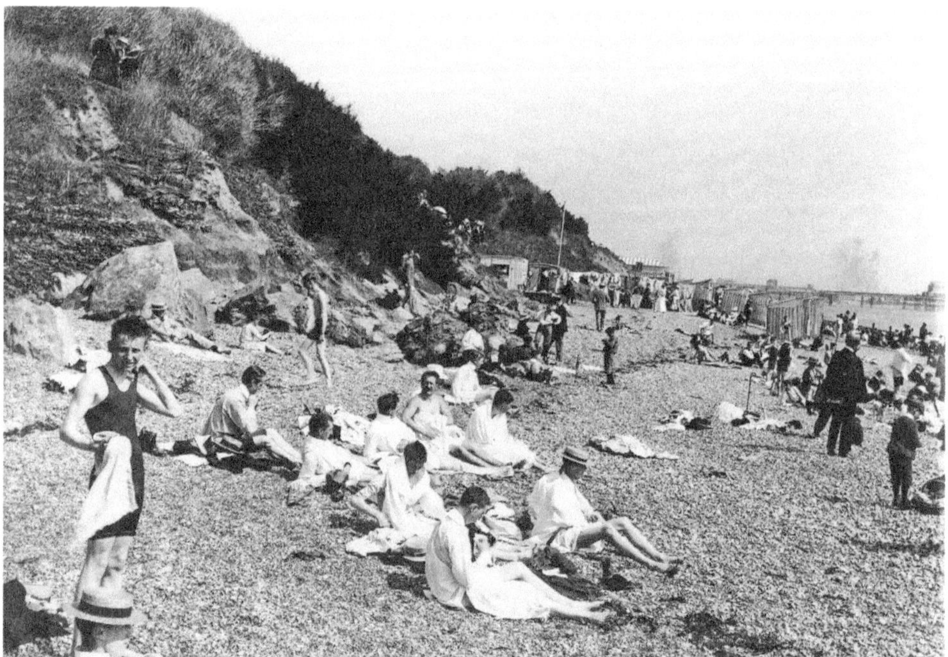

Holidaymakers and locals alike are taking advantage of a nice sunny day in the summer of 1900. The promenade, which one can walk along today, was not built until 1910. The Victoria Pier, which opened in 1888, can be seen in the distance.

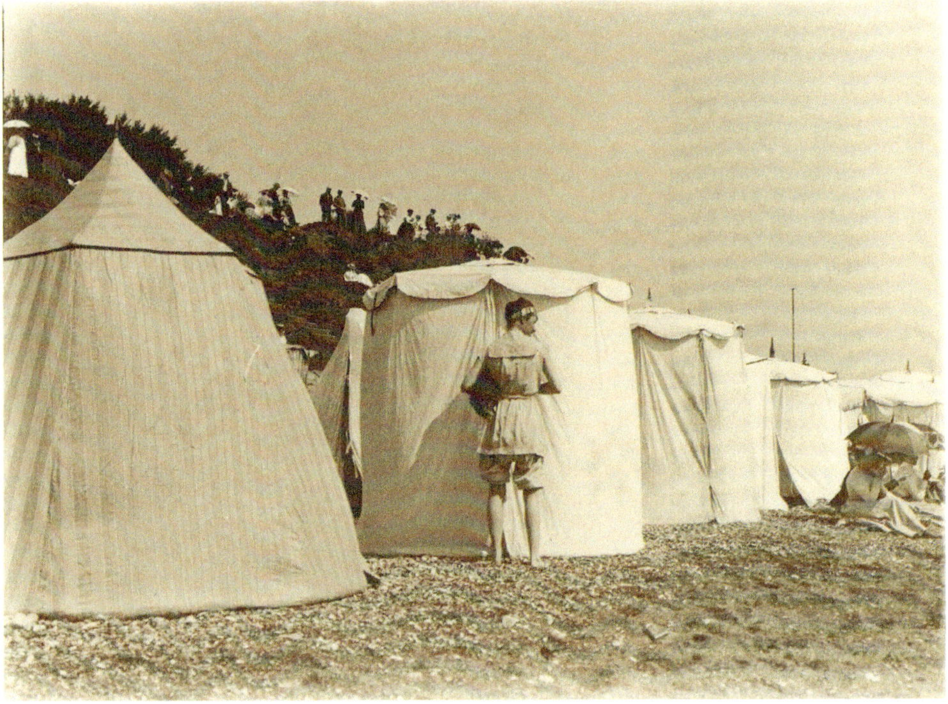

Undressing on the beach was not permitted, so if you were wealthy you could hire a bathing machine, which operated between the harbour and Victoria Pier, or one of these changing tents. This photograph was taken in the summer of 1900.

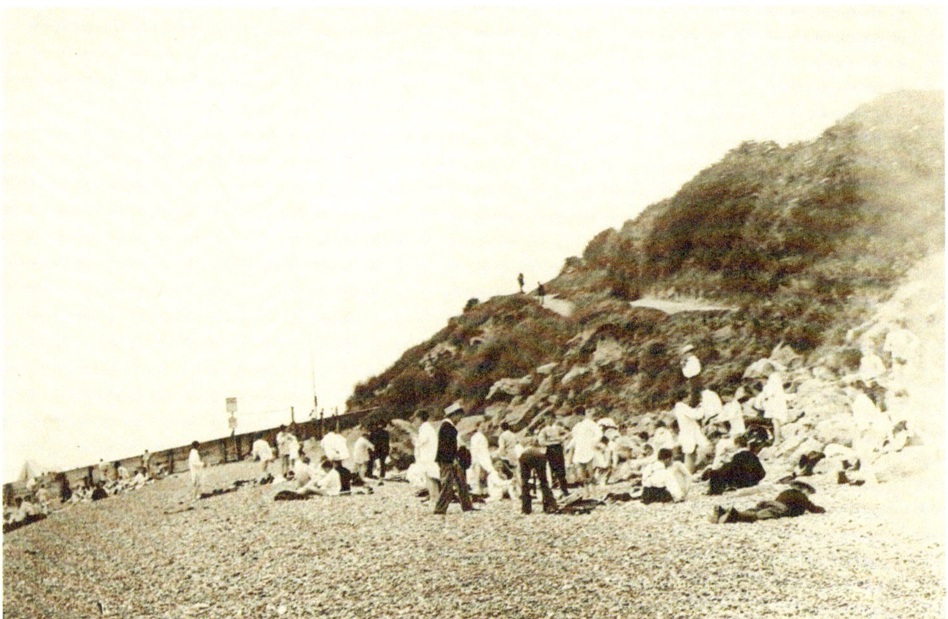

Another view on the beach in 1900 looking towards Sandgate; the position would be around where the Mermaid café is today.

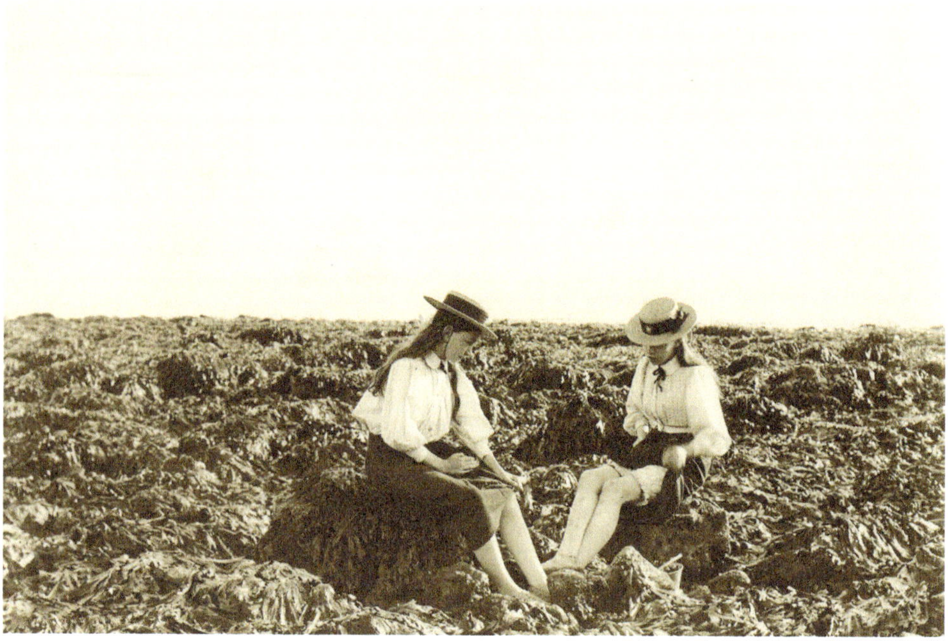

Two teenage girls sitting on the rocks at Mill Point in 1900; the one on the right-hand side is rather daringly showing her knickerbockers.

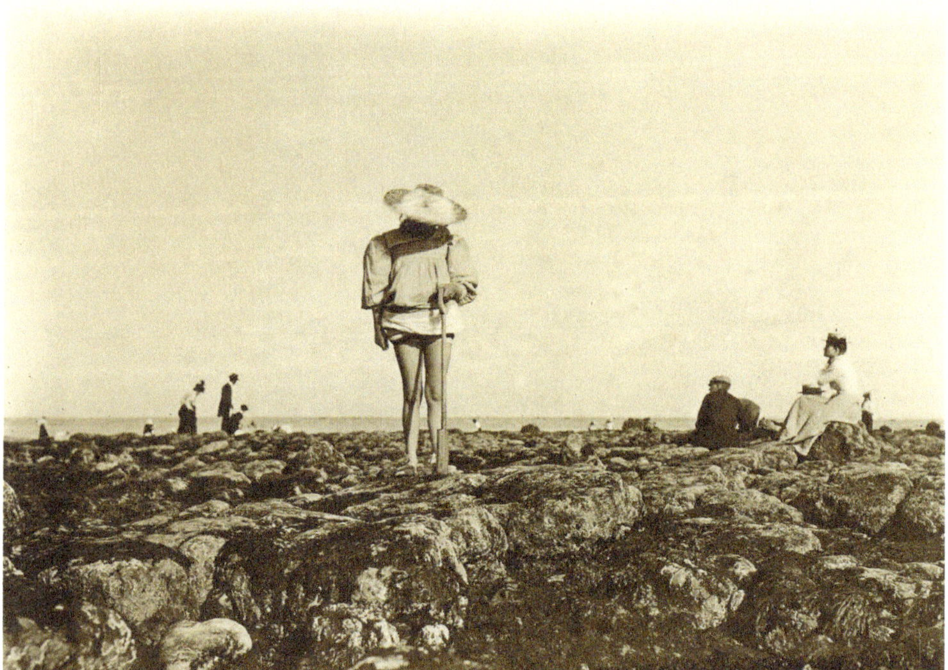

The late Victoria people seen here are foraging on the sandstone rocks at Mill Point where they could find adder crabs, Spanish crabs brown crabs (*Cancer pagurus*), green crabs (*Carcinus maenas*), prawns, winkles, limpets and sea anemones.

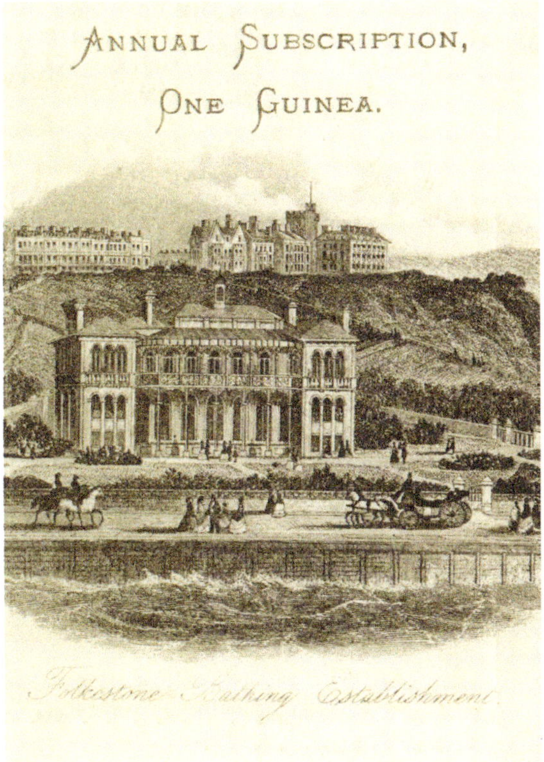


This is a copy of an original subscription card that outlines many facilities and terms at the Bathing Establishment. It dates between 1874 and 1878, when William Hills was manager.

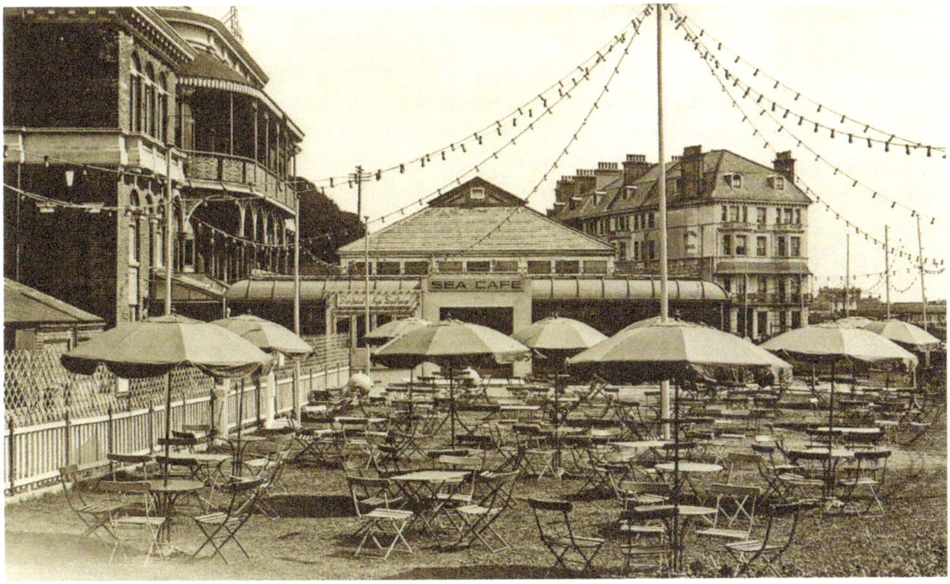


The building on the left is the Bathing Establishment which was just left of Marine Crescent; it was opened on 20 July 1869. It had many attractions on offer including hot and cold sea water baths, medicated baths, vapour baths, a swimming pool, billiard, reading and refreshment rooms and a large saloon with balcony. The extension was added at the front in 1888 to accommodate a larger swimming pool, which was later covered over and used as a dance floor.

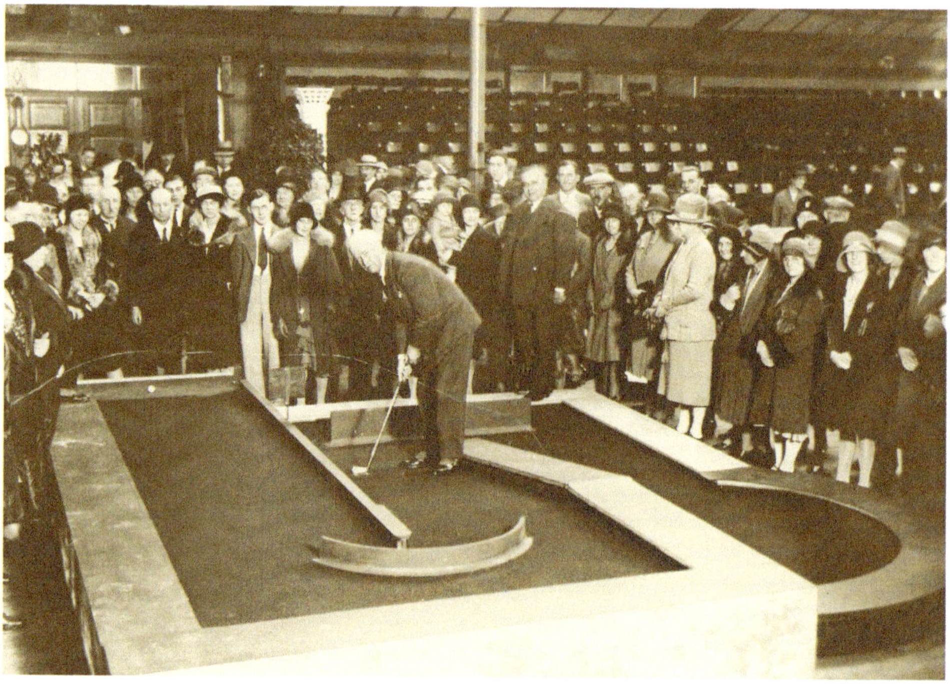

Alderman Albert Castle is seen here opening the Marine Gardens Pavilion on 1 March 1926. It was built by the local builder Otto Marx at a cost of £15,000. It hosted concert parties, variety shows and a skating rink, with live performances in 1981 and the building being divided into a café bar, pub and nightclub. The building was demolished in 2015.

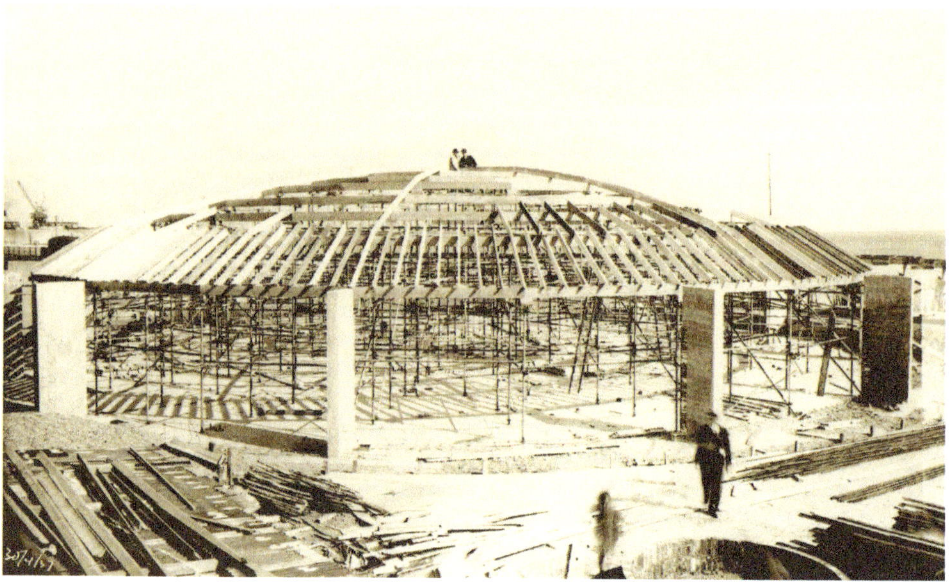

*The Folkestone Herald* for 8 May 1937 reported that, 'the framework and shuttering for the rotunda now in course of erection on the foreshore at Folkestone is being carried out by Messrs C. Jenner and Son, Ltd, with the remainder of the contract'. The Rotunda was demolished in December 2002.

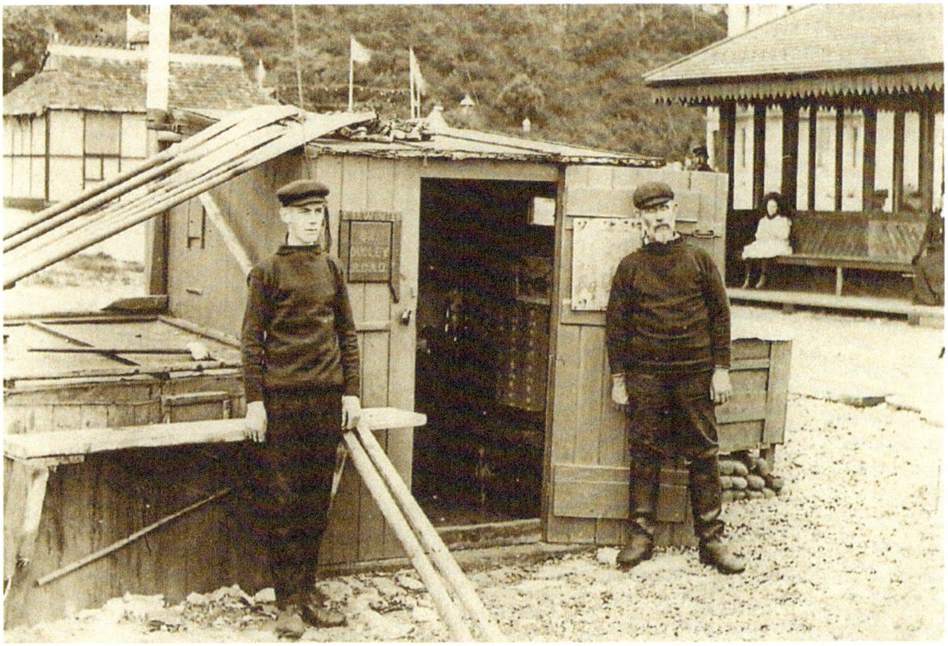

In 1936 Lord Radnor, Lord of the Manor cleaned up the beach in order to make it a leisure area. At the time many fishermen had huts on the beach like this one, owned by Edward D. Winter, seen here on the right, with his son Thomas Marsh Winter on the left. The photo was taken between 1906 and 1926, when the family lived at No. 32 Dudley Road.

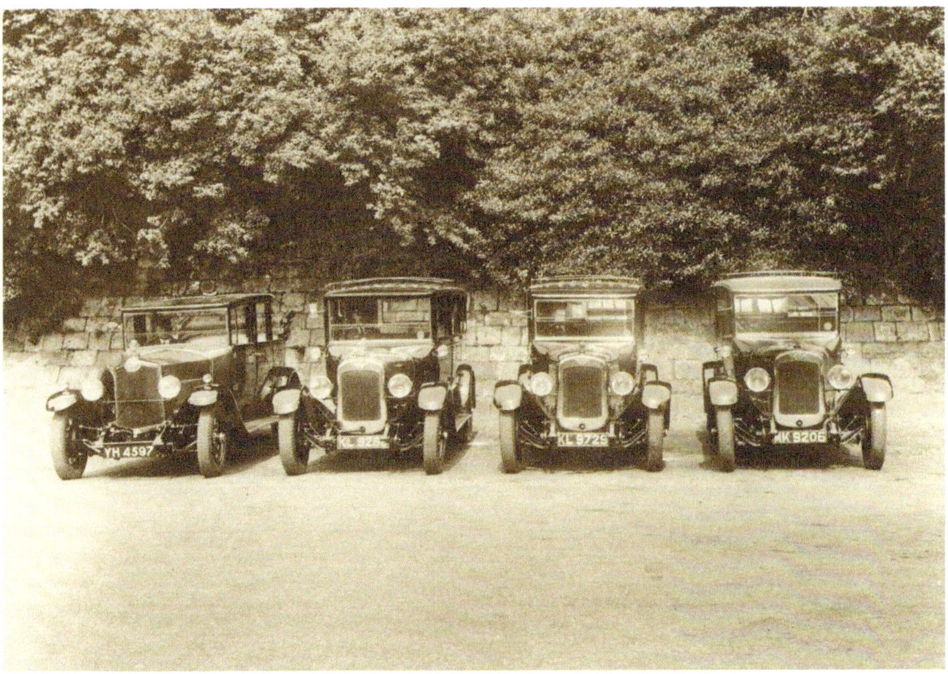


The fleet of Charlie Robert's taxis parked at the bottom of the Road of Remembrance. Mr Robert's garage was at Nos 3–4 Marine Terrace. He specialised in weddings and long-distance journeys.

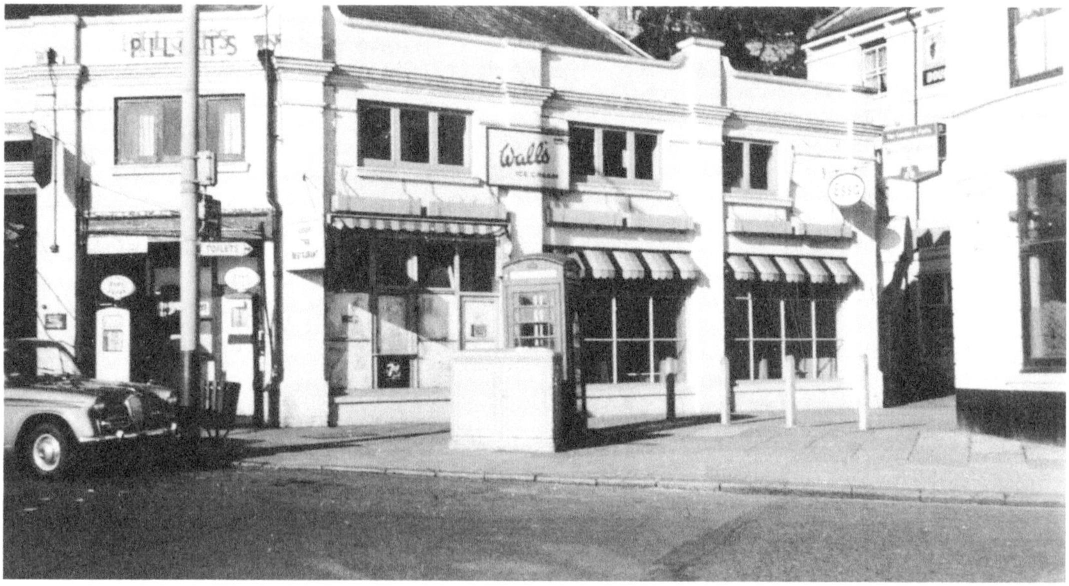


Auto Pilots Garage, Lower Sandgate Road was formerly the County Rink, opened by Mr Robert Forsythe in 1911. Mr H. E. Savery converted it into the Harbour Garage in 1920. The name was changed to Auto Pilots in 1930 and the building was demolished in 1971 to build a filling station. The filling station was demolished in 2001 and a car park was built on the site.

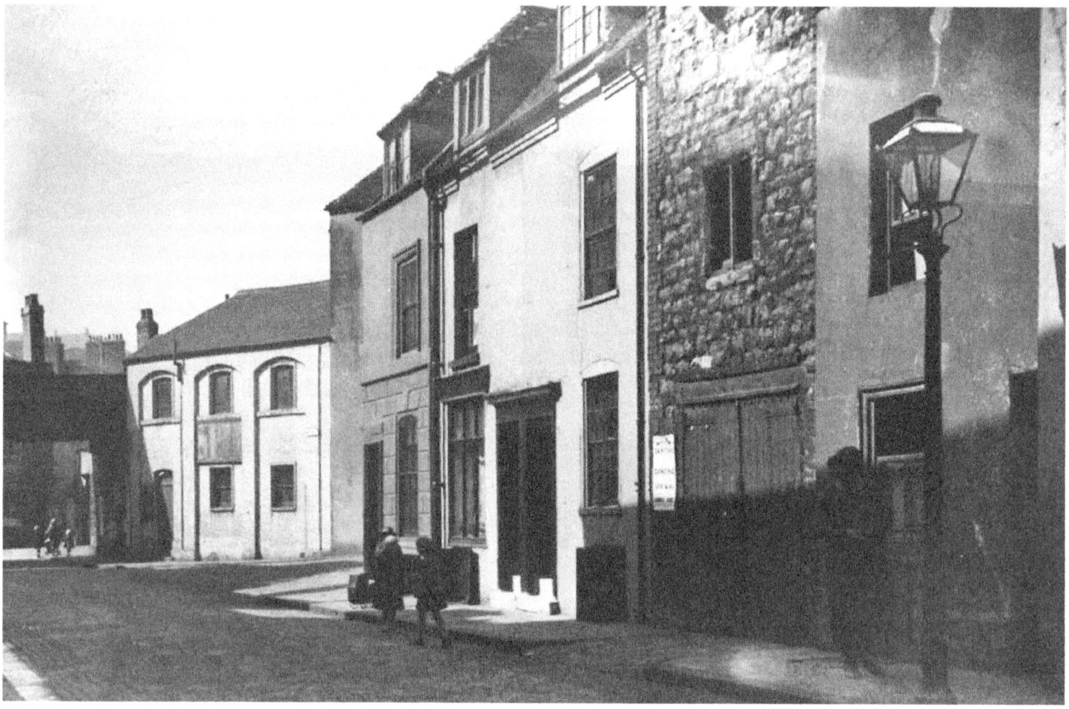

The building at the bottom of North Street at the junction with Radnor Street was in 1891 St Peter's Baptist Mission Hall for fishermen's children, primarily run by the Revd Clark family. They moved to Harvey Street Mission Hall *c.* 1936.

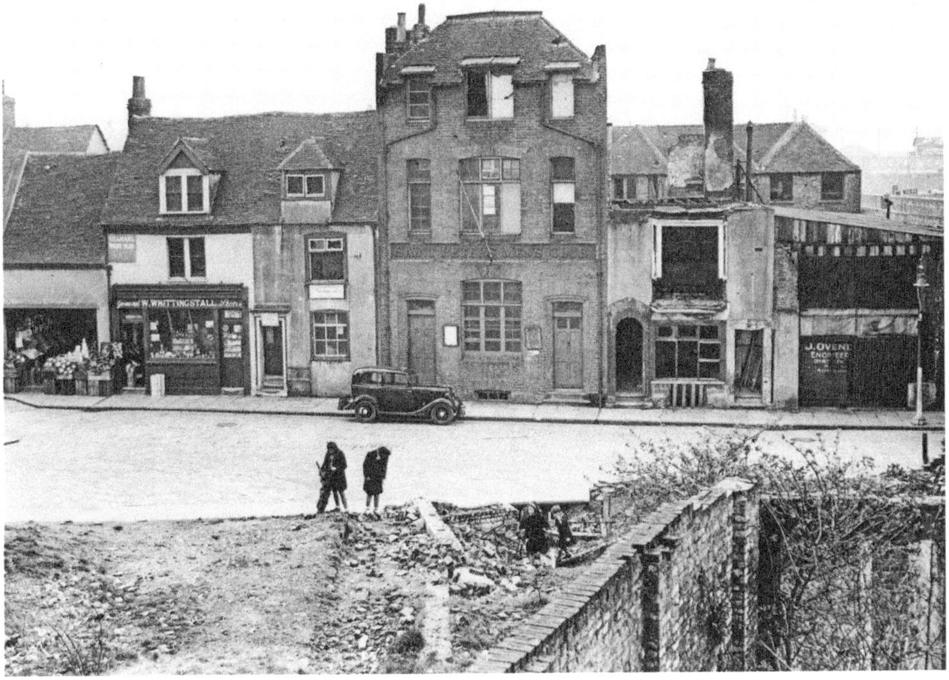


Radnor Street from North Street *c.* 1950. From the left are Mr W. Whittingstall, general Shop Francis Care, St Peter's Men's Club and Ovenden & Son, blacksmith. It's interesting to note that some of the properties have been damaged by enemy action in the Second World War. In the right foreground was St Peter's Baptist Mission Hall, now the site of the yacht club car park.

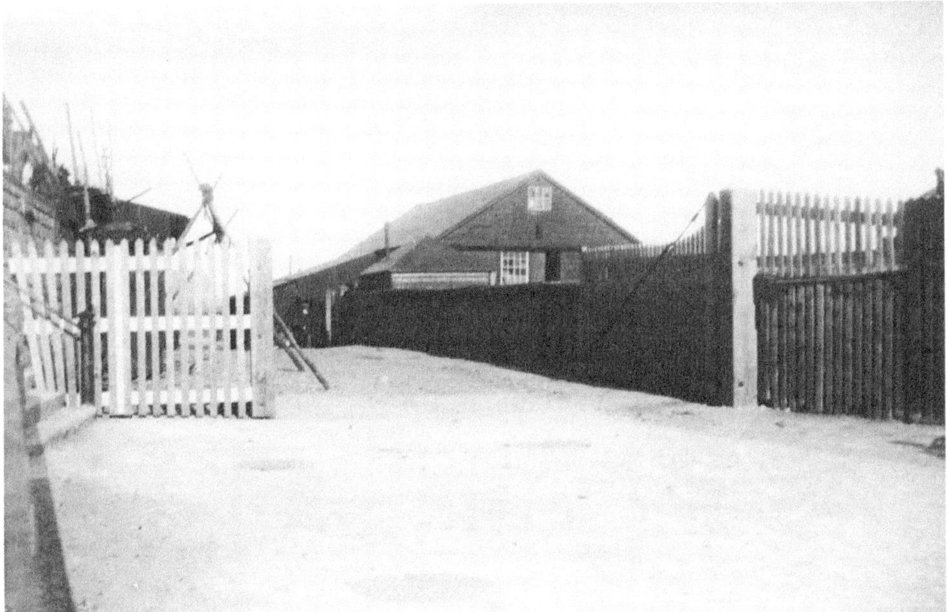

This is the entrance to the new sewer works at the east end of the Stade, 1923.

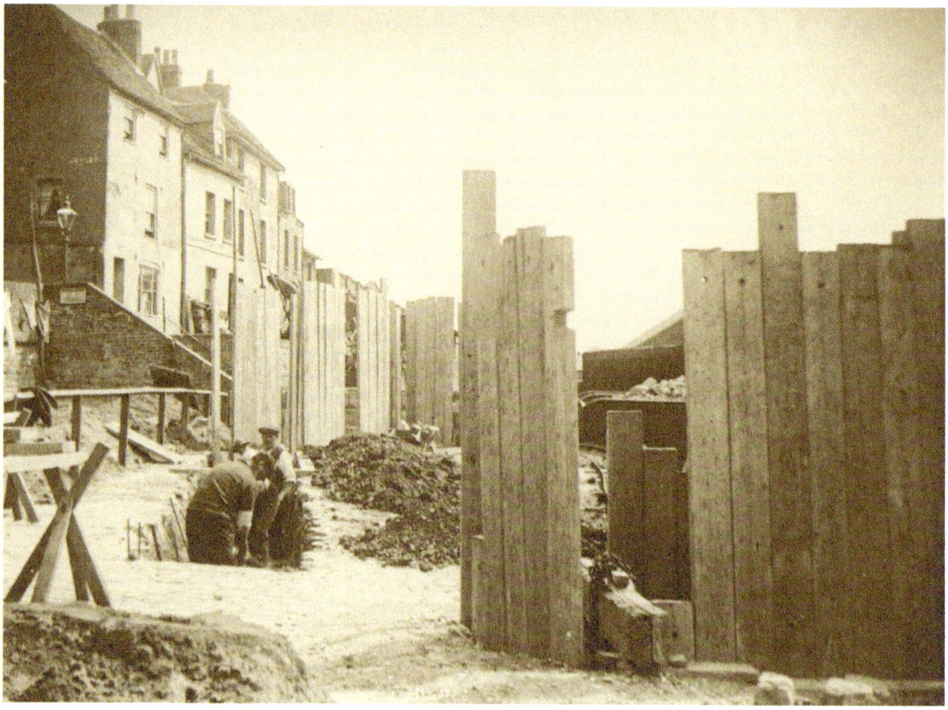

Work in progress laying the new sewer pipes at the east end of the Stade, July 1923. The buildings on the left-hand side are in East Street and they were demolished in 1935.

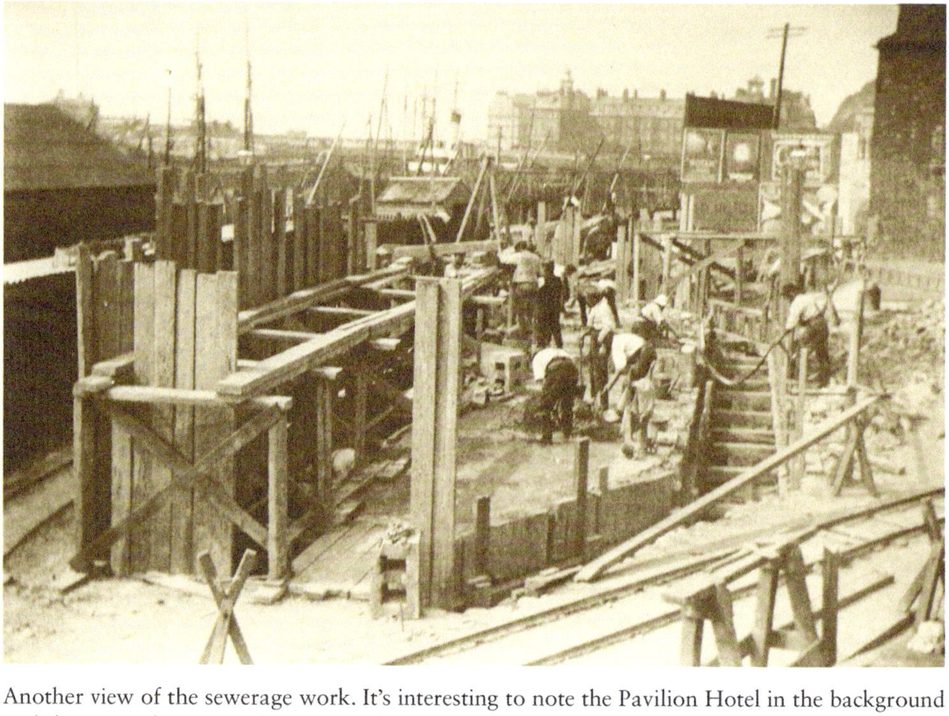

Another view of the sewerage work. It's interesting to note the Pavilion Hotel in the background and the cargo ship moored alongside the Jetty.

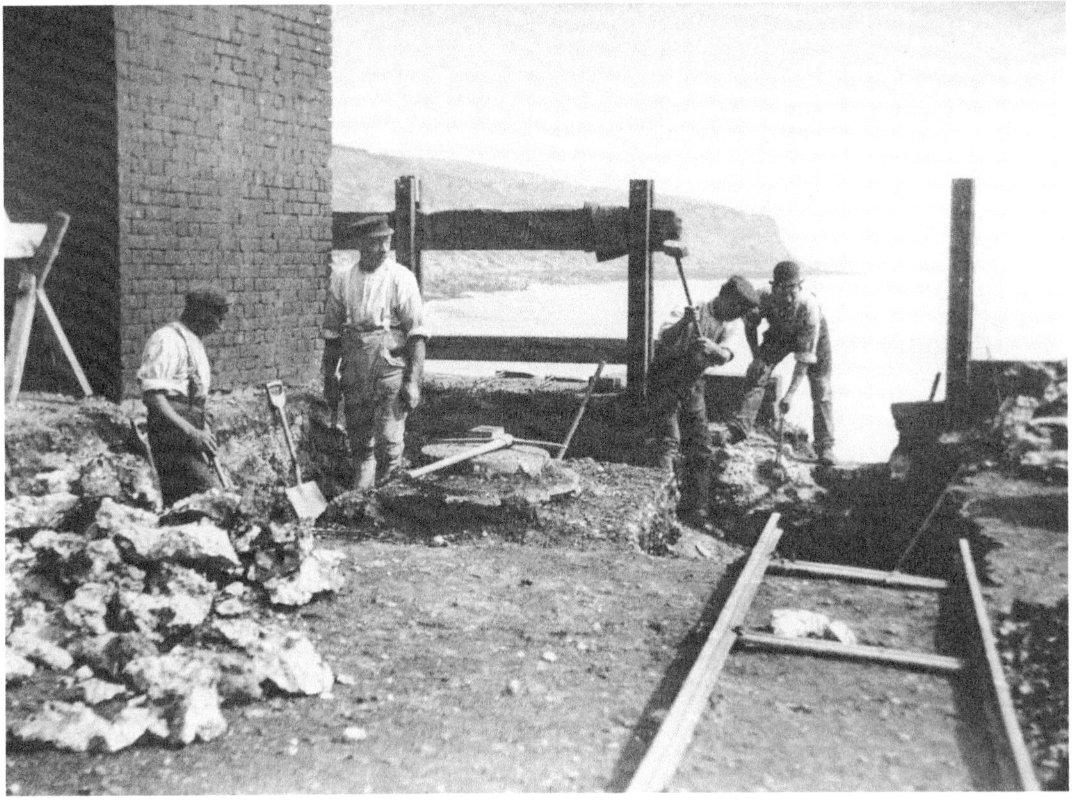

The sewerage work nearing completion at the eastern end of the Stade in 1924.

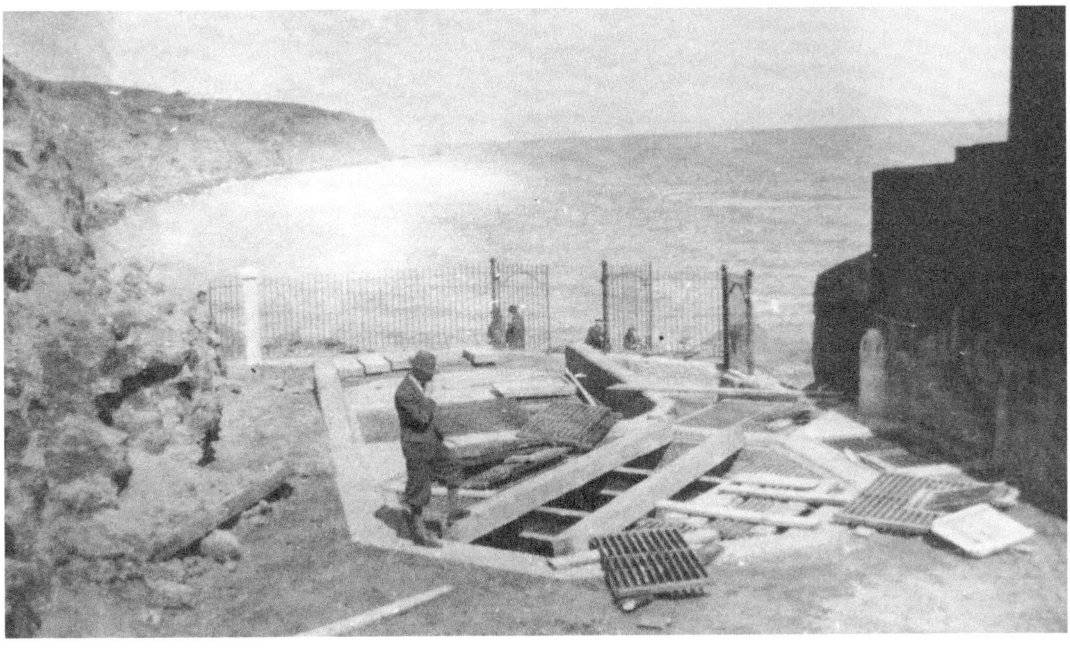

Sanitary inspector Mr Herbert Gill inspecting the new sewerage work.

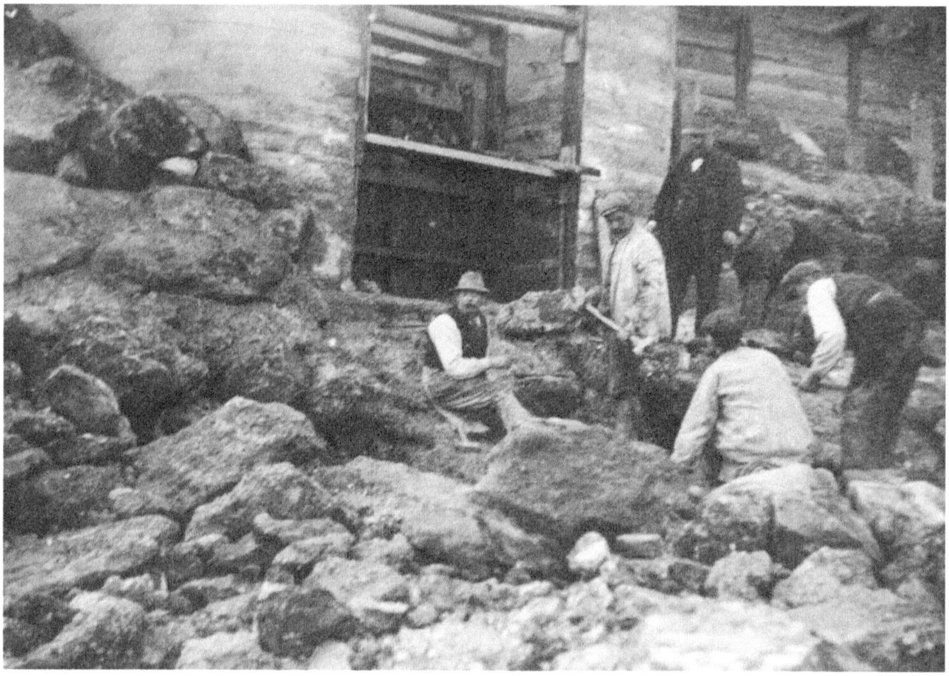

These men are working on the storm water outlet that would discharge onto East Cliff sands when the sewer was unable to cope with the volume of rainwater.

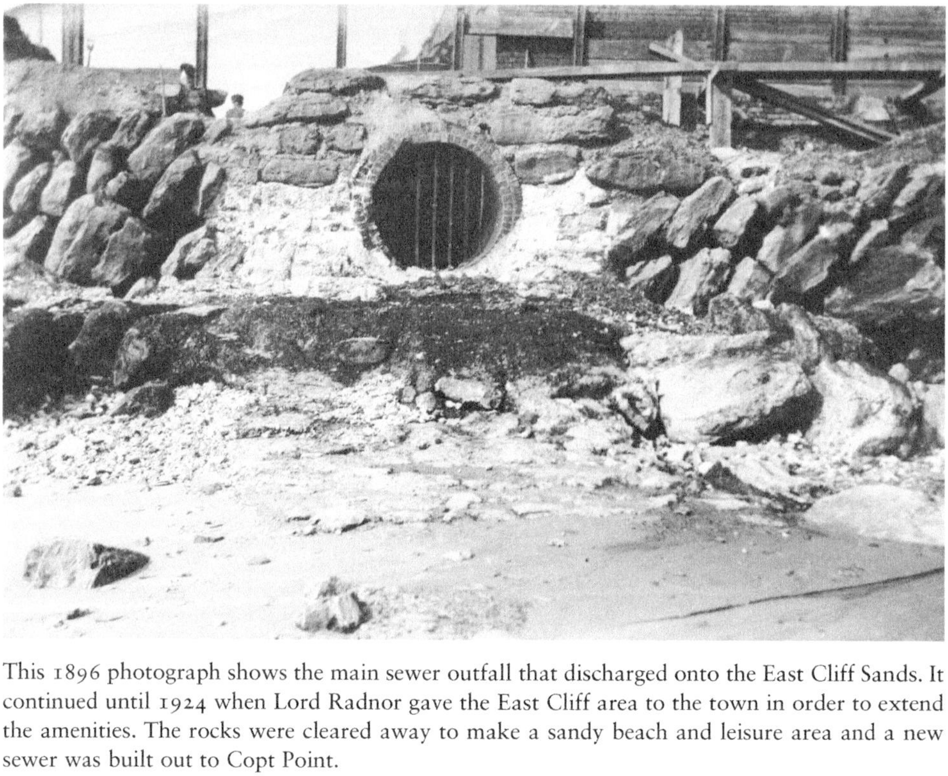

This 1896 photograph shows the main sewer outfall that discharged onto the East Cliff Sands. It continued until 1924 when Lord Radnor gave the East Cliff area to the town in order to extend the amenities. The rocks were cleared away to make a sandy beach and leisure area and a new sewer was built out to Copt Point.

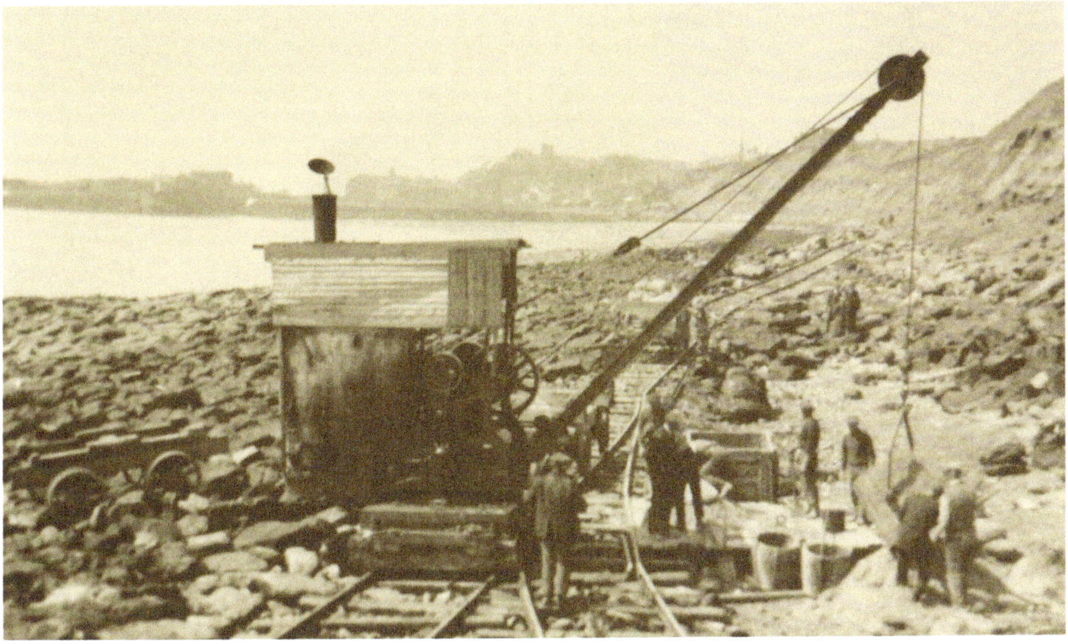

A rail track has been laid to run this steam crane along the rocks below the East Cliff in preparation to lay the sewer pipes in 1924.

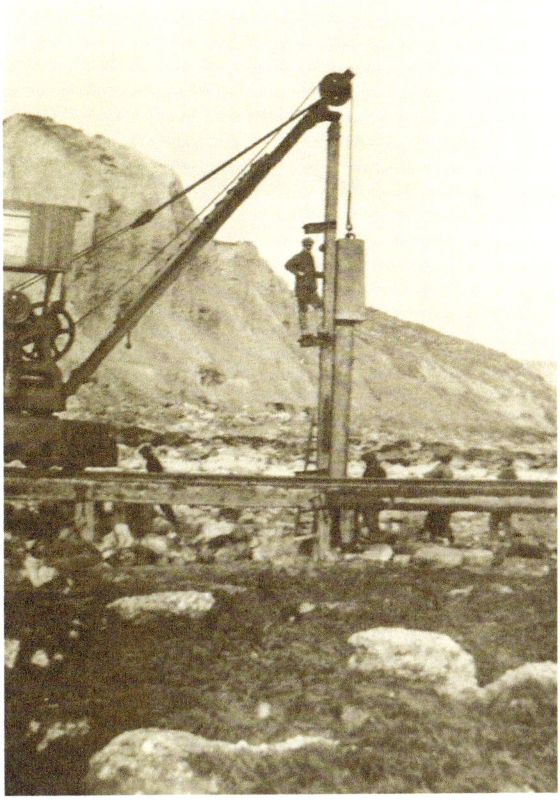

This steam crane is pile-driving at Copt Point, preparing for the laying of sewer pipes.

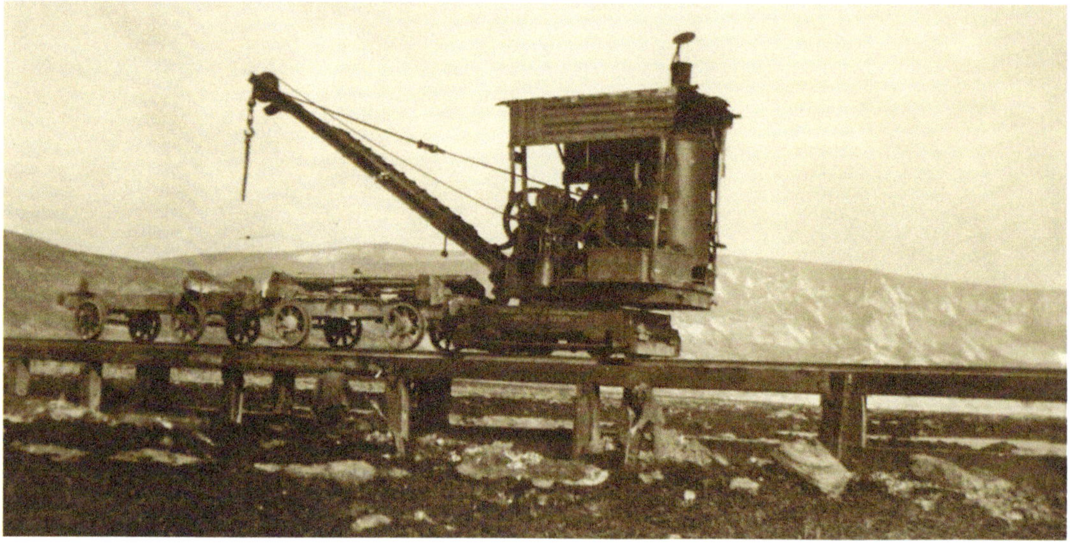

Sewer pipes being carried along the temporary rail track in 1925 at Copt Point.

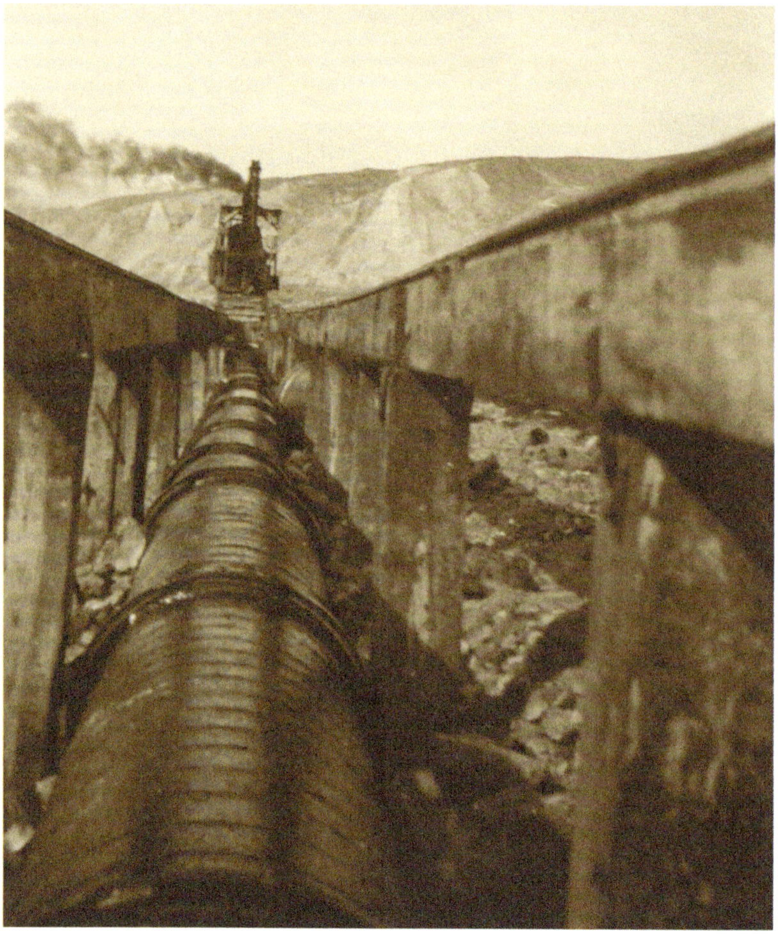

This view shows the new sewer pipes at Copt Point.

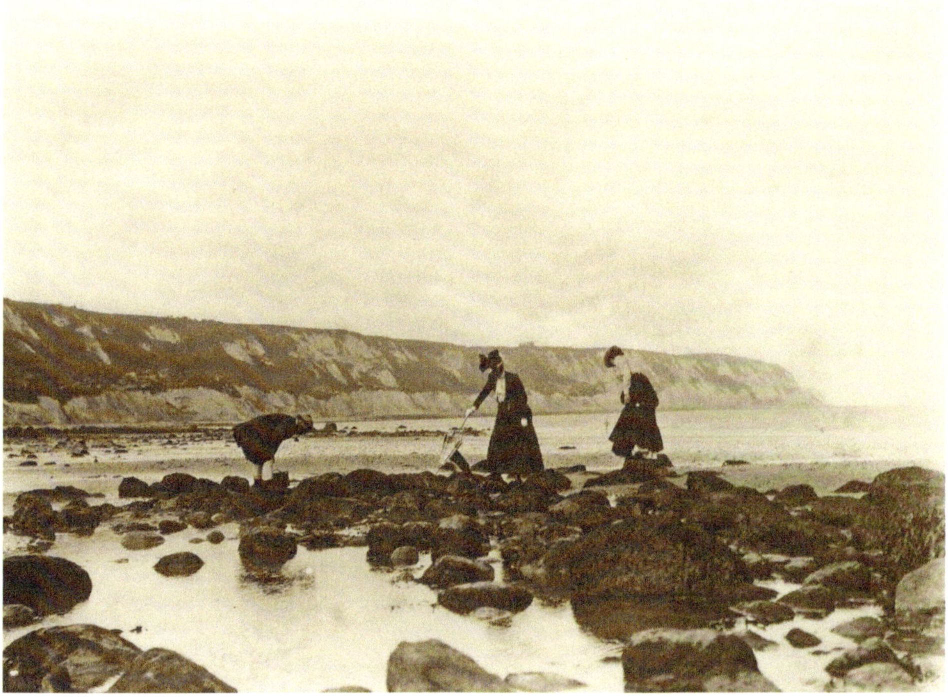

The ladies in their Victorian finery are seen here at Copt Point, foraging among the rocks.

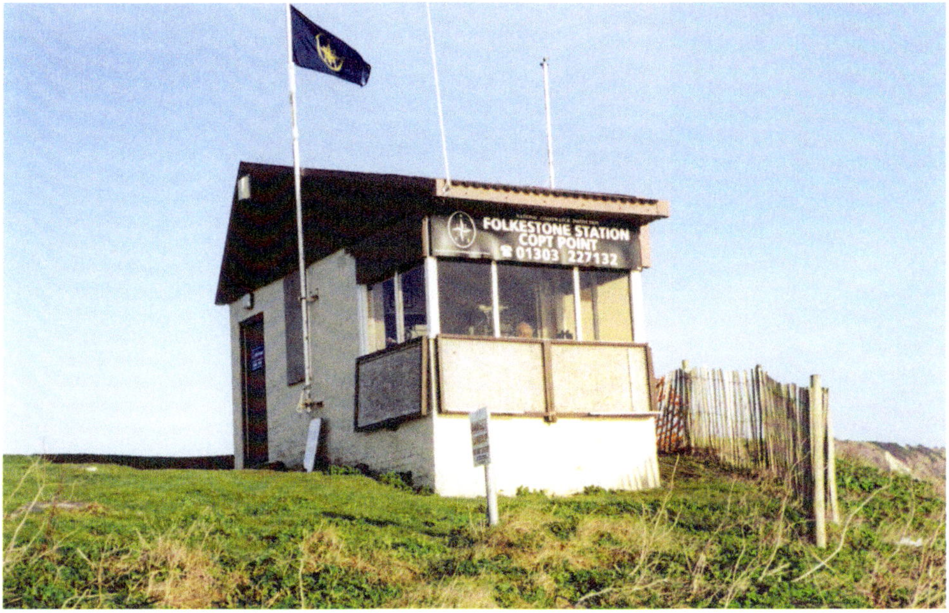


The National Coast watch Institution was formed in 1994 as a charitable organisation. This disused coastguard station at Copt Point became a coast watch station manned by volunteers recruited by John Mill-Baker. It was opened by weatherman Ron Lobeck in October 1998. Due to cliff erosion the station was abandoned in 2001; they now operate from a Second World War gun emplacement on East Cliff.

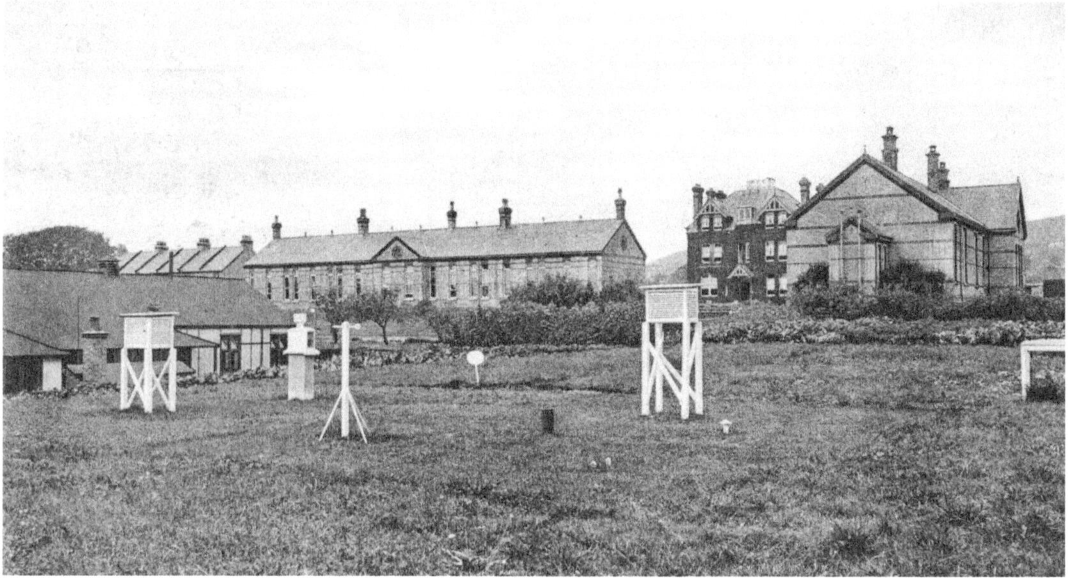

The Folkestone Borough Sanatorium was situated in Warren Road, East Cliff, in grounds having an area of 4 acres. The foundation stone was laid on 9 December 1877 by the Mayor Stephen Penfold. It opened with eight wards with fourteen beds. The buildings were bombed in the early hours of 6 July 1940 and subsequently demolished in June 1959. The site is now occupied by St Mary's school.

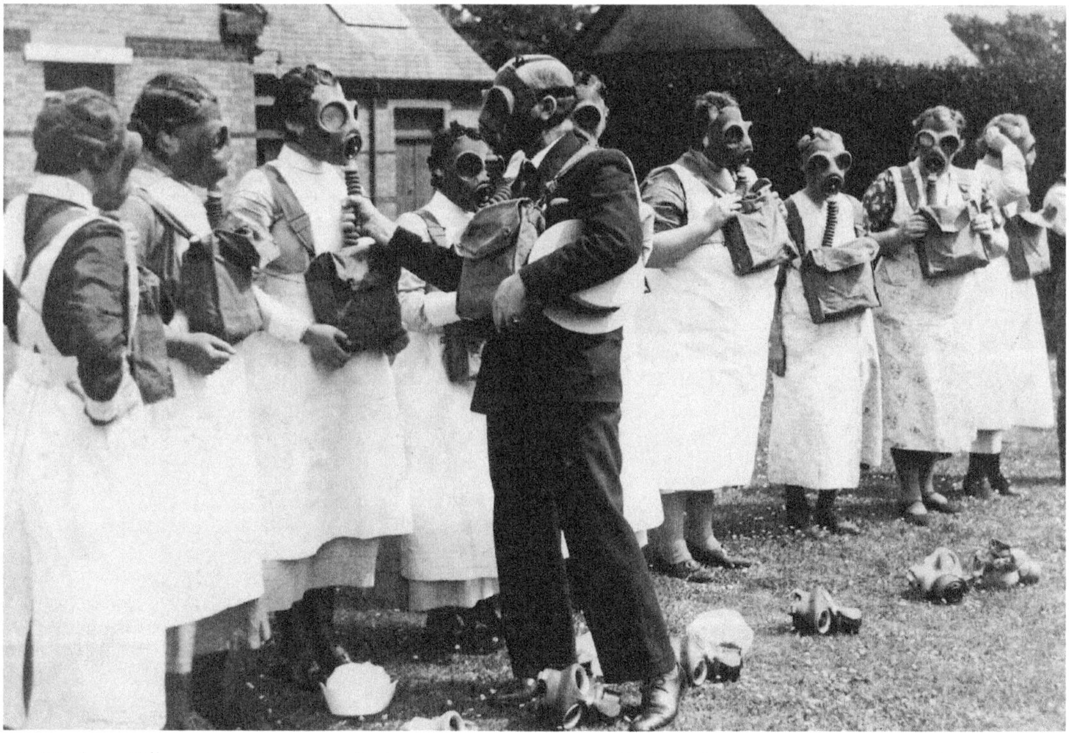

Mr Herbert Gill, sanitary inspector, is demonstrating to the staff of the Folkestone Sanatorium how to put on their gas masks in the 1940s.

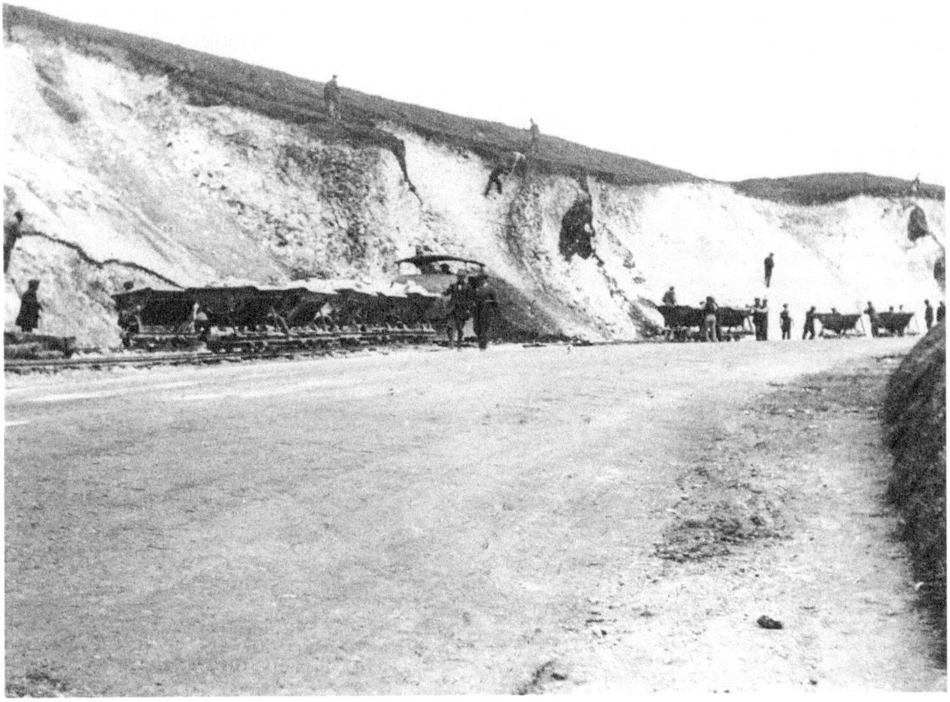

Work to widen the road at the top of Dover Hill is in progress, 17 May 1923.

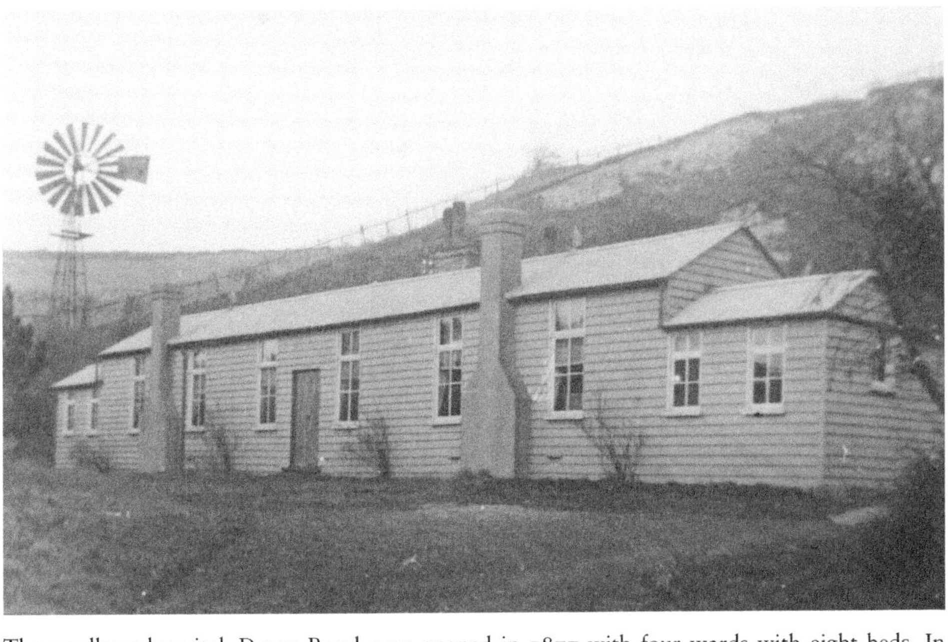

The smallpox hospital, Dover Road, was opened in 1877 with four wards with eight beds. In 1940 Austin Priestman was the medical officer and Henry and Mrs Marsh were caretakers, after which the buildings were taken over by the army during the Second World War and didn't open again afterwards.

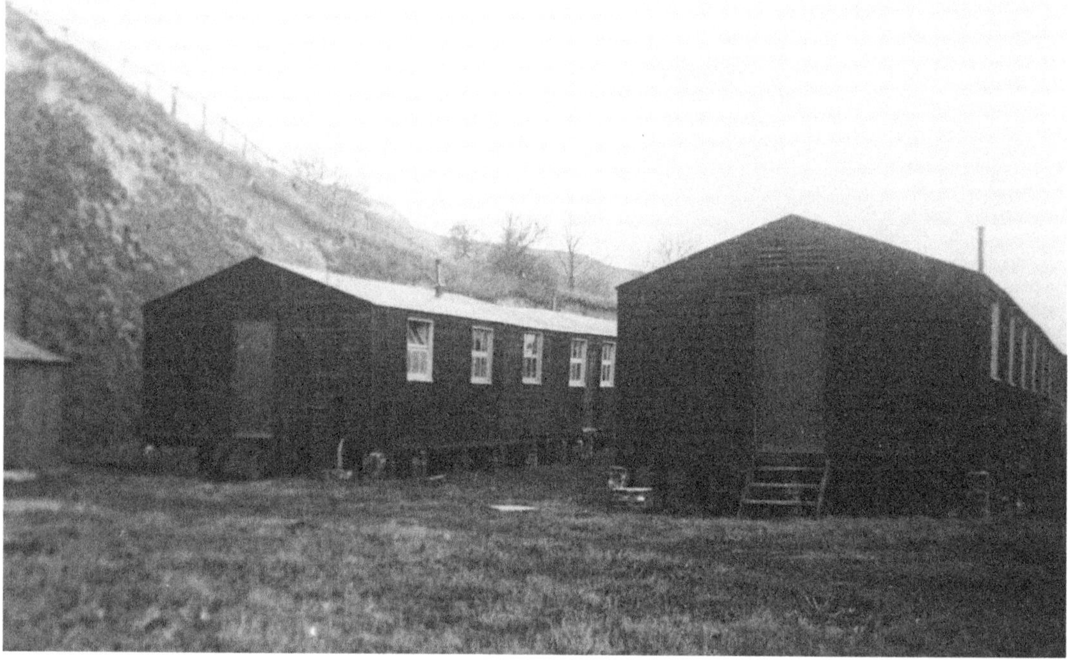

Another image of the smallpox hospital.

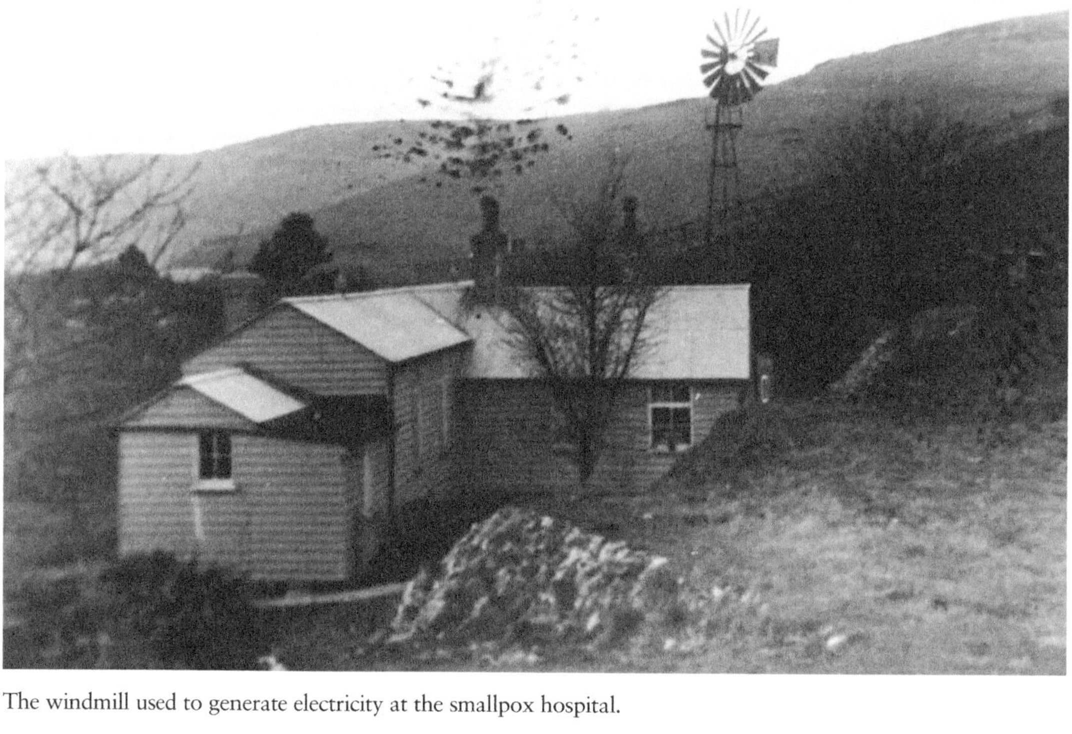

The windmill used to generate electricity at the smallpox hospital.

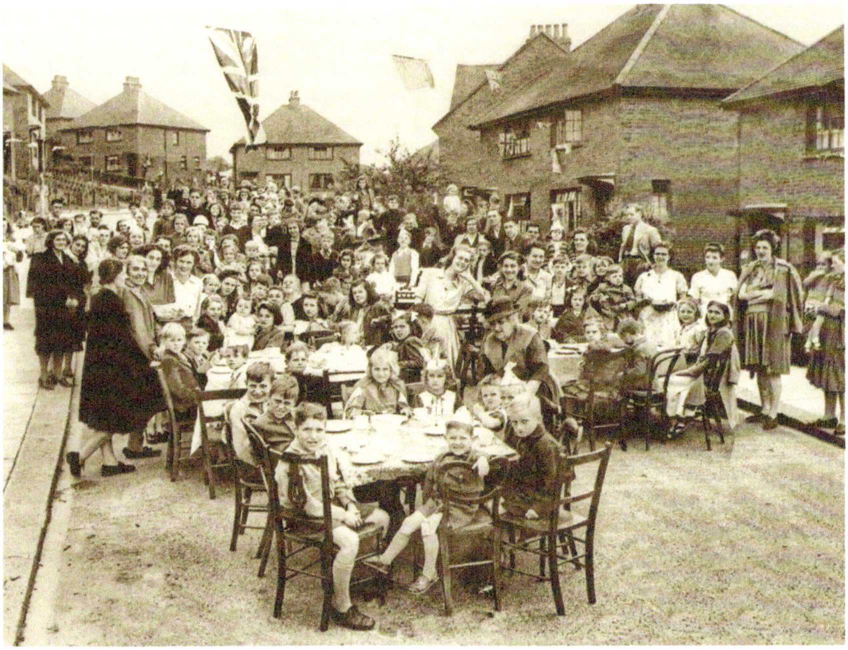

Victory in Europe, generally known as 'V-E Day', was on 8 May 1945. It was declared a public holiday and to celebrate street parties were held; this one is in Dallas Brett Crescent. Our family lived in Joyes Road, which was a semi-main road, so we could not have a party. My sister and I went to the one in Tyson road with our cousin Michael who lived at No. 10 Joyes Road on the corner of Tyson Road.

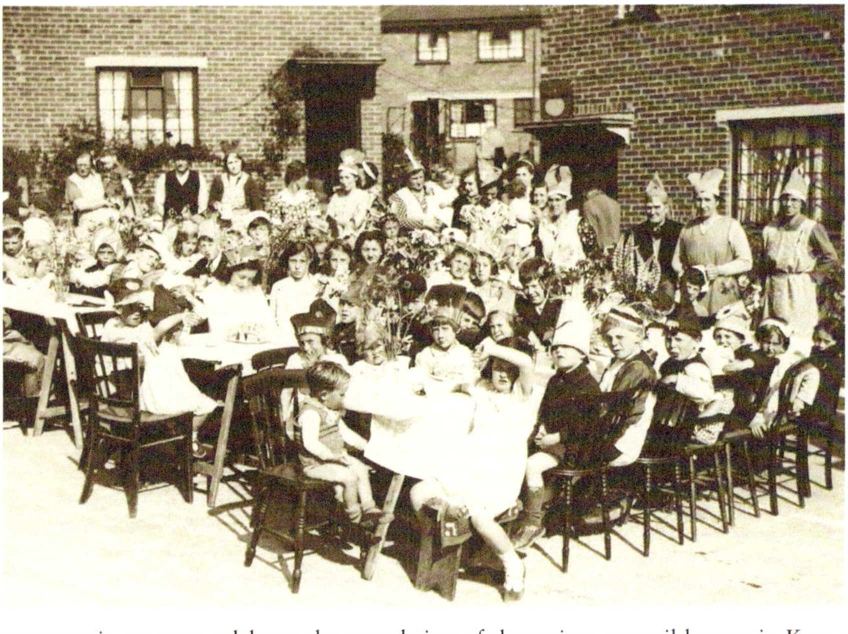

A street party in 1939 to celebrate the completion of the artisan council houses in Keys place. Some of the house was occupied by families who were rehoused from the houses in East Street, The Stade and Radnor Street, which were being demolished to make way for new council houses.

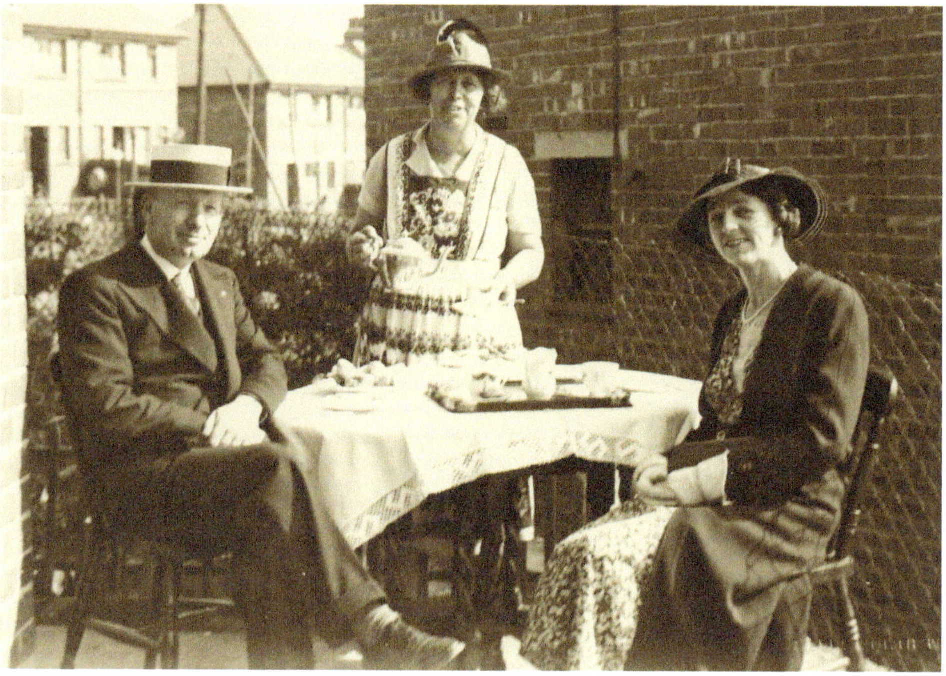

Mr Herbert Gill, Chief Sanitary Inspector, with his wife at a tea party for the opening of the new council houses at Keys Place in 1939.

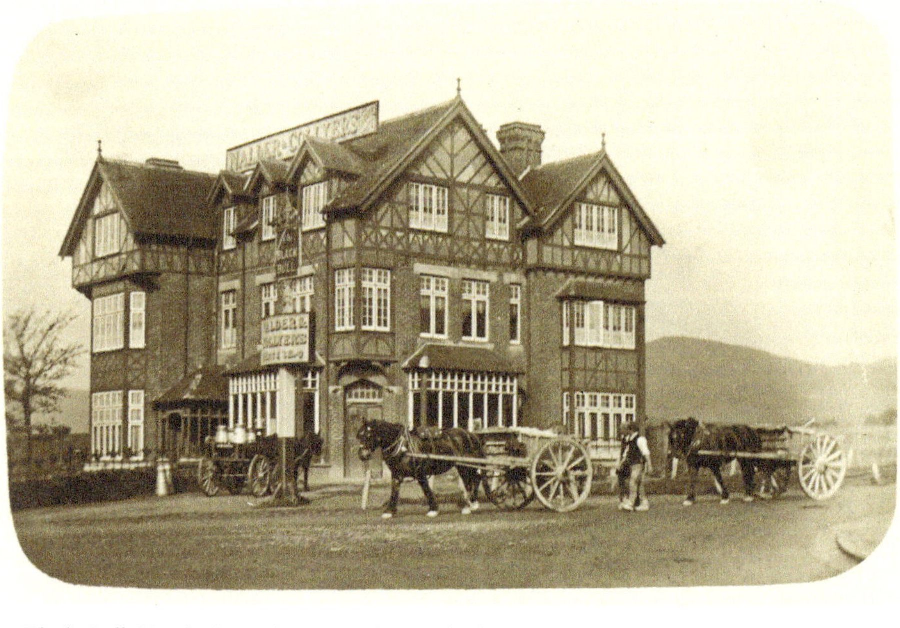

The Black Bull Hotel, Canterbury Road, was built in 1881 to replace an earlier pub of the same name. It is seen here in 1900. At the time of writing it is owned by Green King, who have refurbished the pub and restaurant under the 'Hungry Horse' brand, which opened in September 2013.

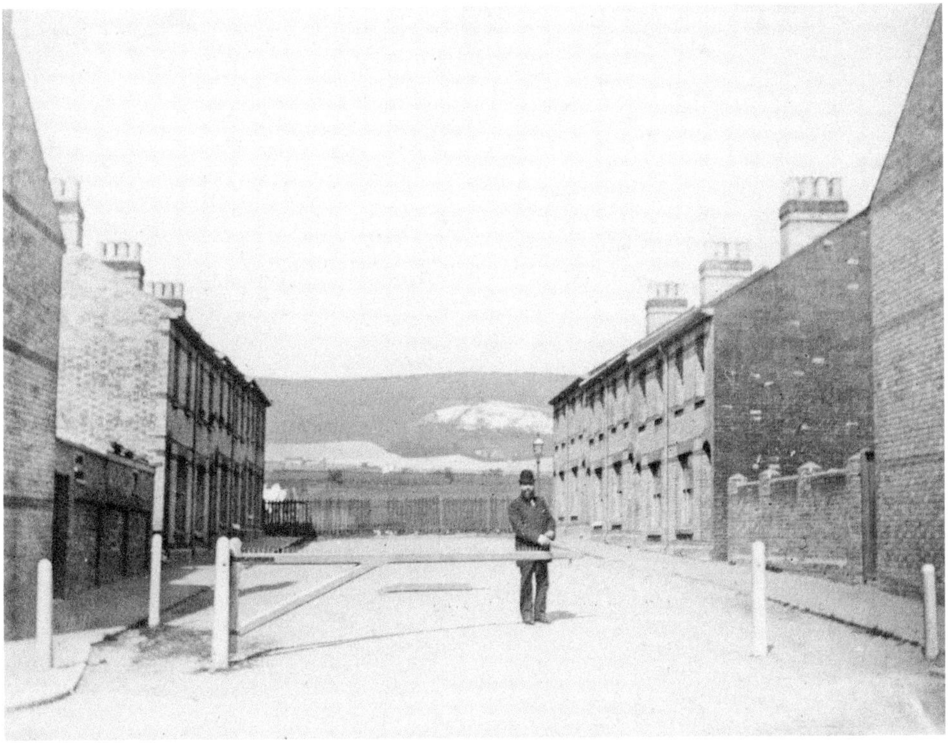

This is James Street built in 1878 seen here in 1893, a cul-de-sac, which would appear to be a private unmade road. It's interesting to note the lack of development in the back ground and the chalk pit on Canterbury Road. The road is much the same today and still unmade!

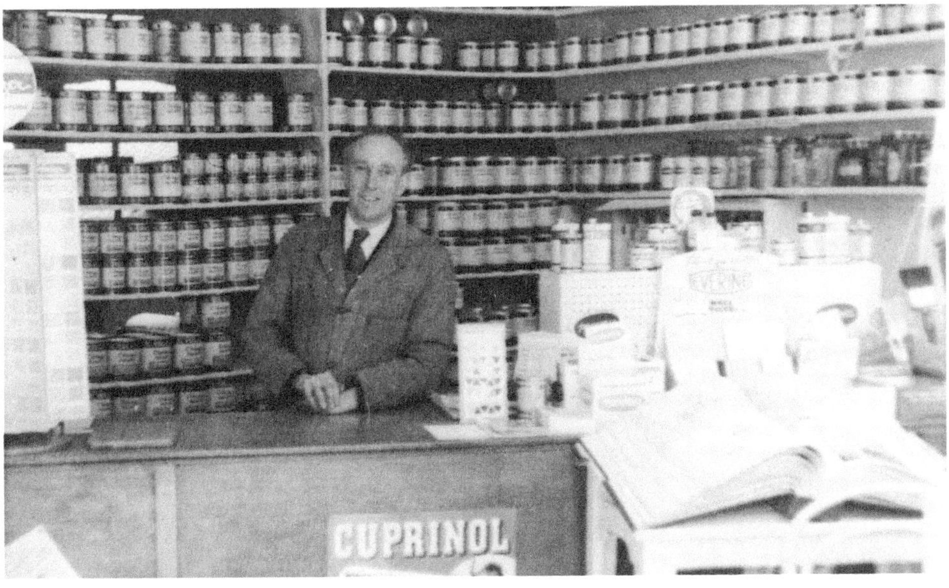


Clarke Bros, No. 1a Sidney Street. Wallpaper and decorator's merchants, they occupied these premises from between 1949/52 to 1968/70. Posing for the camera is employee Frederick Crouch, who lived at No. 6 Ship Street, Folkestone.

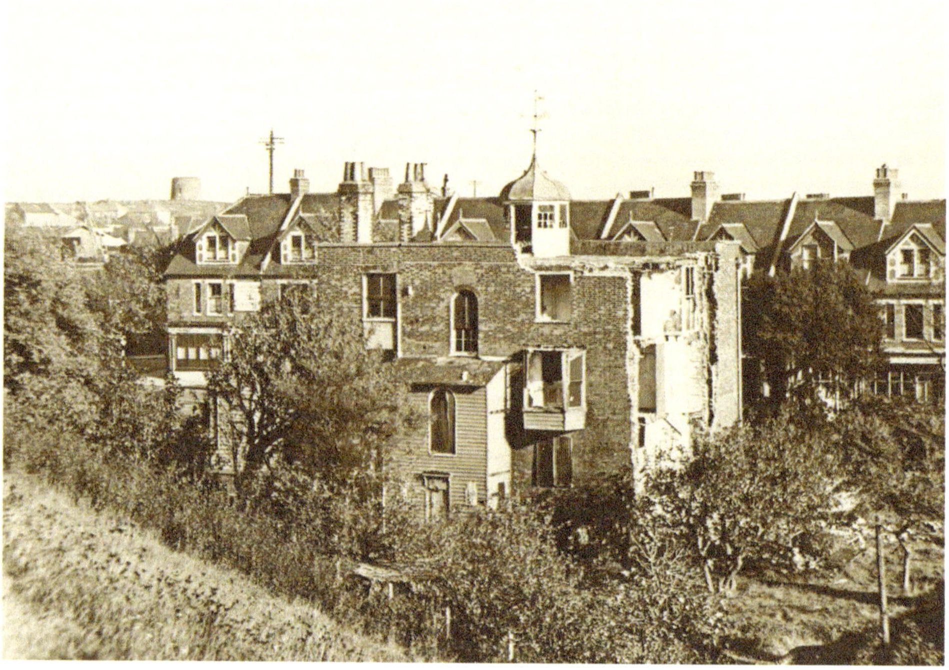

A view showing the back of Cupola House in Dover Road, occupied by Dr Robert Lindsay, and damage from an HE bomb, 6 October 1940.

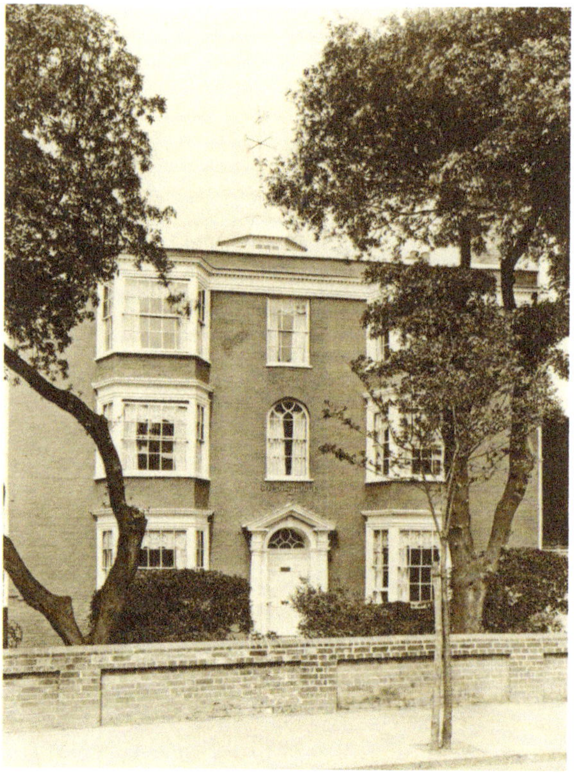

Cupola House was occupied by a mineral water manufacturer, Dr Billing, and Dr Lindsay. Dr Lindsay moved to Canterbury Road after the bomb damage. The building was demolished and Hall & Co., builder's merchants, built their offices on the site in 1952, calling it 'Cupola House'. These offices were demolished in 1970 and Pembroke Court was built on the site in 1972.

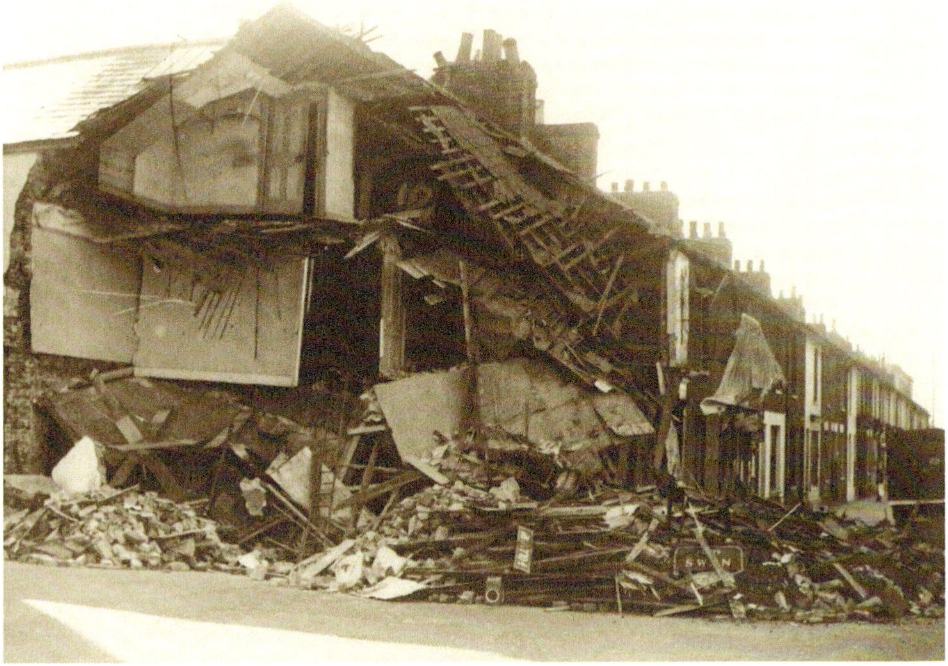

The Swan public house opened in 1847 was in Dover Road on the corner of Folly Road (now Rossendale Gardens). A HE bomb destroyed the property along with neighbouring houses on 6 October 1940. A large complex of flats named Rossendale Court now covers the site.

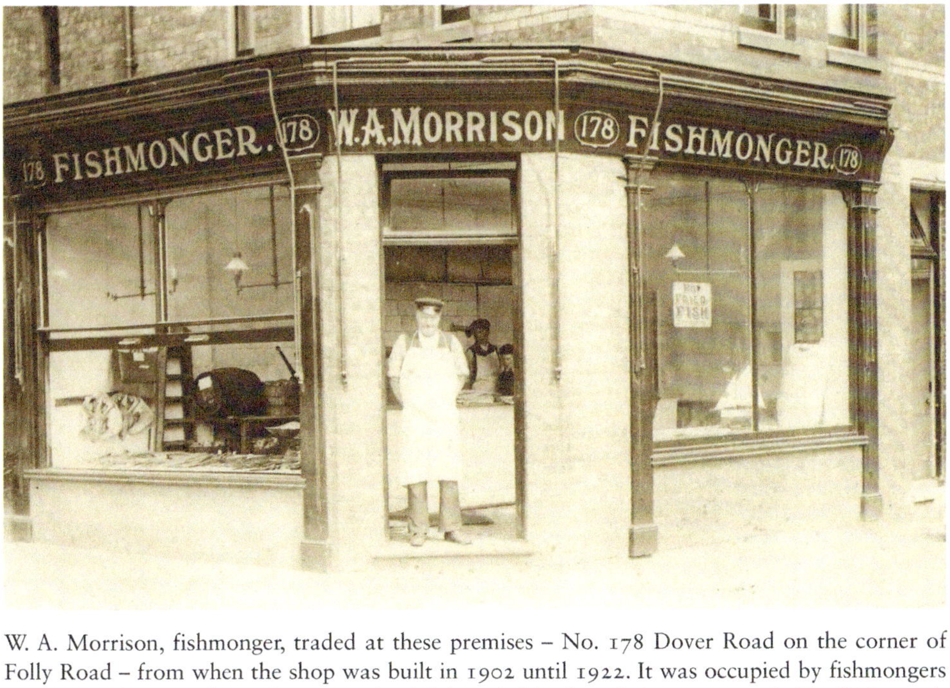


W. A. Morrison, fishmonger, traded at these premises – No. 178 Dover Road on the corner of Folly Road – from when the shop was built in 1902 until 1922. It was occupied by fishmongers until around 1945 when it became a fried fish and chip shop. It is now occupied by D'Agnostis Fish & Chips.

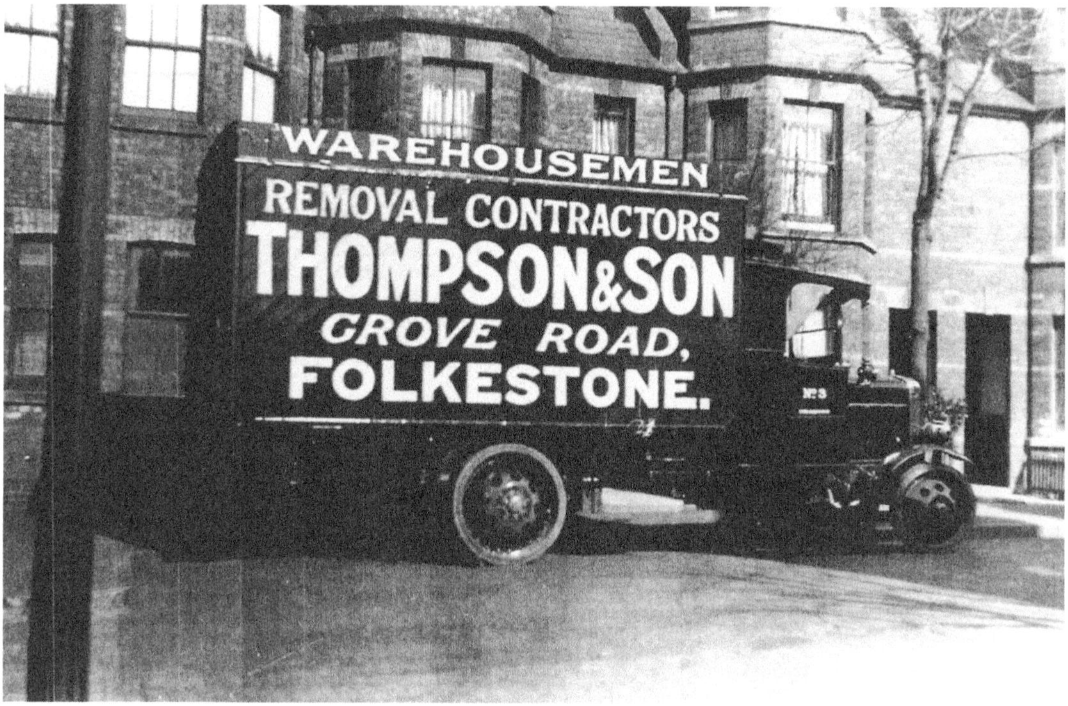


Thompson & Son removal contractors were in business from 1920 to sometime between 1940 and 1947. Their vehicle is seen here parked in Grove Road.

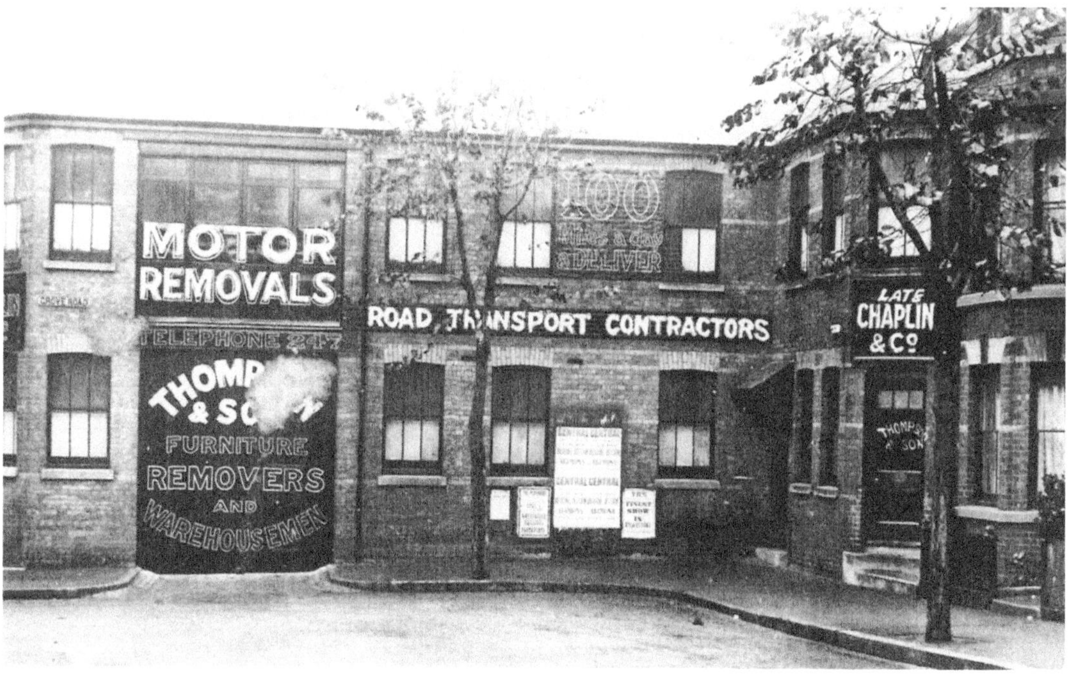


This is Thompson & Sons store in Grove Road. The premises have now been demolished to build three town houses.

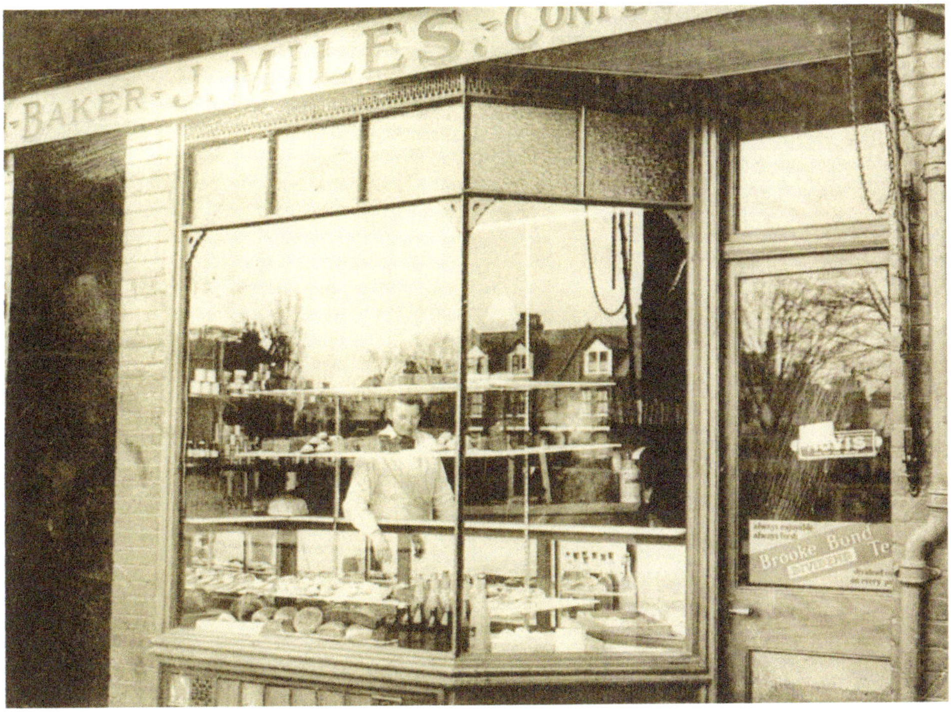


J. Miles, baker and confectioner, No. 143 Dover Road, traded at these premises from between 1940–47 and 1947–49. It has now been converted into a house.

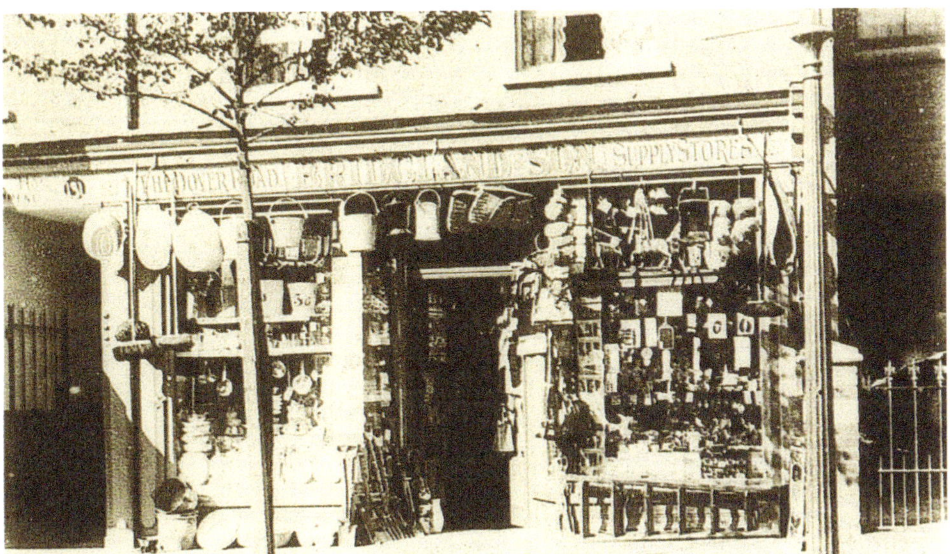


Bridgland J. & Son, china, glass dealers and newsagents, No. 133 Dover Road, traded here from 1885 to 1930. St John's were there from 1931 to 2008 when they sold the building, and it has now been converted into flats.

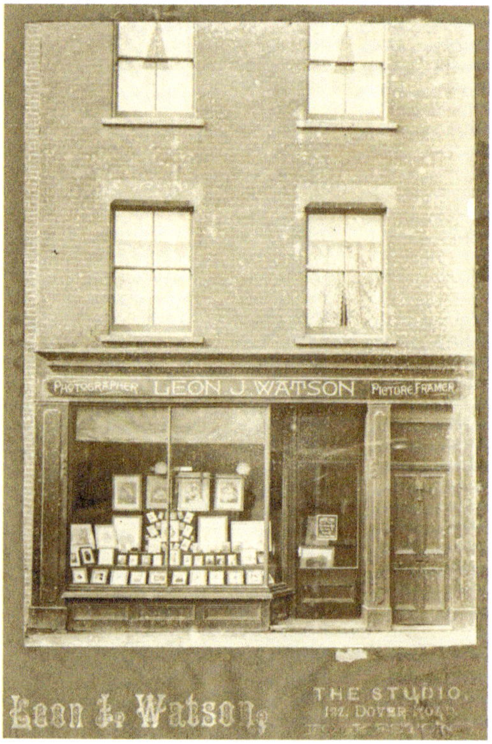


Leon Watson, photographer, occupied this shop, No. 127 Dover Road, from 1901 to 1905. It is now Lacies.com – lingerie and footwear.

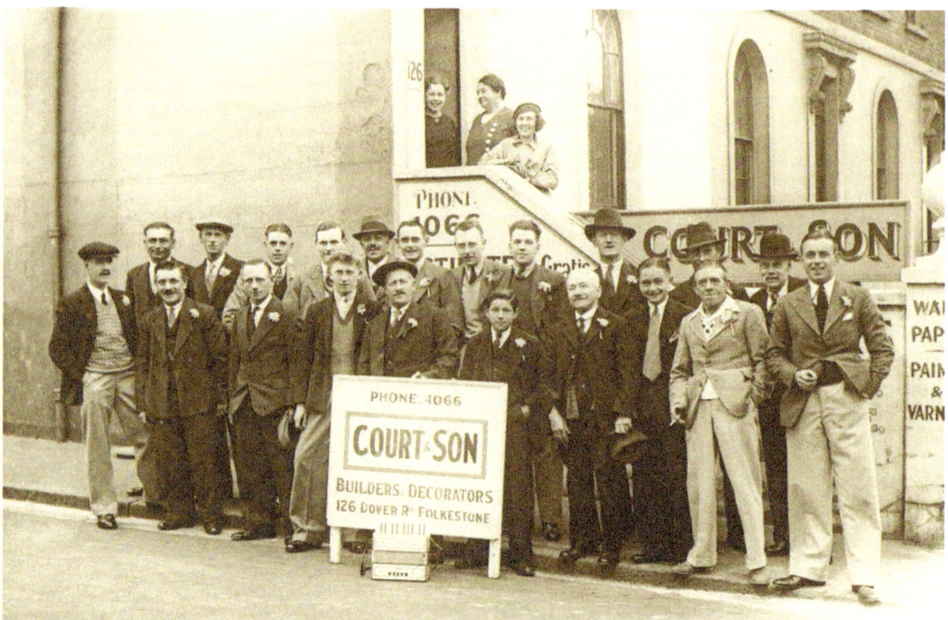


Arthur Henry Court, builder and contractor, No. 126 Dover Road, on the corner of Martello Road. This house was his office and his works were in Martello Road from 1928 to sometime between 1949 and 1952. The staff are seen here posing for the camera before leaving on a firms outing.

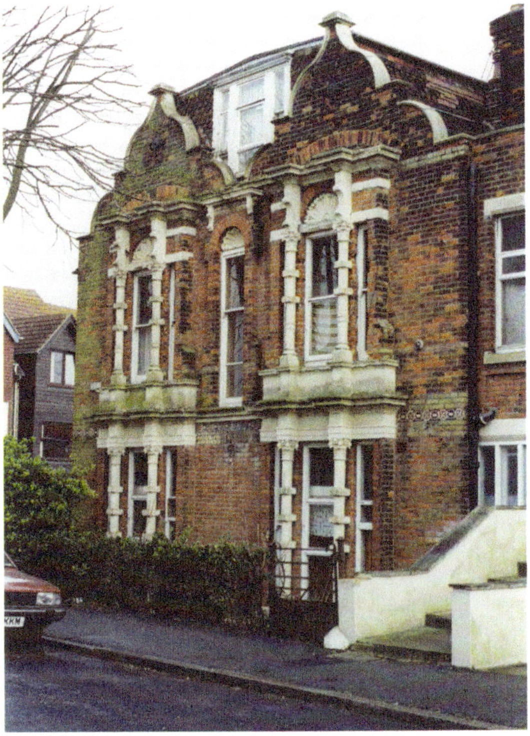

This highly decorated Victorian villa, No. 10 Lennard Road, was demolished in 2000 by Ashtone Property Services, Cherry Garden Lane, to build a four-storey block of flats.

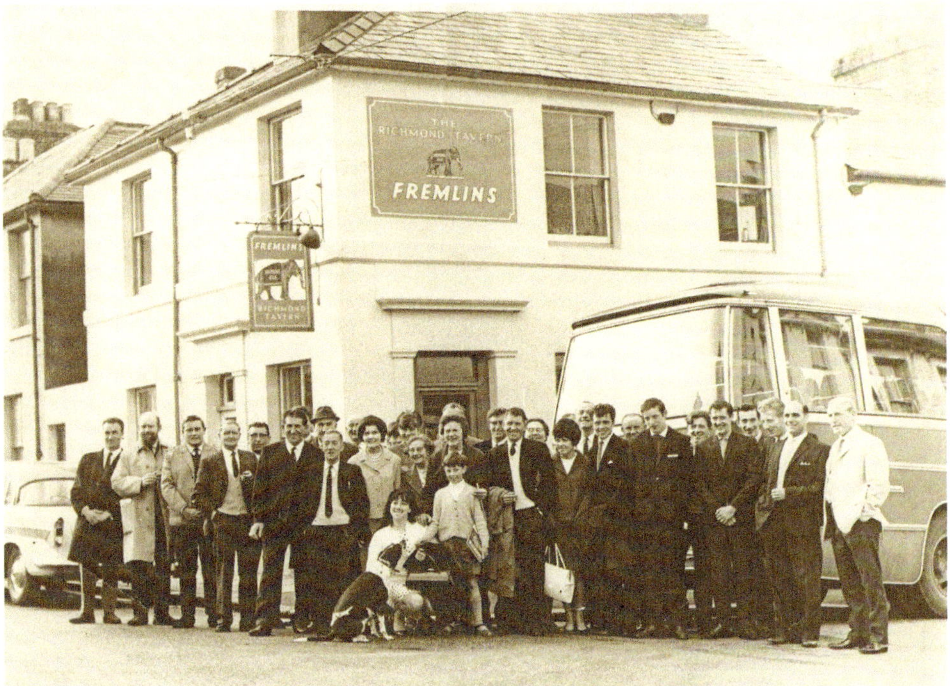


An outing from the Richmond Tavern, Margaret Street – formerly Richmond Street – in the 1960s. It was taken over by Shepherd Neame in 1972, but has now been converted into flats.

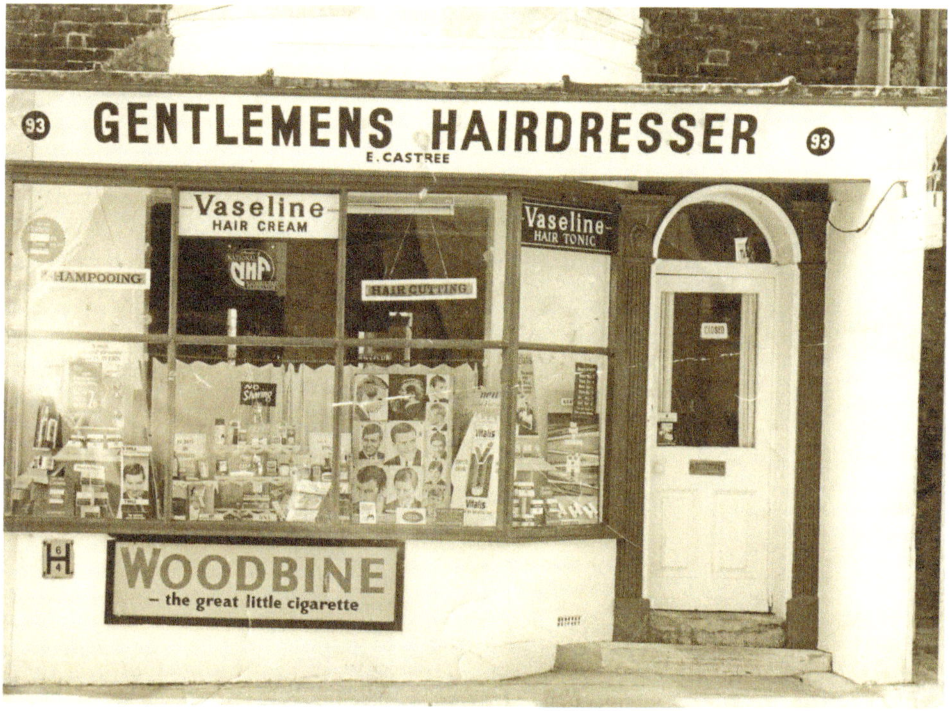


Ernest Castree, Gentlemen's Hairdresser, No. 93 Dover Street (Harbour Way), was in business here from around 1948 until he retired, after which the shop was occupied by Russell & Wheeler, electrical contractors. The shop was converted into living accommodation in 2013.

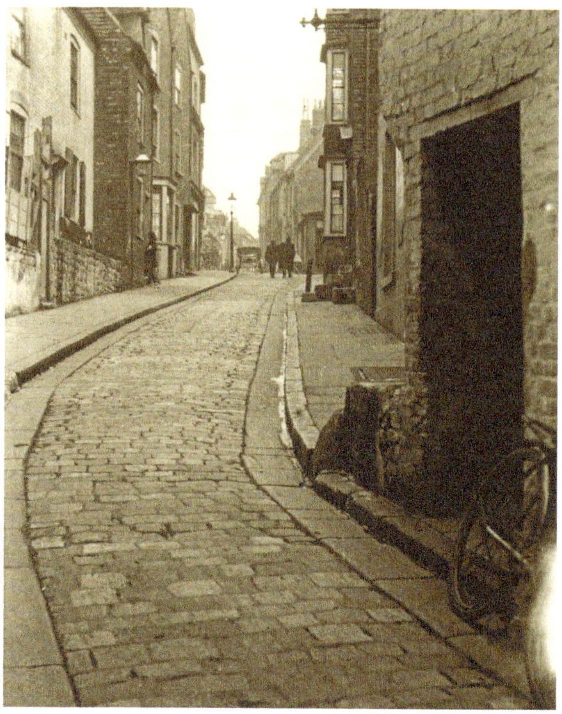

A view from the middle of Dover Street looking towards Dover Road in May 1923. The street was renamed Harbour Way in 1955 after these houses had been demolished to widen the road and build new council houses. The two people are by the junction with Saffron's Place where there are two old houses called 'Rosemary Cottages'.

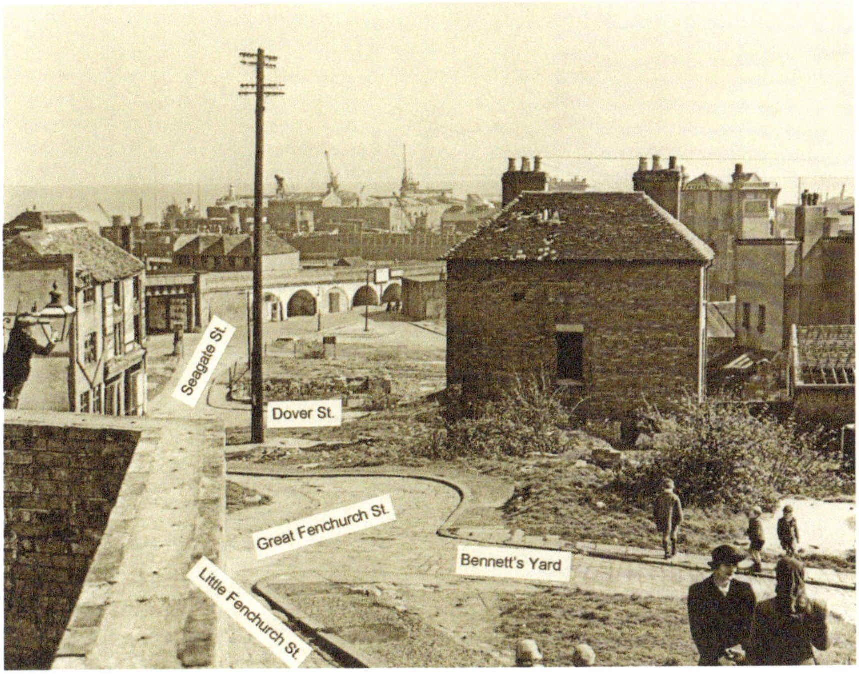


This photograph shows the layout of the roads *c.* 1950 after damage sustained during the Second World War. The names of all these roads have now gone!

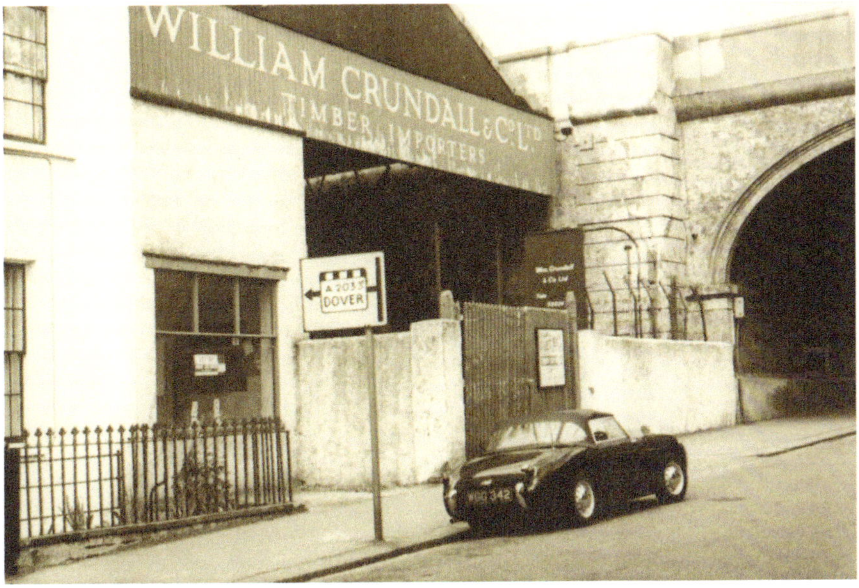


Tram Road. The building in this yard next to Radnor Bridge was occupied by WHSmith's Ice Company, listed in Kelly's Kent Directory for 1887. It was used as a garage from 1928, Dixson's builder's yard from *c.* 1947, and then George Stone builder's yard and workshop from *c.* 1951 to 1958. It was then taken over by William Crundall & Co. Ltd, timber merchants, followed by South Coast Engineers in 1973. The site is now occupied by a block of flats called 'East Cliff Heights'.

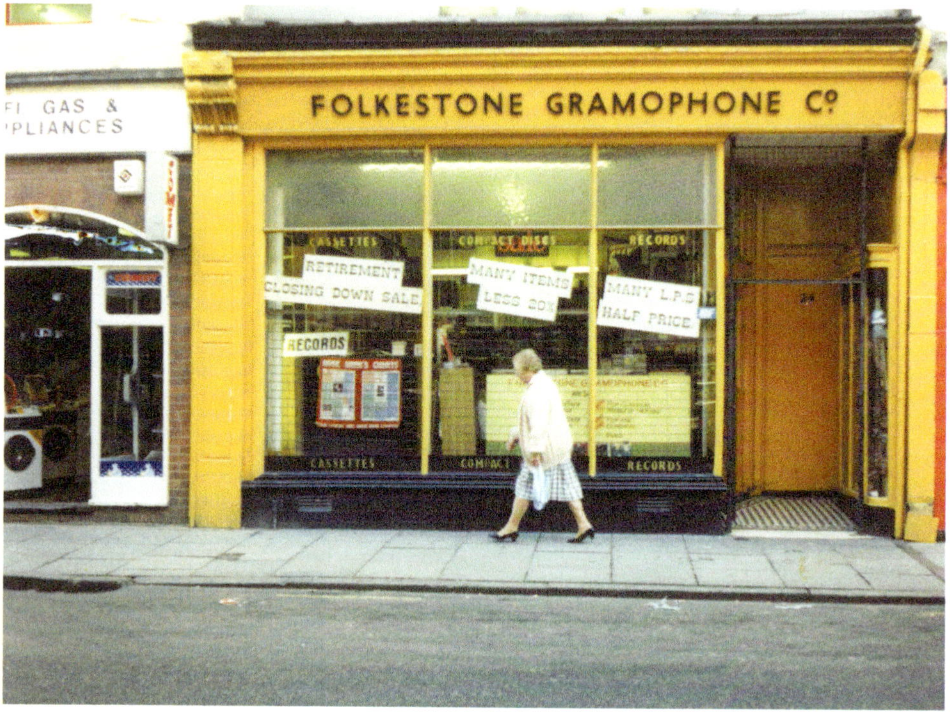


Folkestone Gramophone Co. at No. 24 Tontine Street closing down sale 14 November 1988. Formerly B. V. Chard gramophone dealers, the business changed hands sometime between 1940 and 1947.

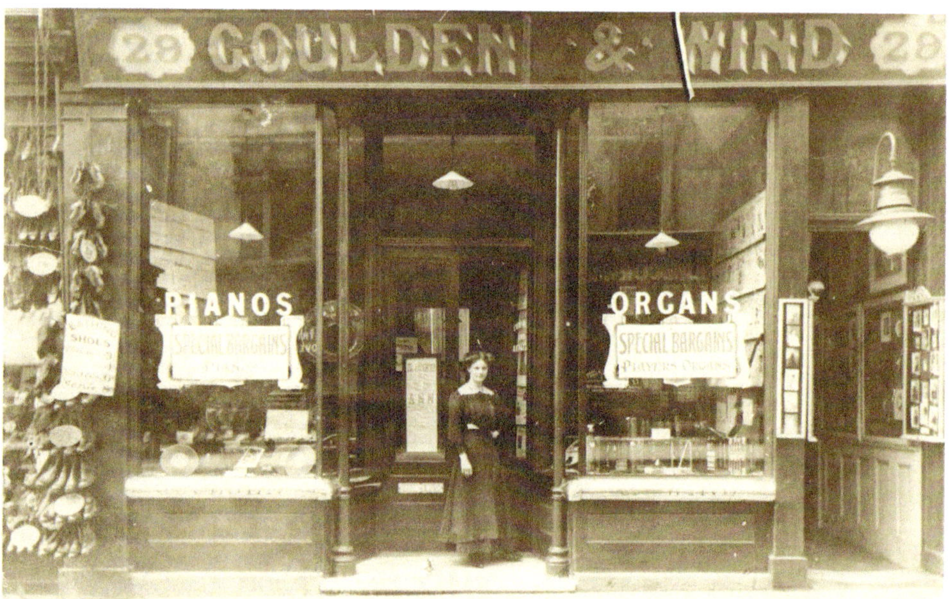


Goulden & Wind, music sellers, No. 29 Tontine Street, traded from these premises from 1893 to 1962/3. It was formerly Marsh's music warehouse. Goulden & Wind also had shops at Dover, Canterbury, Ashford, Maidstone and Tunbridge Wells.

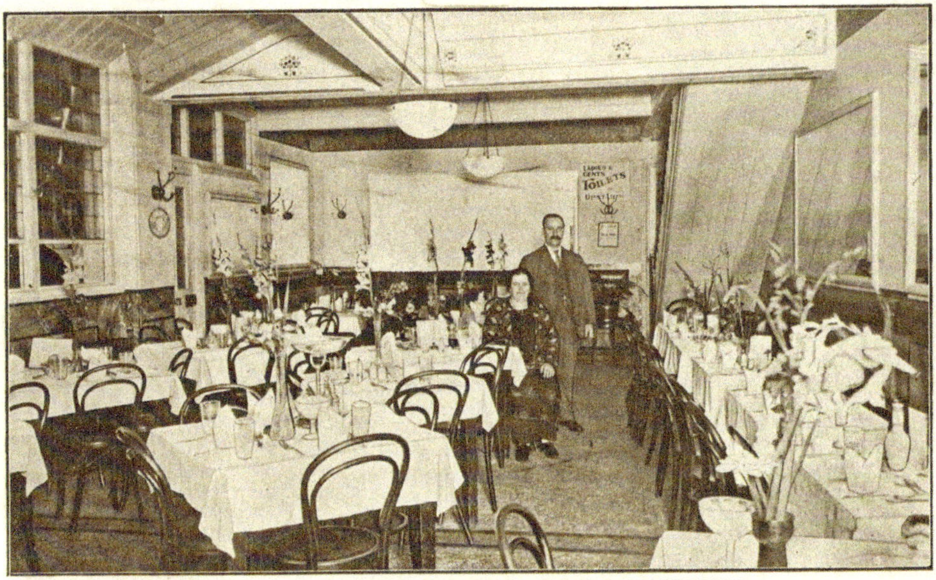

ROSSI'S RESTAURANT, 54, TONTINE STREET, FOLKESTONE.

The interior of Rossi's restaurant at No. 54 Tontine Street with Mr and Mrs Rossi posing for the camera. They started their business at this shop in 1909, where they continued until 1958. The premises are now the Curry House Restaurant.

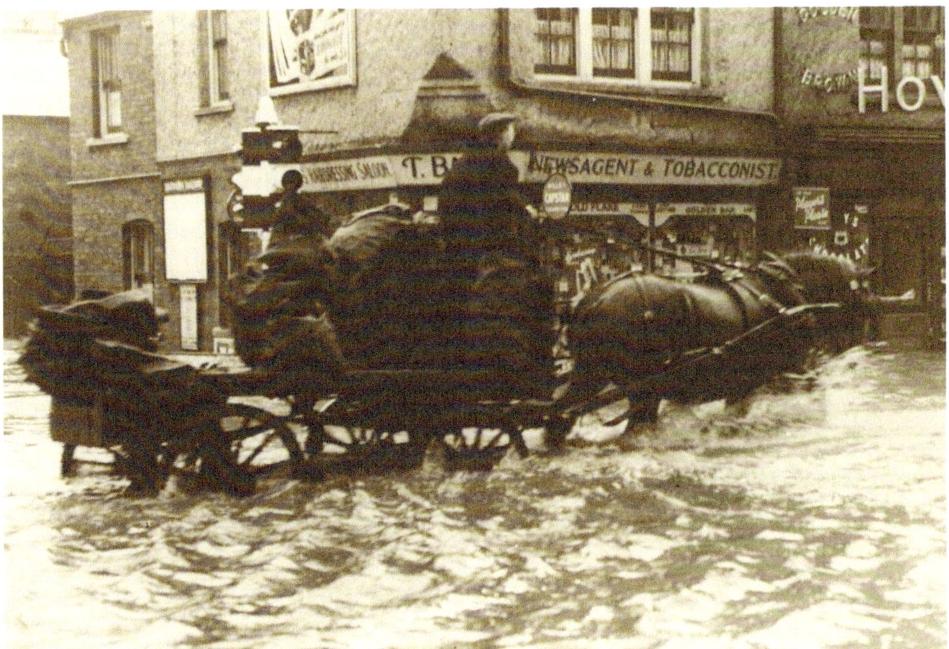


Black Bull Road and Foord Road have always suffered with flooding. This flood happened on 31 October 1939. The horse-drawn coal cart is opposite Mr T. Bates, newsagent and tobacconist shop, which was on the corner of Bradstone Avenue. The shop has now been converted into living accommodation.

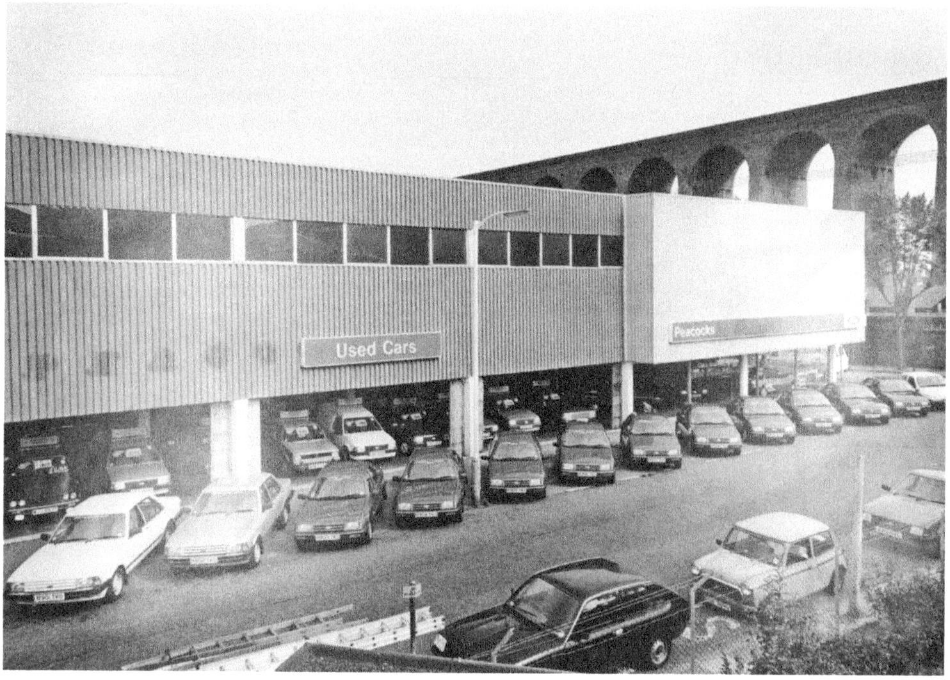


Peacocks, main Ford dealers, No. 104 Foord Road, occupied these premises from 1928 to 1988 when they were taken over by Doves, who were then taken over by Invicta motors. They closed this branch in December 2004. The premises are now occupied by Red Devil Storage Depot.

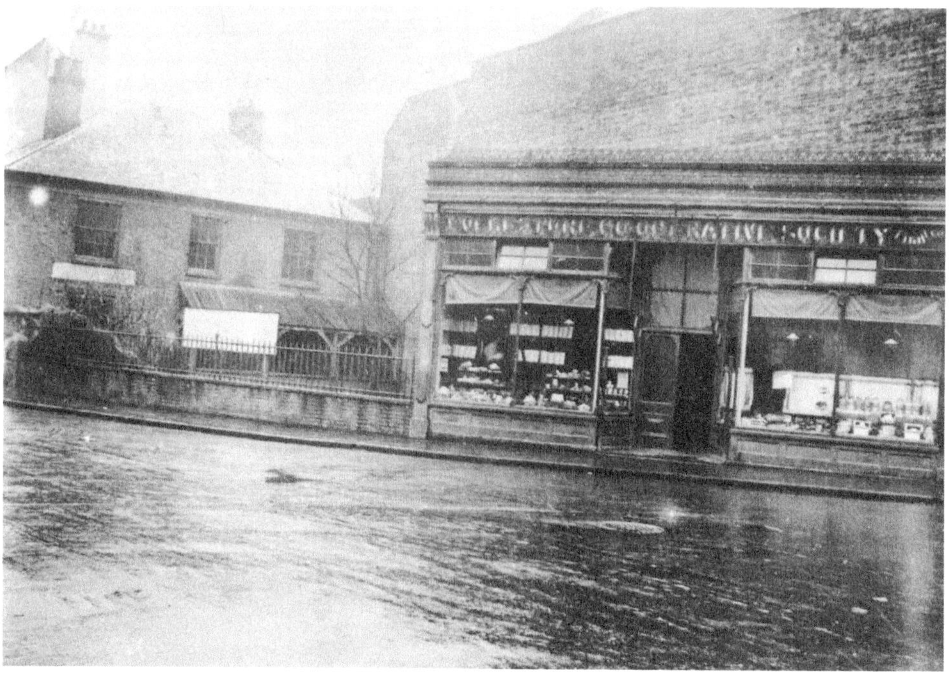

On the left-hand side can be seen the back of Mr Couch's shop in Tontine Street, while on the right is the Co-operative Society's first shop (1892) at No. 34 Dover Road.

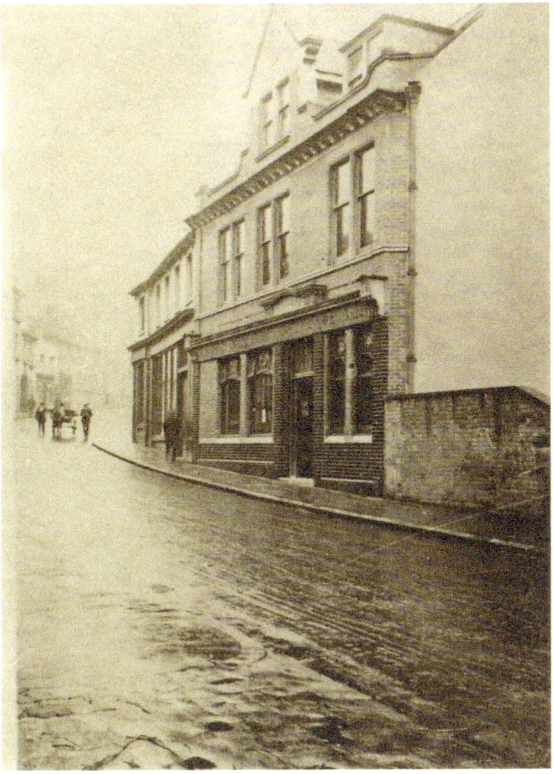

In around 1915, the Co-op built these premises at No. 34 Dover Road. A new facade was built on all these shops in 1923.

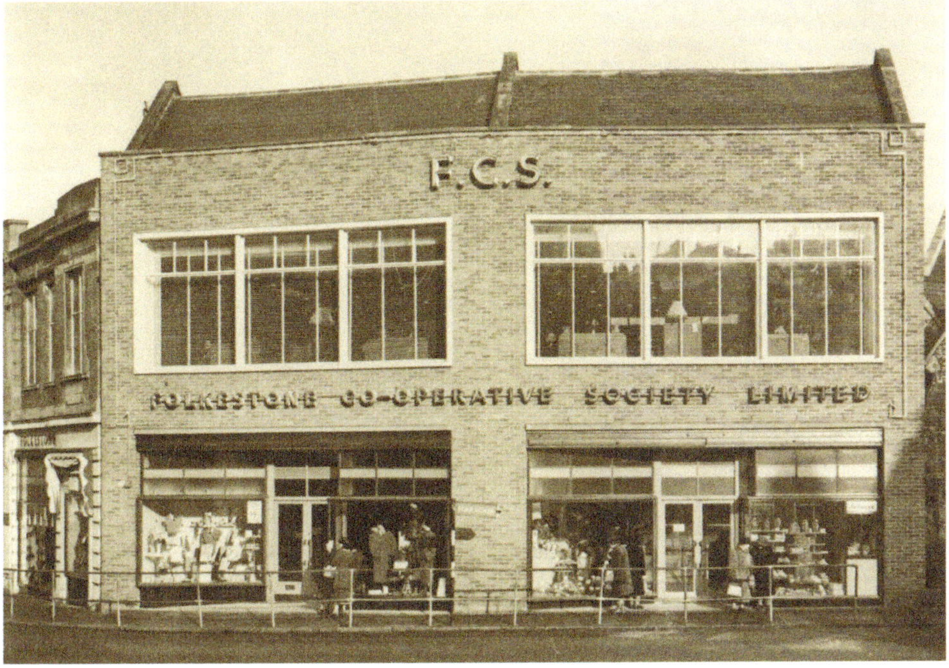


F.C.S, No. 28 Dover Road, which had a new facade built after the Second World War. The Co-op occupied Nos 28–34 Dover Road until they closed this branch in 1972.

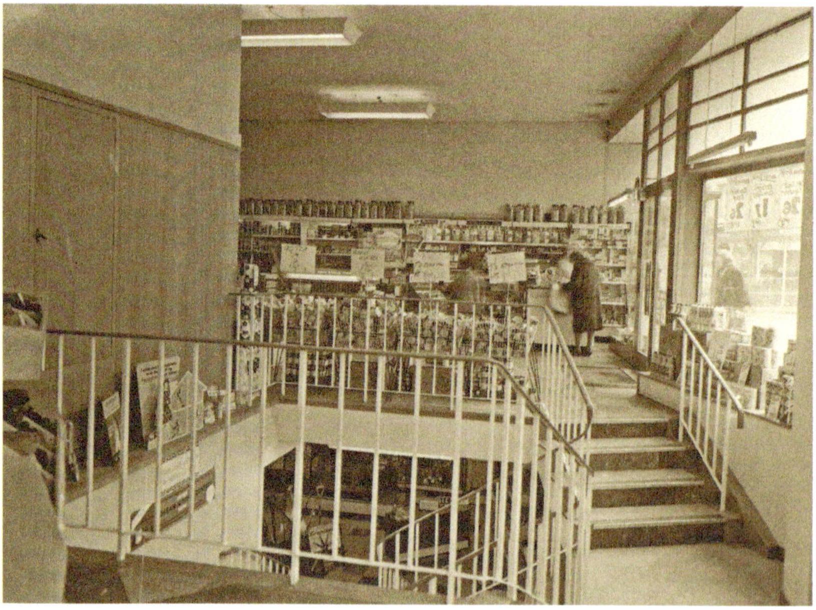

The interior of the Co-op grocery department on the first floor, Dover Road.

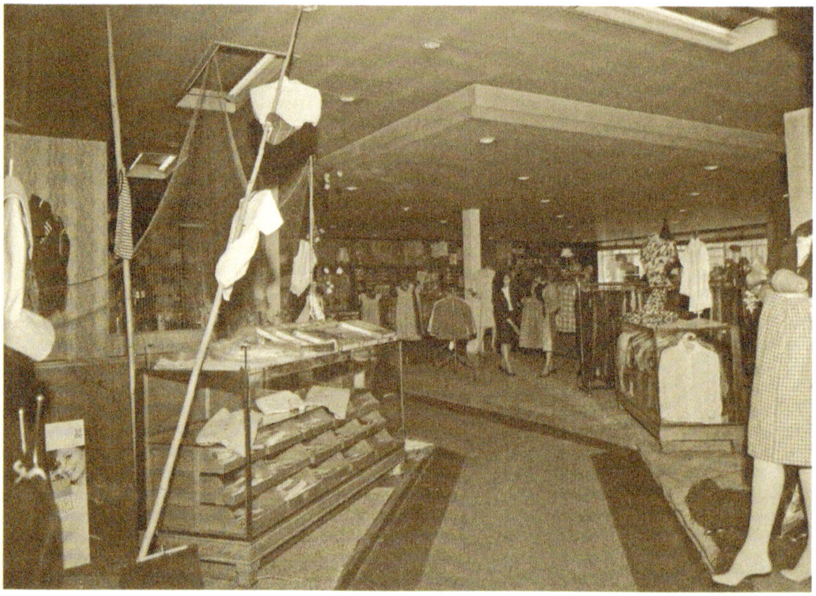

The interior of the Co-op clothing department. This branch of the Co-op at Nos 28–34 Dover Road closed in 1972 and Crouch plumbers and hot water fitters at Nos 81–85 Tontine Street also closed down in 1972. Nos 81–85 Tontine Street became Pains nightclub, while Nos 28–34 Tontine Street (at a later date) became Bar Luxor and Deluxe Bingo Hall. On 11 July 2013 the whole site was put up for auction. The *Folkestone Express* reported on 1 August 2013 that the properties had been sold and could be turned into flats or housing, with parking spaces. The property changed ownership to Roger de Haan Charitable Trust who got planning permission to demolish the buildings and build a multistorey Sports Park. At the time of writing the Sports Park was under construction and should be open in 2017.

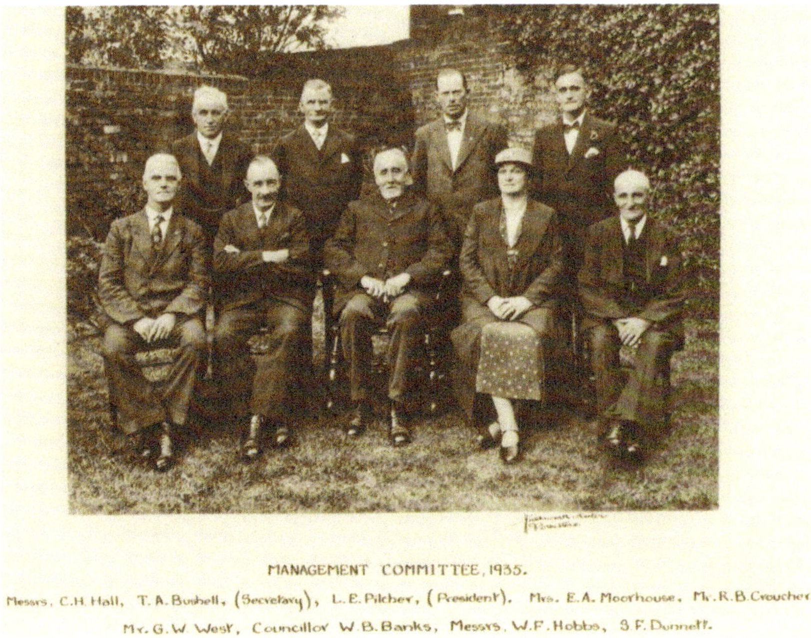


The management committee in 1935 for the Co-op were: Messrs, C. H. Hall, T. A. Bushell, (secretary), L. E. Pilcher (President), Mrs E. A. Moorhouse, Mr R. B. Croucher, Mr G. W. West, Councillor W. B. Banks, Messrs, W. F. Hobbs and S. F. Dunnett.

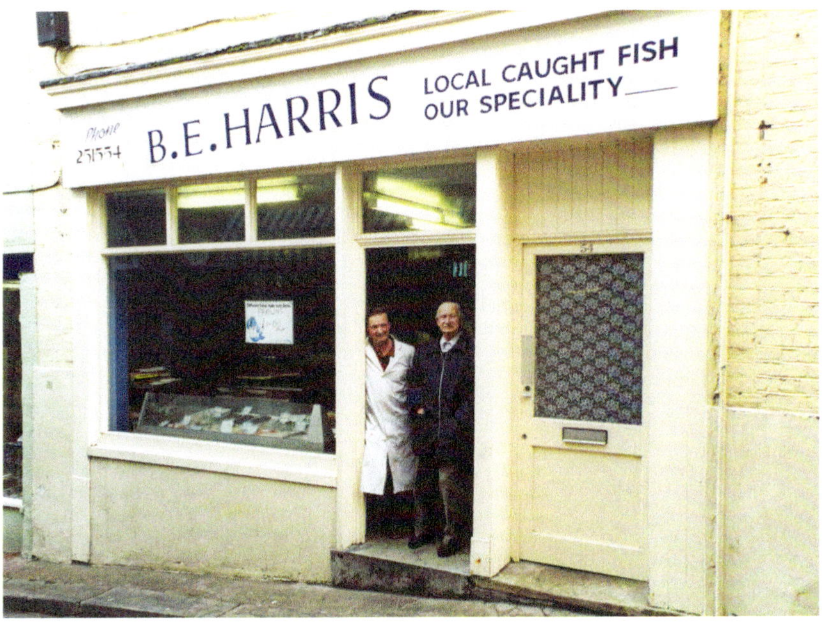


Mr Ernest Harris standing in the doorway with his son, Brian, started as a fish-hawker, pushing his barrow round the streets selling fish. After he came out of the Navy he took a stall in Fryatt Ward's indoor market No. 15 Tontine Street, which went through to No. 67 High Street. Mr Harris and Mr Holloway opened this shop, No. 54 High Street, in 1950. Ernie's son, Brian, came into the business in 1963; the business closed on 1 November 2000 due to the decline in trade.

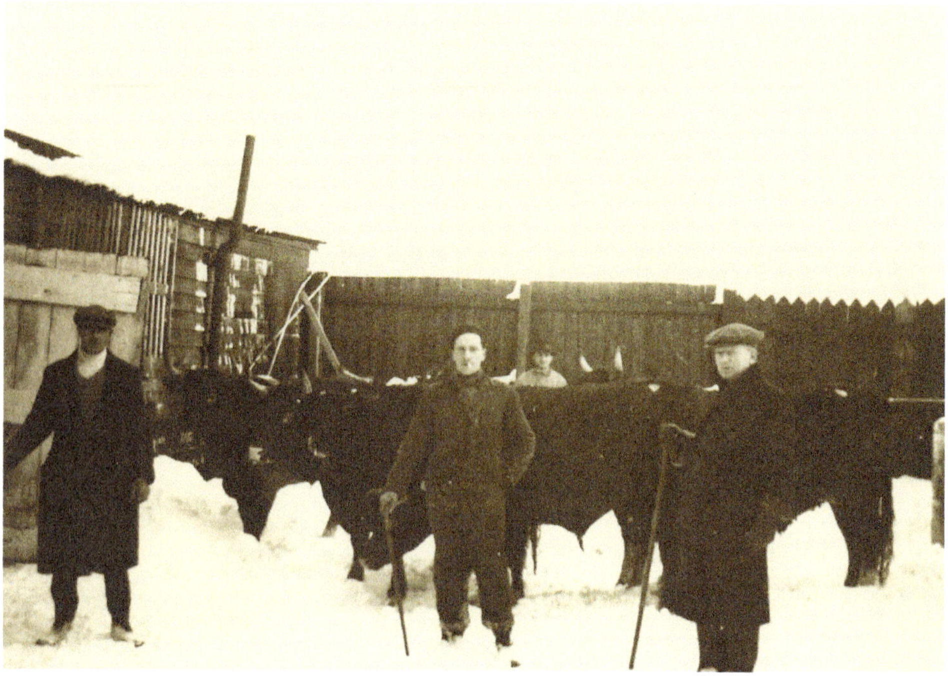

An abattoir in Payer's Park belonging to Mr William Worsell, butcher at No. 3 High Street. From left to right are: G. Harris, J. Price and Herbert Gill, Chief Sanitary Inspector. The photograph was taken in January 1940.

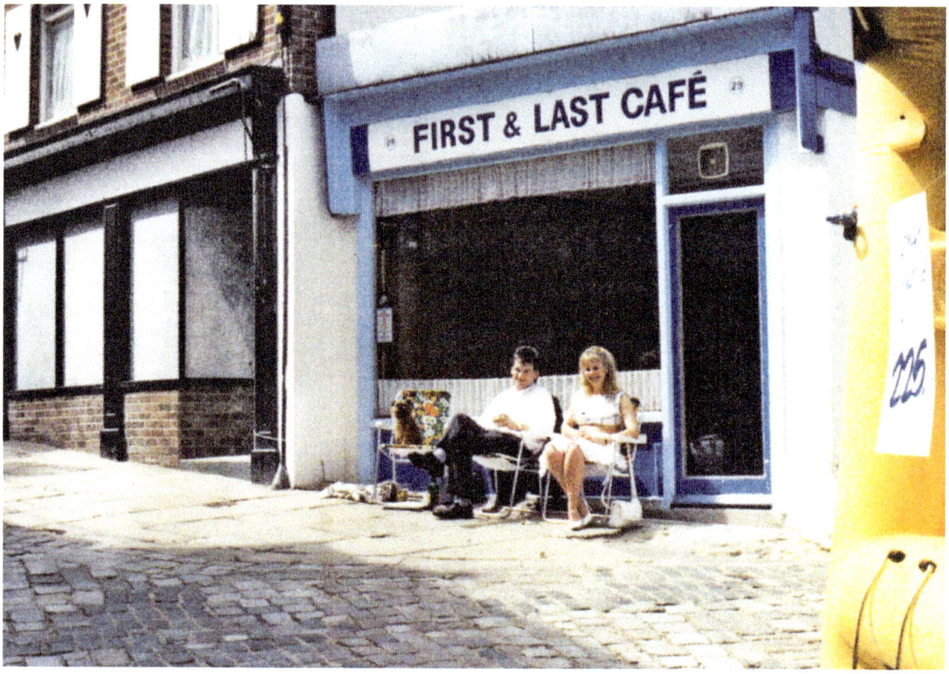


The First and Last Café, No. 29 The Old High Street (on the corner of the access to Payer's Park), the photograph was taken in around 1990 and the building was demolished in 2002.

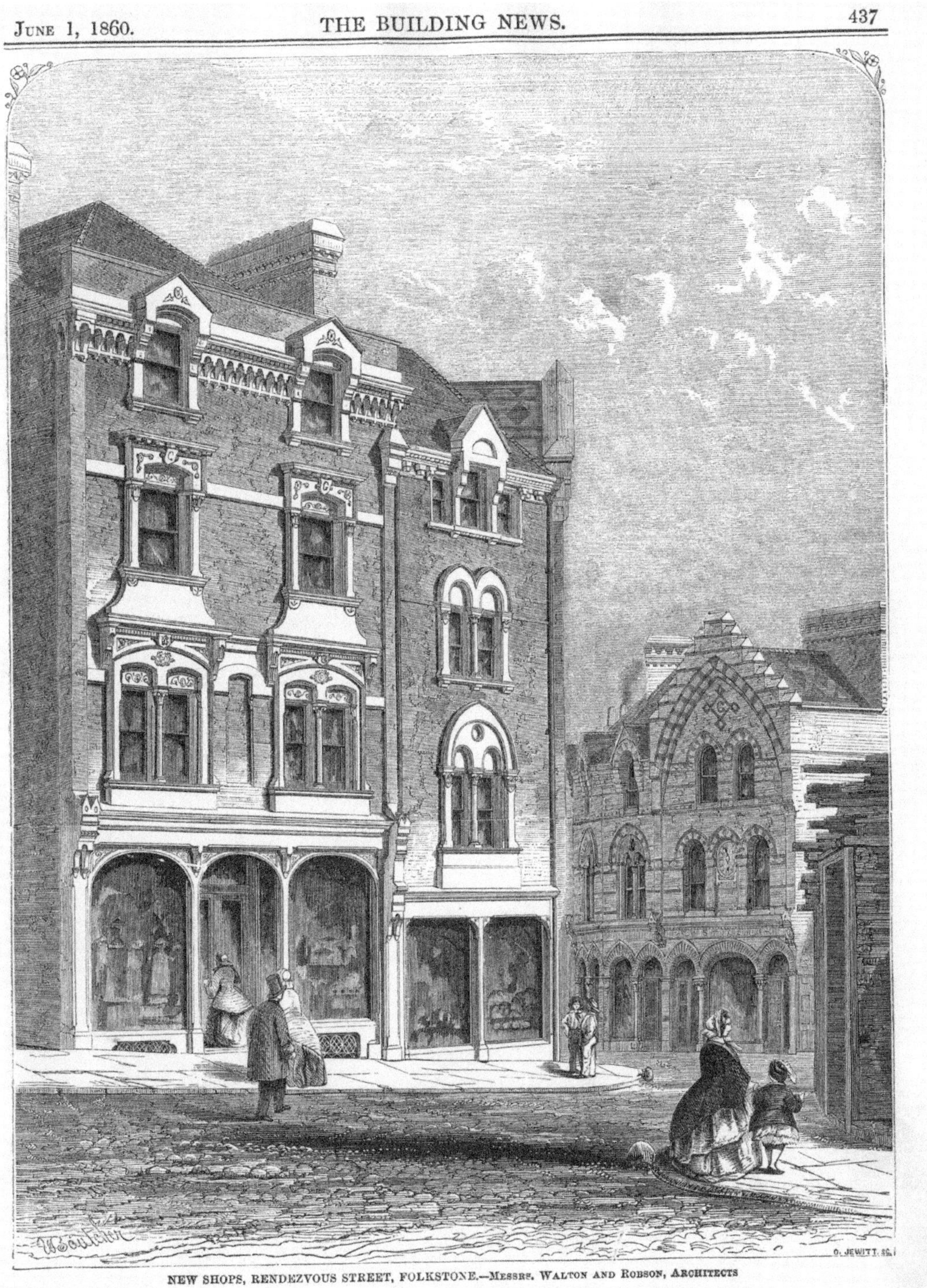


This engraving was published in the *Building News* dated 1 June 1860. The caption reads: *New shops, Rendezvous Street – Messrs, Walton & Robinson, architects.* The site was previously occupied by Market–Place and the Town Prison.

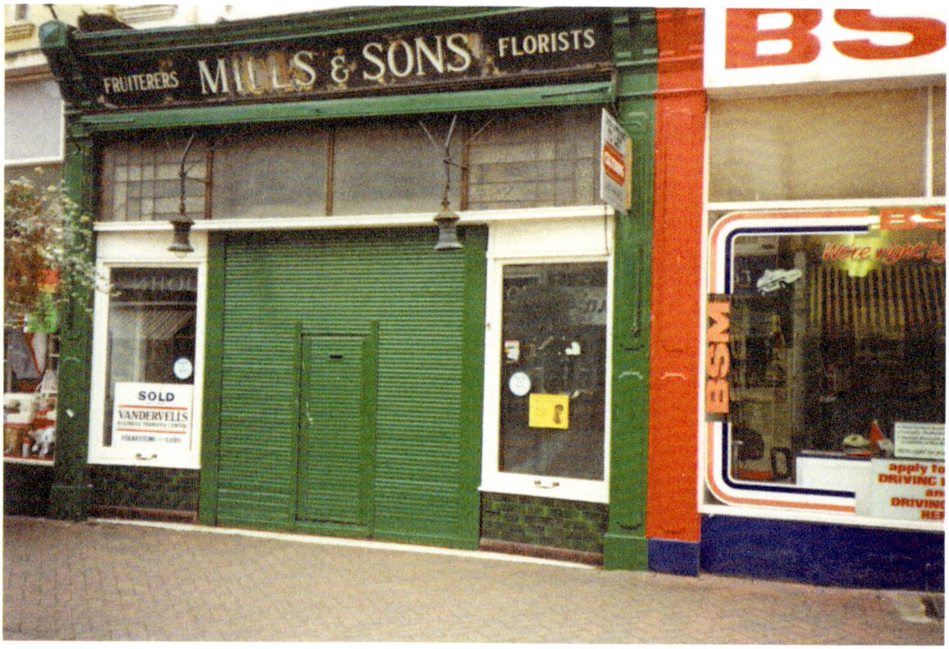


James William Mills, fruiterer, traded at a shop in Harbour Street that was damaged by a parachute mine on 18 November 1940. The family continued trading at these premises, No. 9 Guildhall Street (which opened in 1932), until closing in 1988.

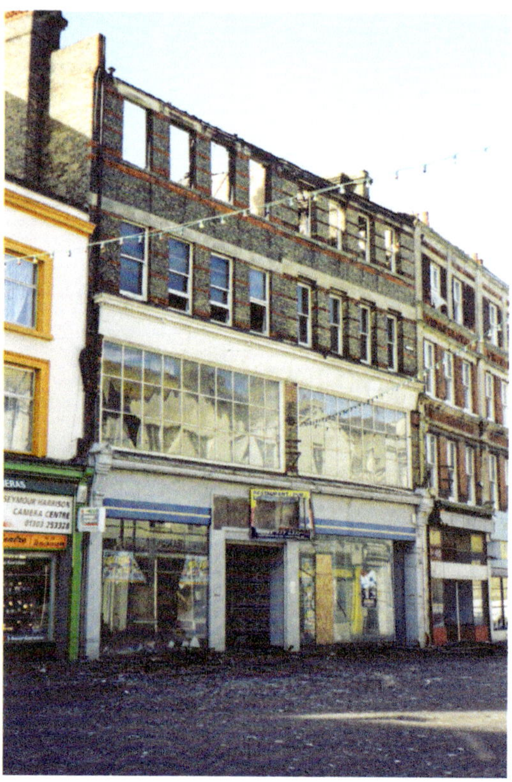

A fire above an empty shop, 27 Guildhall Street (the former Courts shop), on Sunday 2 February 2003 at 3 a.m., which was tackled by twenty-five soldiers in four Green Goddesses and two Navy crews. This was due to the firemen being on strike.

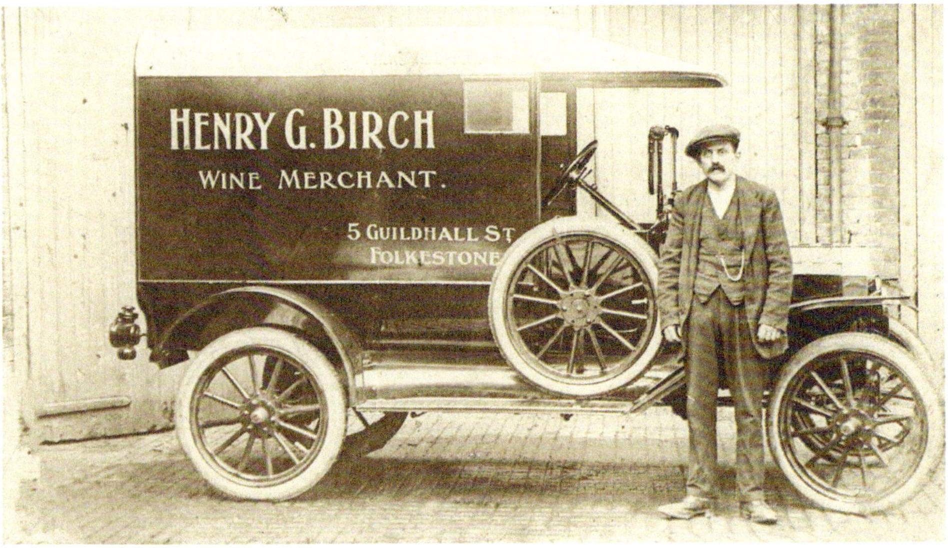


Henry G. Birch, Wine and Importer of No. 5 Guildhall Street, established 1885, was taken over by Prentis and Sons in 1924. It continued as an off-licence until the late 1980s.

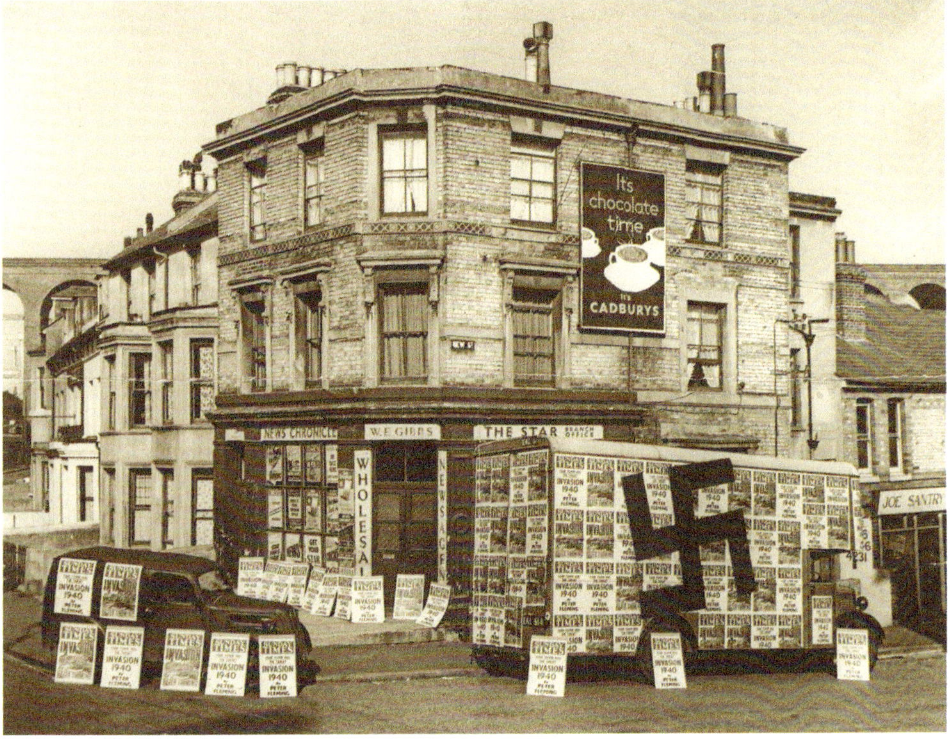


*Invasion 1940: An account of the German Preparations and the British Counter-Measures* by Peter Fleming, first published by Rupert Hart-Davies (1957). The photograph is of a serialisation of the book published in *The Sunday Times* in 1957. W. E. Gibbs, No. 30 Foord Road, wholesale newsagents, traded from this shop from 1948 to 1960. No. 1 New Street is occupied by Joe Santry, turf commission agent.

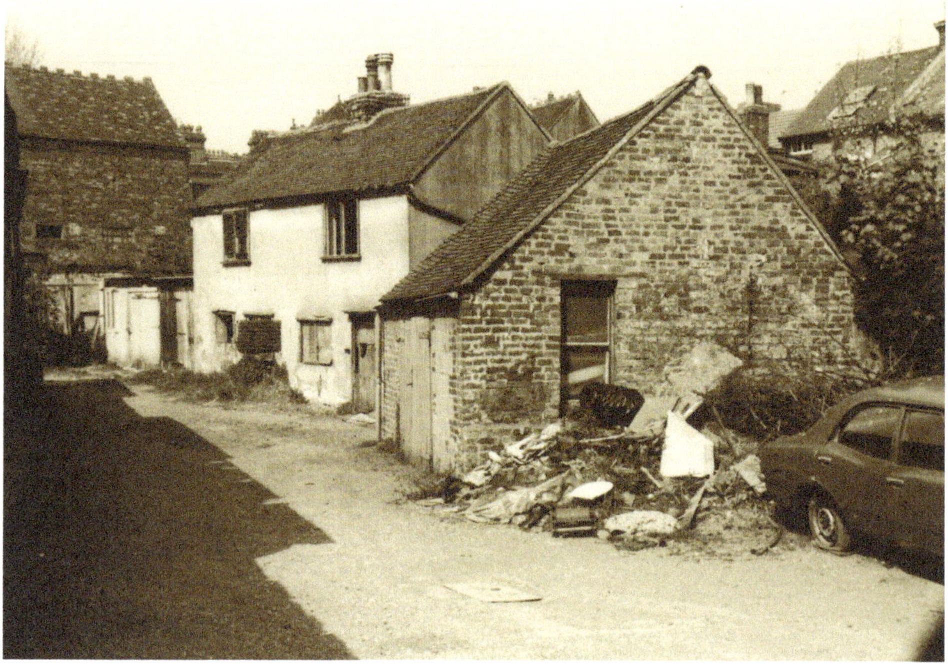

These rundown workshops are at Valebrook Mews known as 'Norrington's Hole'. The access is by a narrow lane in Broadmead by the junction with Bournemouth Road. The photographs were taken in 1982, but the buildings still look the same today.

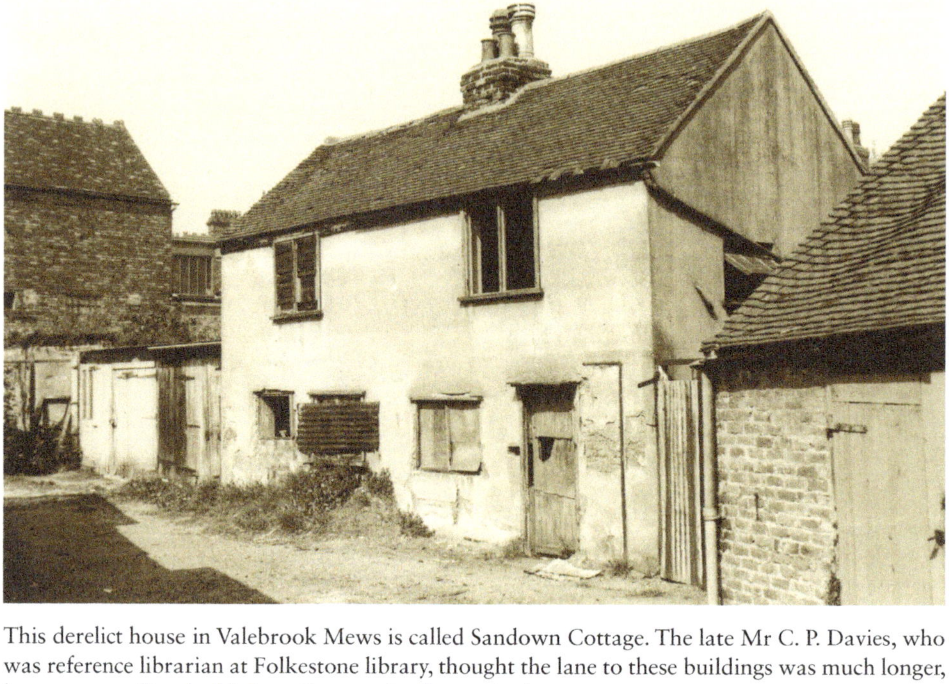

This derelict house in Valebrook Mews is called Sandown Cottage. The late Mr C. P. Davies, who was reference librarian at Folkestone library, thought the lane to these buildings was much longer, but was cut off to build the railway embankment in the 1840s.

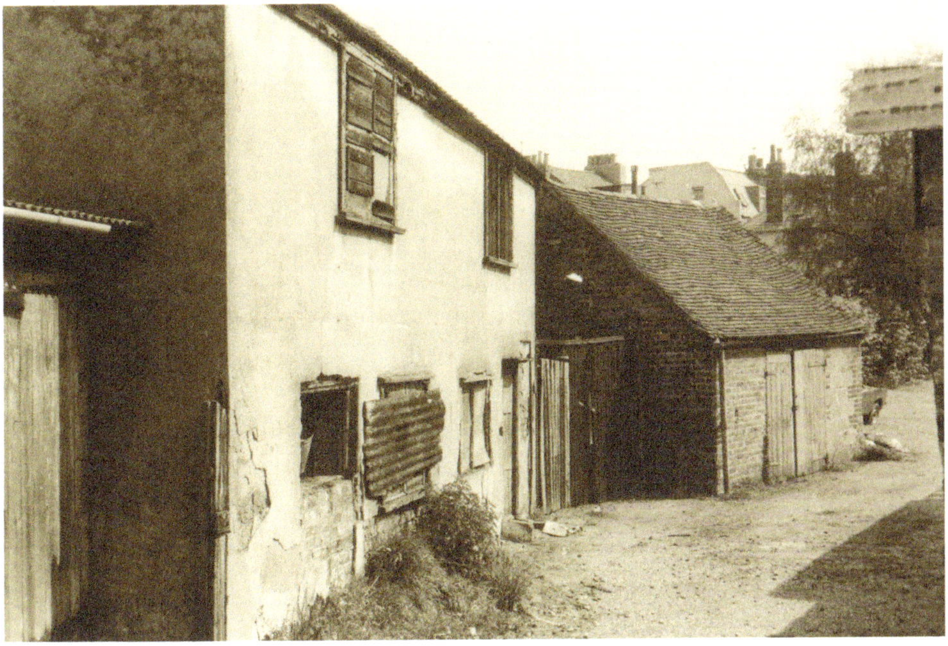

This cluster of workshops are set back off Broadmead Road. The buildings contain many period features reflecting their historic use. These include find timber joinery, external workshops, lifting arms and vaulted timber ceilings.

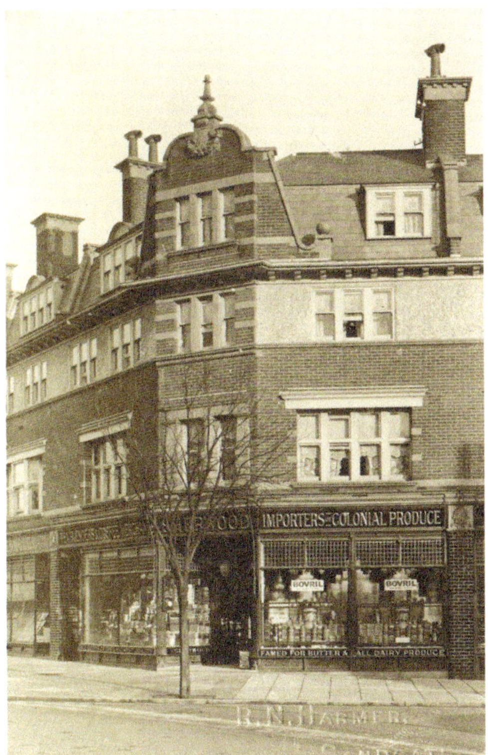


Sherwood & Son, Grocer & Provision Merchants, No. 100 Cheriton Road on the corner of Brockman Road, were in business here from 1903 to 1906 when the business was taken over by Howard & Co. who traded there until 1970. The shop is now Co-op Welcome.

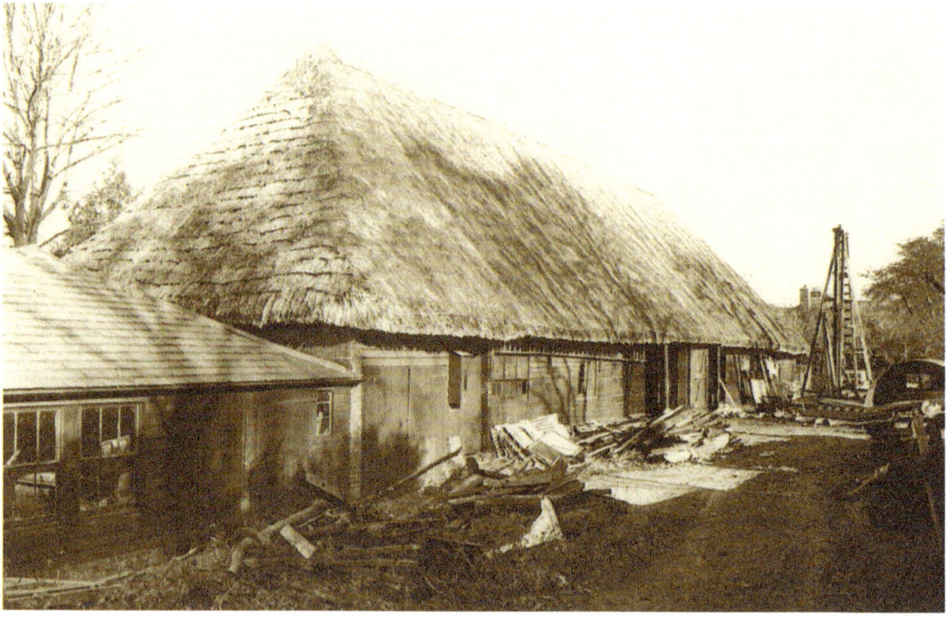

Eighteenth-century Ingles Manor Barn, Castle Hill Avenue, was built in 1710 and was an eight-bay barn. It was owned by Lord Radnor's Folkestone estate and was one of the last thatched buildings of its type and size in Shepway. The barn was 40 metres long and made entirely of wood.

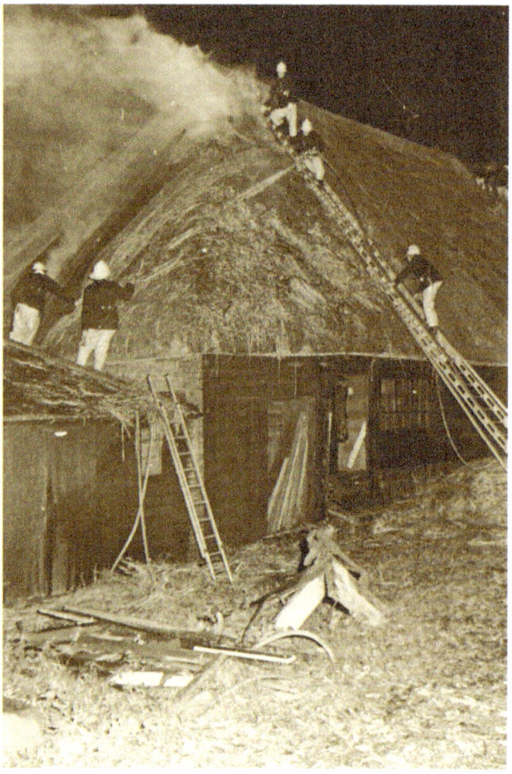

The barn was destroyed by fire on 15 March 2001. It was being used for storage by arts company Strange Cargo, who used the barn to store sculptures and arts materials.

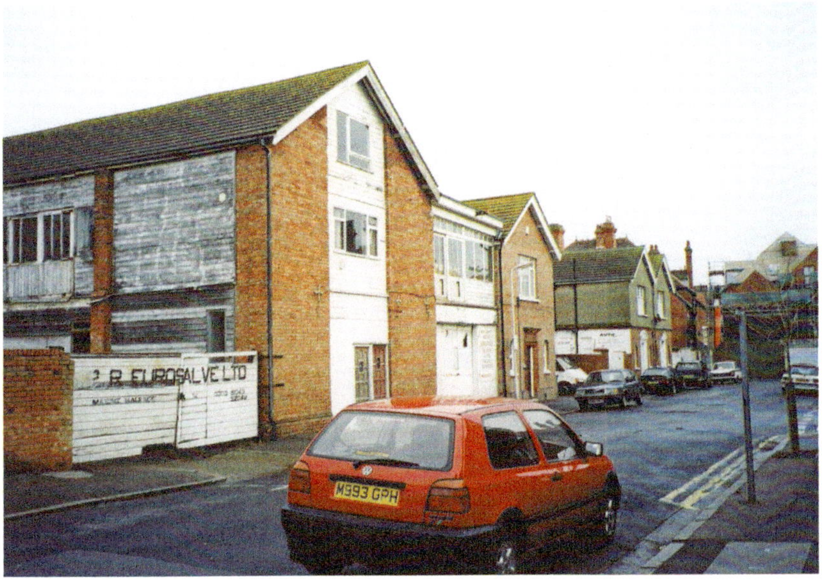


P. R. Eurosalve Ltd and Gerald Swaffer, Auto Services, traded from these properties in Plain Road until planning permission was granted to build six houses and two apartments by Shepway District Council in June 2006.

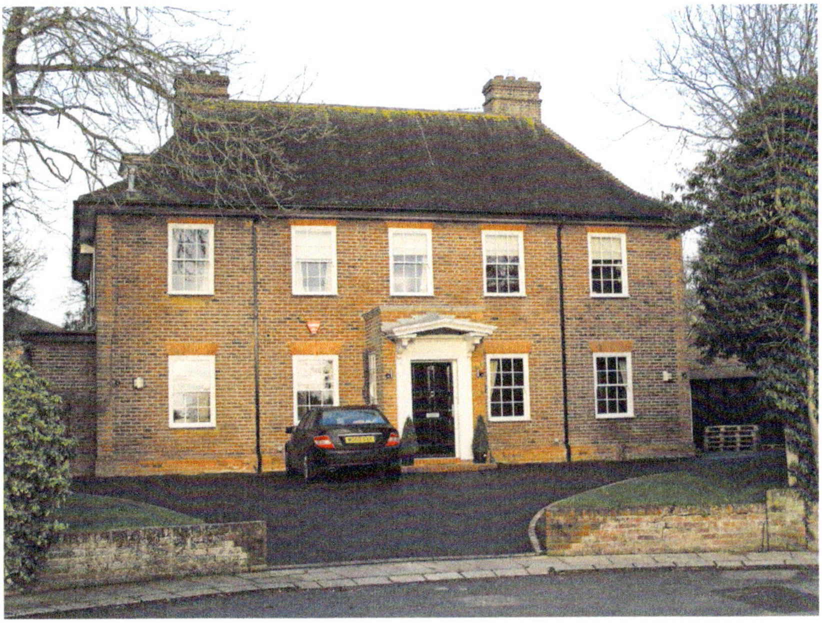

Pelham Court, No. 9 Pelham Gardens, was designed by architect Seton Dahl and was built with three reception rooms, six bedrooms and one bathroom, costing £6,000 freehold in 1930 for Revd Harold Barclay Hennell. His home was The Old Rectory, The Street, Ash Cum, Ridley, Sevenoaks, Kent. When he died in 1941 his wife Ethel lived permanently here until she died in 1954. Their son, Thomas Hennell, artist and writer (1903–45), loved to spend time in Folkestone by the sea as a boy; he holidayed with his family annually in Dymchurch and felt Romney Marsh to be a great subject for painting. He was a keen cyclist and often cycled from Ridley to Folkestone.

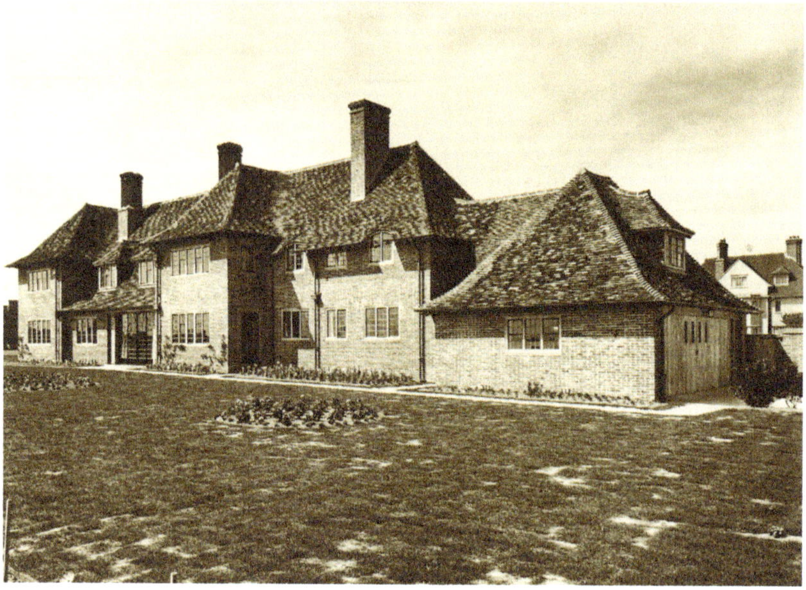

Milden House on Dixwell Road and The Leas was built to designs by Seaton Dahl on land bought from Lord Radnor in 1935/6 for the retirement of Sir Robert Baden-Powell, founder of the Boy Scouts. Two other houses were built in the garden after Baden-Powell died in 1941, leaving Milden to his brother. The beautiful eight-bedroom house, which is completely private, still has many original features, including a square-thatched revolving summerhouse, reminiscent of a South African hut, and previously open loggia where Baden-Powell, who loved sleeping under the stars, was reputed to spend some nights.

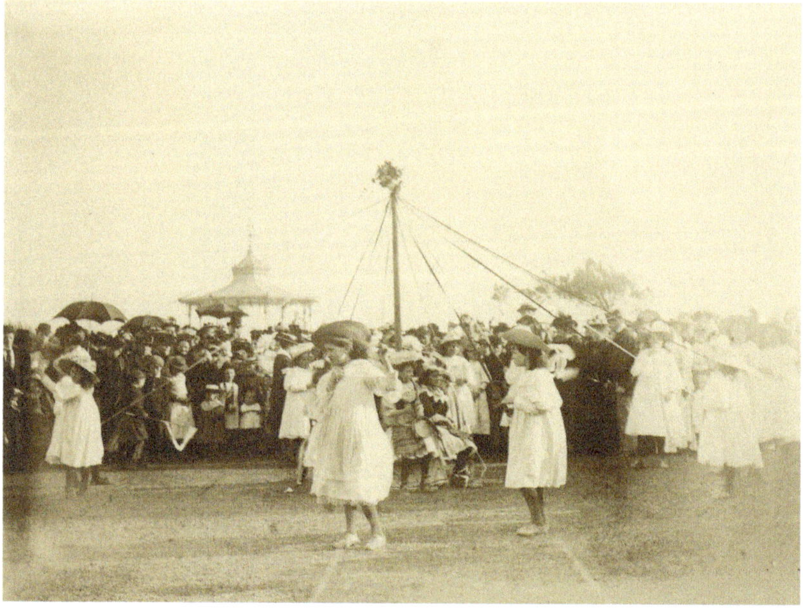

Gone are the days when May Day, 1 May, was celebrated by dancing round the maypole. This celebration took place on The Leas on 1 May 1900. It's interesting to note the Leas bandstand (built in 1895) in the background.

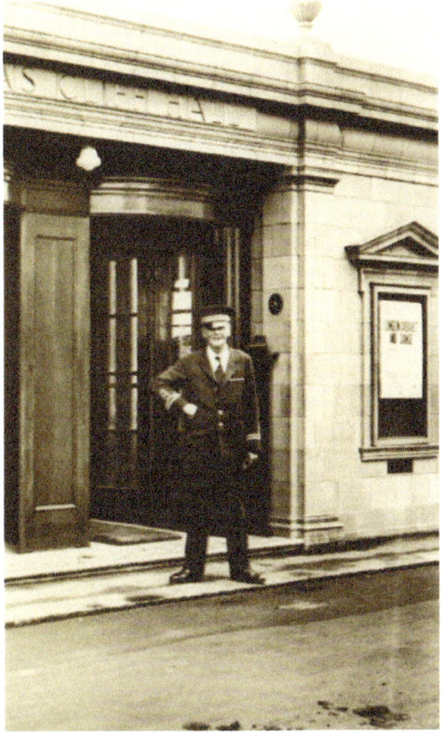

Mr J. Roche, seen here outside The Leas Cliff Hall, is reputed to have been one of Lord Radnor's policemen who patrolled The Leas between the two world wars.

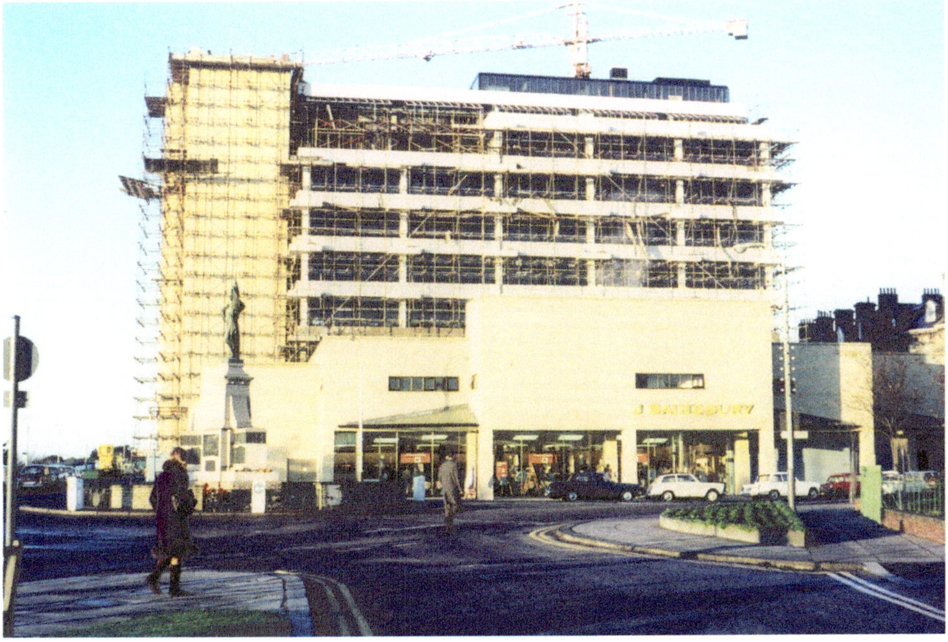

The building under construction in 1970 is Fortune House, an office block built for the Welfare Insurance Company. The Welfare Company moved to Devon in June 1978 and the building remained empty until 1987 when it was converted into flats. In front of the flats is Sainsbury's store, which opened in 1970 and is now occupied by a McDonalds.

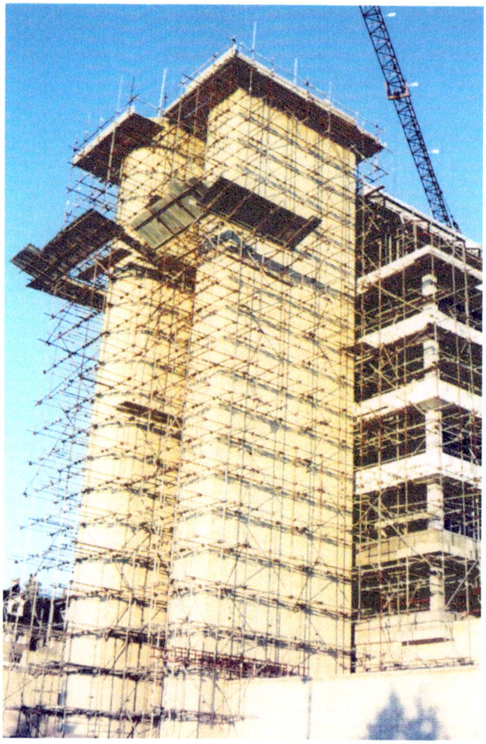

The front elevation of a block of offices being built for the Welfare Insurance Company in 1970 at No. 1 The Leas. They were converted into flats in 1987.

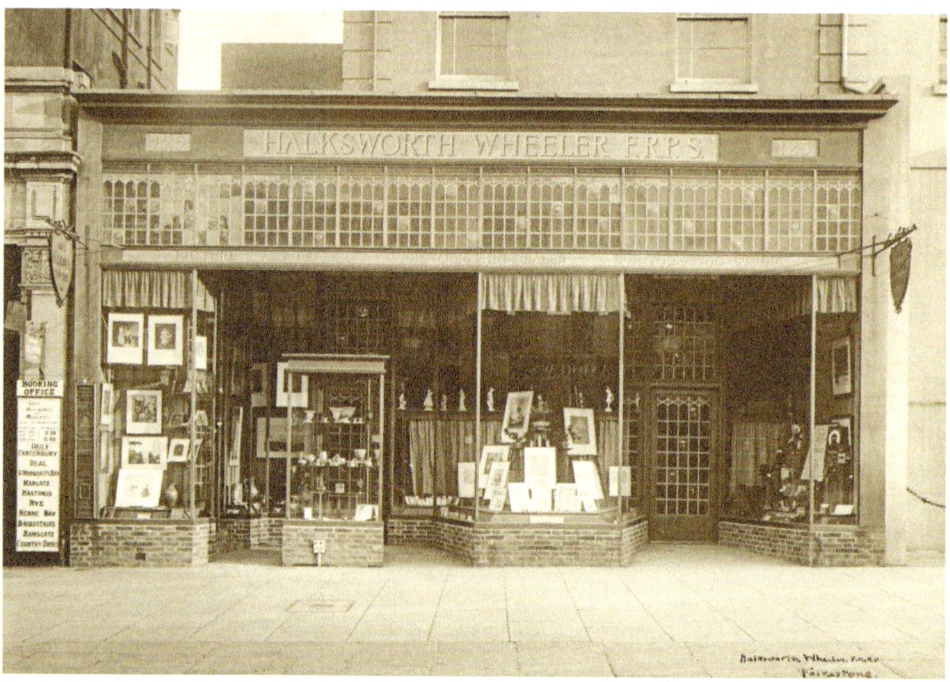


Halksworth Wheeler, photographer, No. 125 Sandgate Road, traded from this shop from 1928 to 1959. The shopfront was designed by local architect Seaton Dahl. The shop is now divided into two, housing Fell Reynolds, the estate agents, and a barbers named 'Top Cut'.

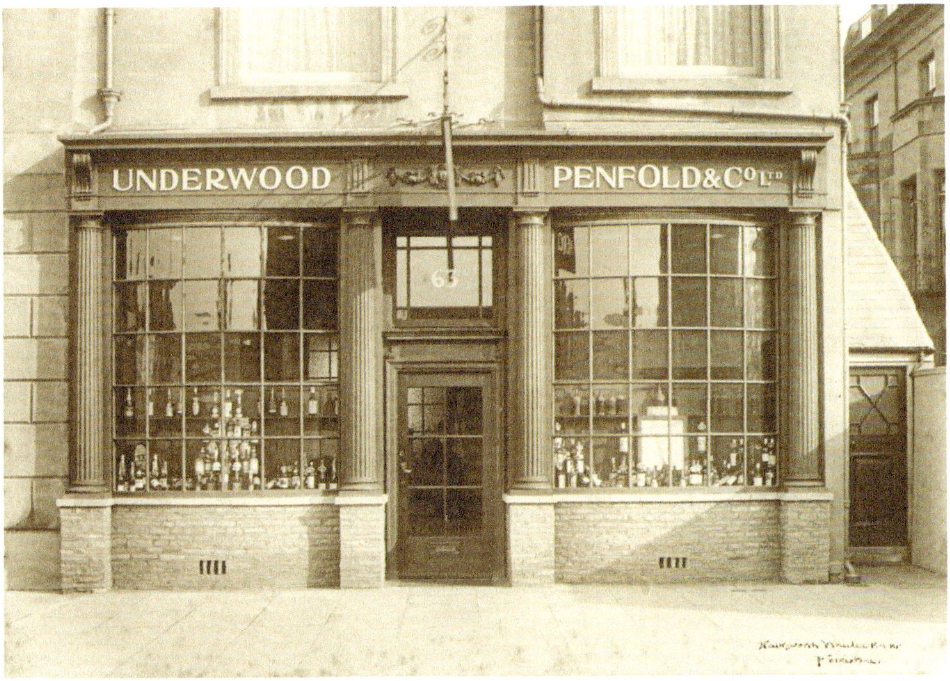


Underwood & Penfold wine & spirit merchants moved to No. 63 Sandgate Road (next to Barclays Bank) in 1929, where they stayed until 1963. The premises continued to be occupied by wine merchants until 1985. The shopfront was designed by Seaton Dahl. The premises are now occupied by Game.

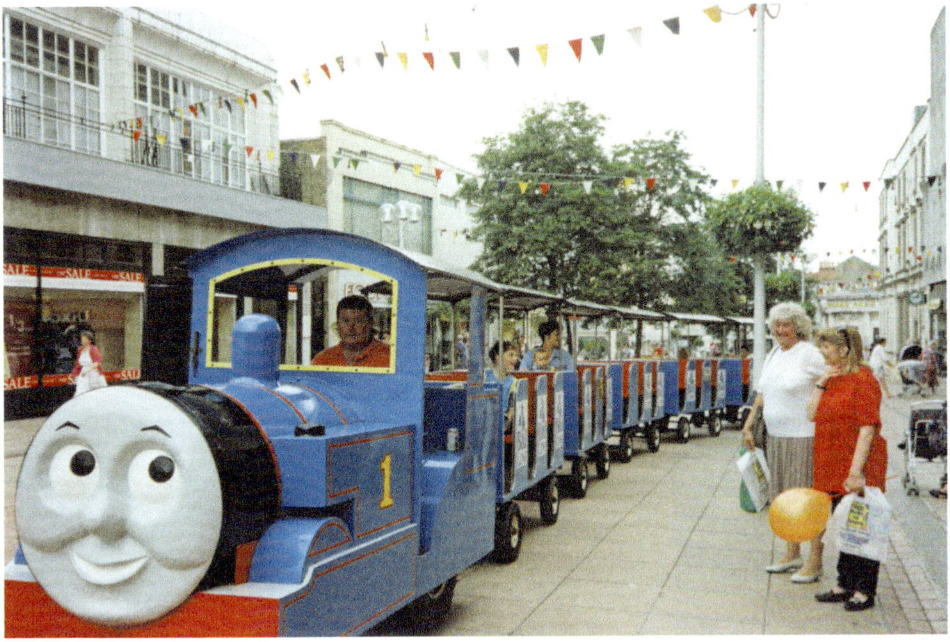


This kiddies train in Sandgate Road was the 'Onward Event' celebrating 150 years of the Railway first coming to Folkestone, held on 25, 26 and 27 June 1993.

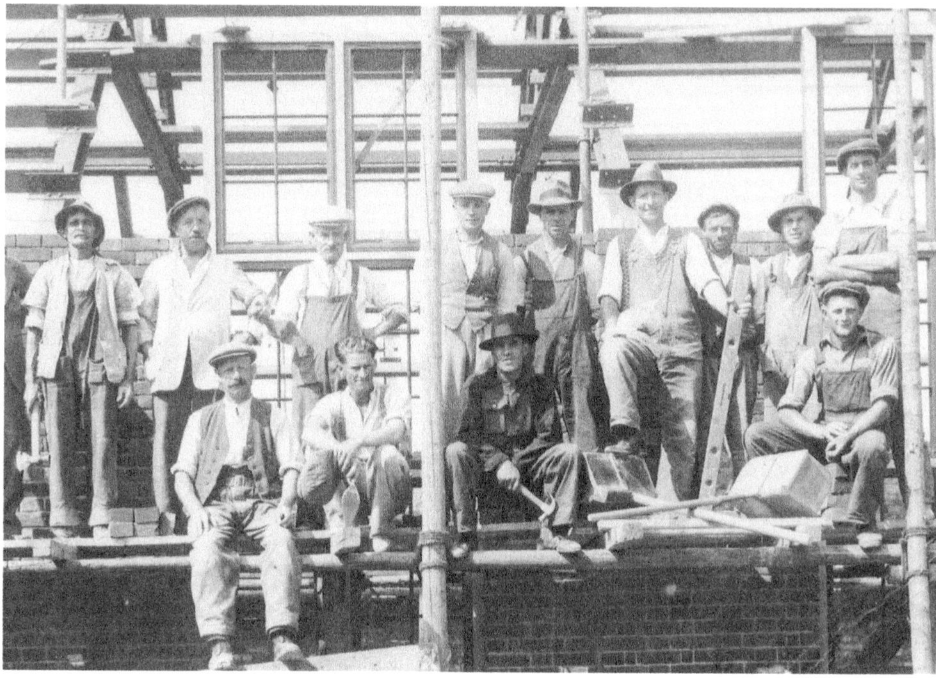

The staff of local builder Hayward & Paramor and seen here building a new post office in Bouverie Place. The official opening took place on Wednesday 30 March, 1938.

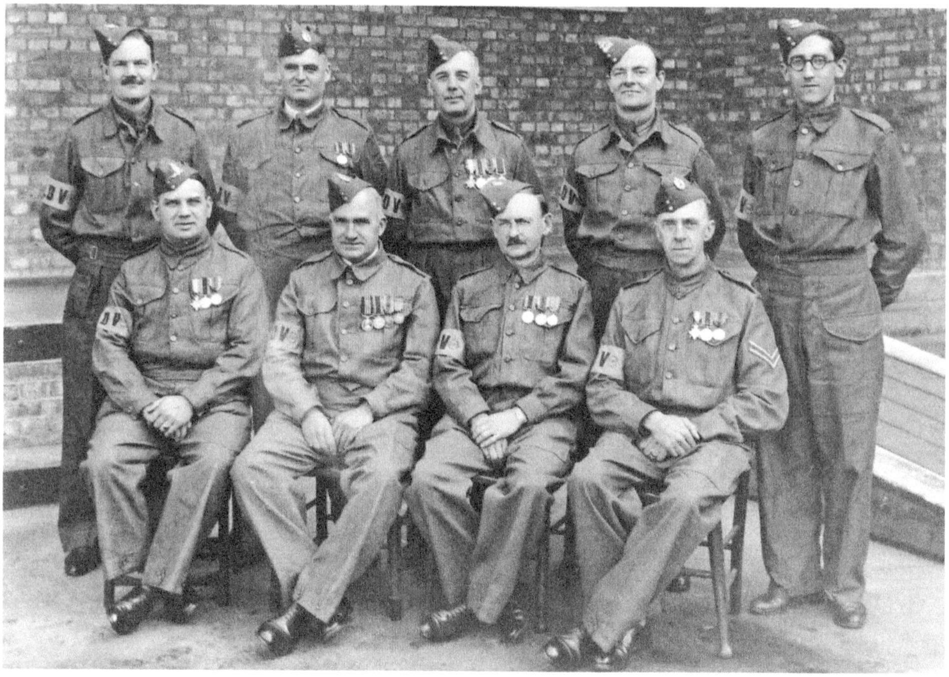

Folkestone Post Office workers parading in their Home Guard uniforms in the Second World War. Back row L to R: Frank Ash, Mr Cox?, Reg Gamage. Front row: Bill Best, Mr Friend, Joe Horton and Bob Ball.

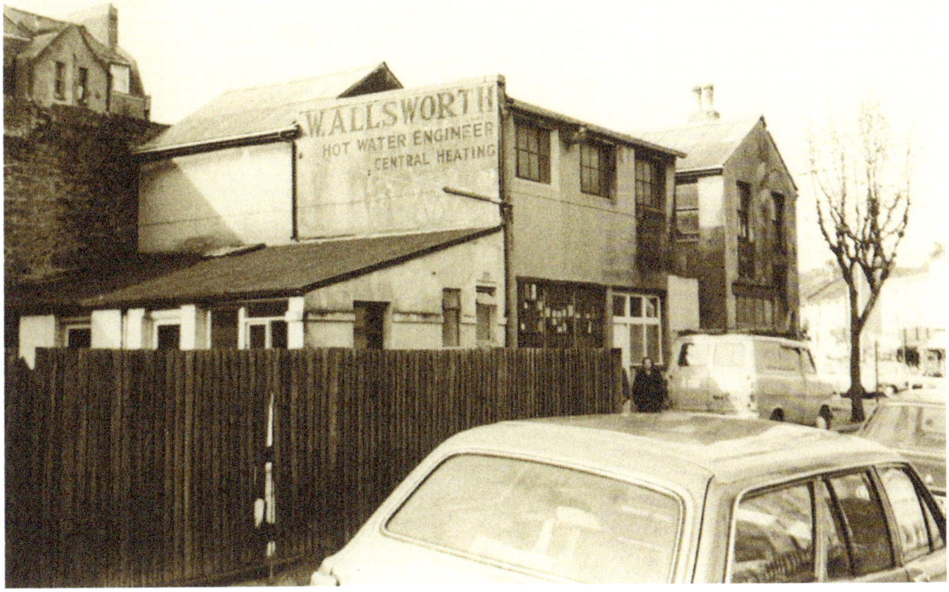


The workshop of W. Allsworth & Son, Ironmongers and Heating Engineers in Gloucester Place. They also had an ironmongers shop at Nos 16–18 Guildhall Street where they traded from *c.* 1905. These premises were demolished in March 1975.

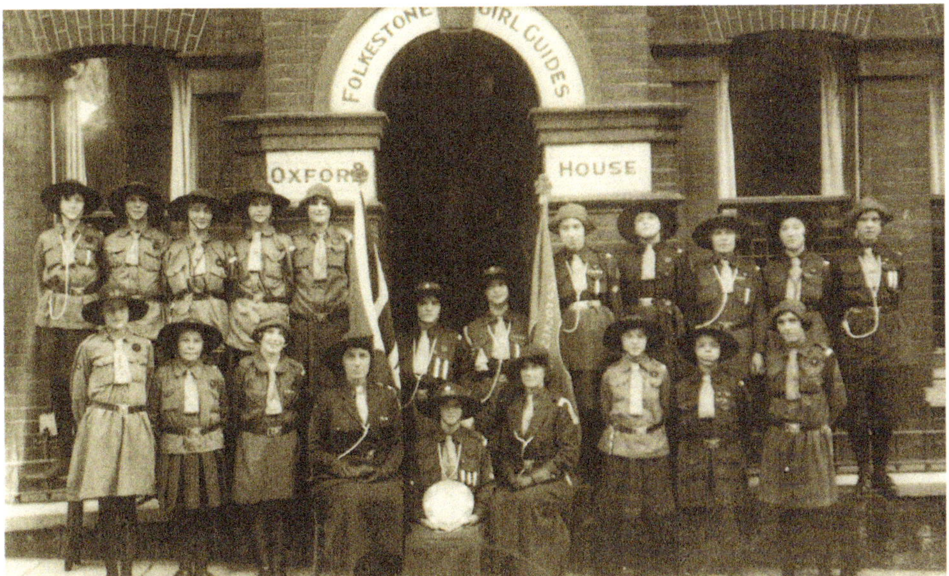


Girl Guides posing for the camera in the 1920s outside Oxford House in Oxford Terrace, which ran from Gloucester Place to Alexandra Gardens. Mrs Thompson (neé Oliver) is under the letter 'E' in 'House'. Oxford House became 'The Oxford Steak House', run by Charlie and Joyce Evens around 1967. The building was demolished in 1975.

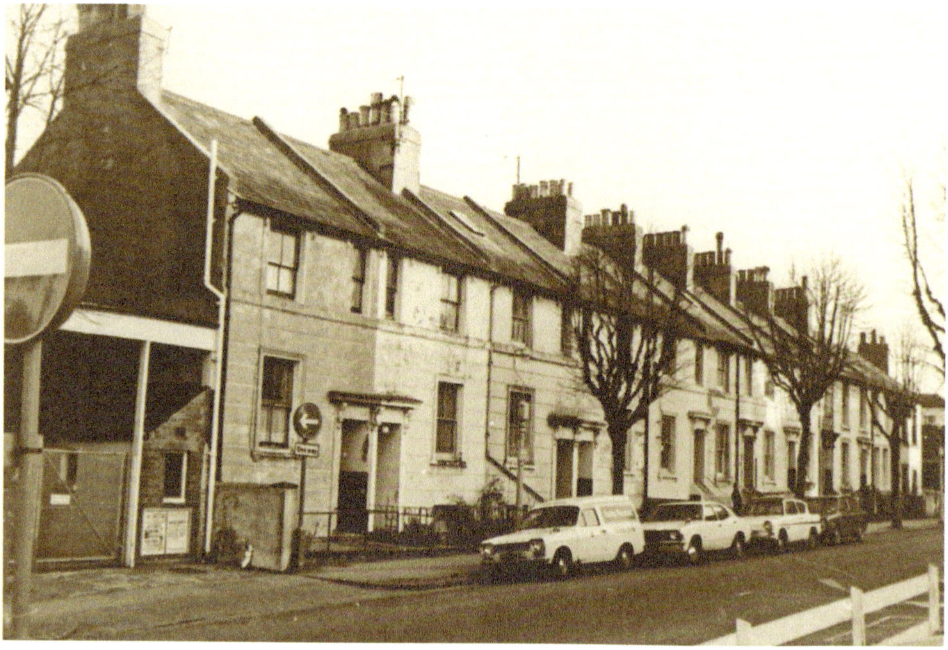

Gloucester Place from Cheriton Road. This terrace of houses were demolished in February 1980 to build a service road at the backs of the shops in Guildhall Street because Guildhall Street was being pedestrianised. It was widened in 1998 for the construction of the new shopping centre.

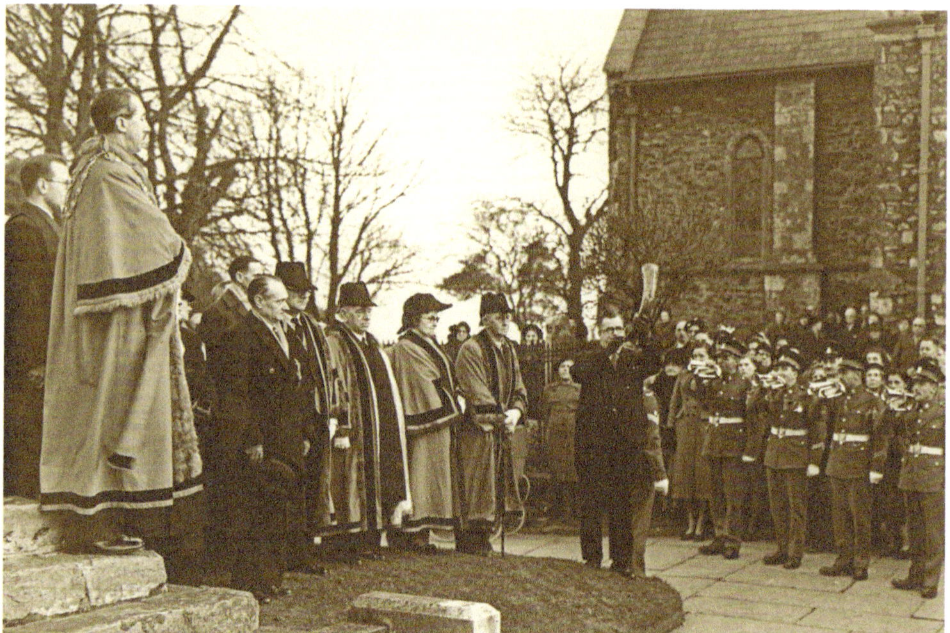

Blowing the Horn is to summon the people entitled to vote on electing a person to serve as Town Mayor and it goes back to 1313. Alderman John Moncrieff here is being installed as mayor at the Church Yard Cross. He was mayor from 1951 to 1954.

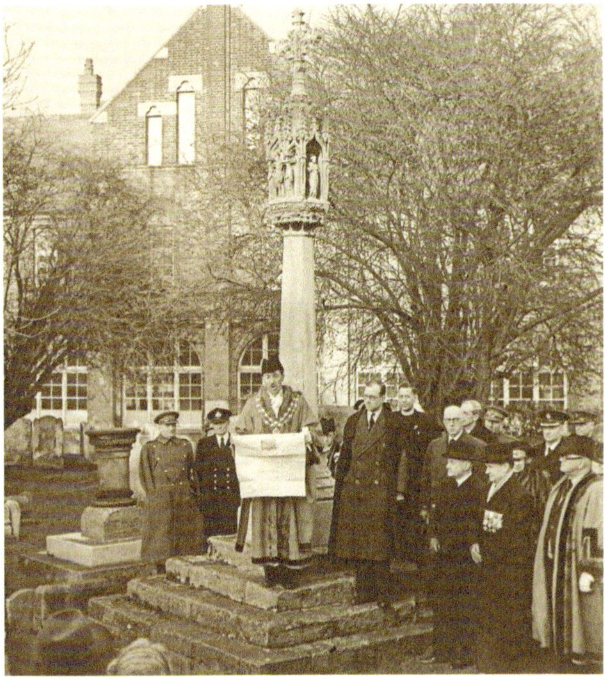

Today the councillor to be installed as mayor with the rest of the council and vicar meet in the Woodward Hall then walk to the Church Yard Cross and into the church. John Moncrieff installed as mayor with the other dignitaries at the Cross.

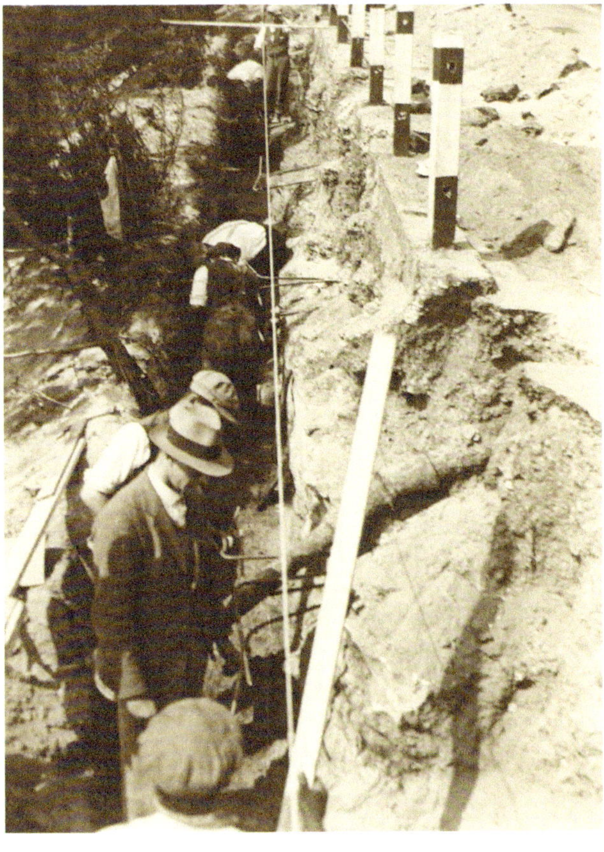

Widening the Road of Remembrance, formerly 'The Slope Road'. The name was changed in 1924 in memory of the service personnel who marched down it during the First World War to the Western Front, many of whom never returned.

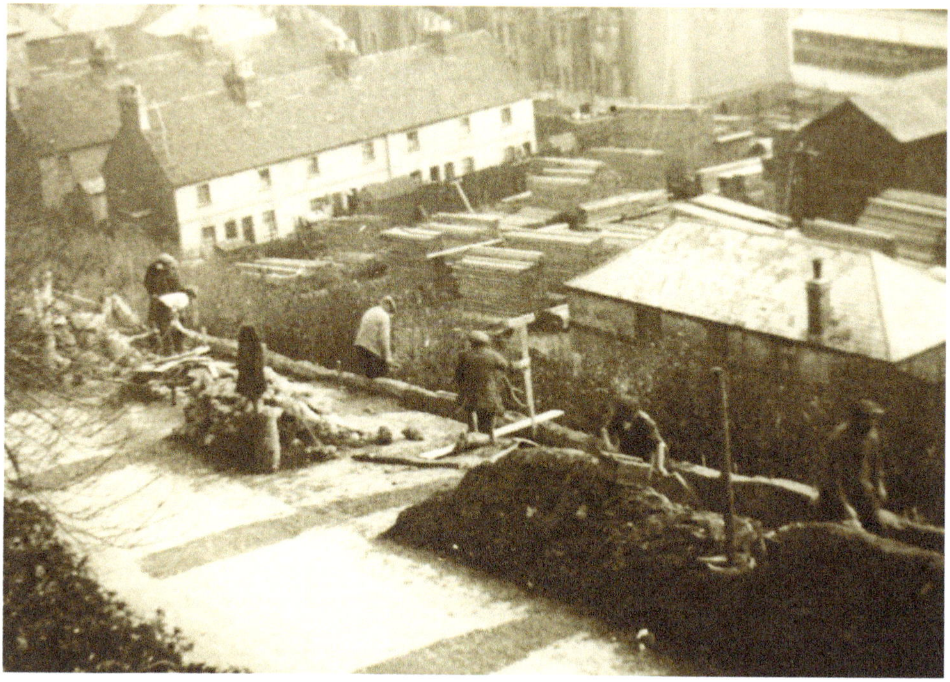

The workmen seen here are widening the Road of Remembrance, formerly 'The Slope Road', in 1924. The row of houses were the Coast Guard Cottages, which were destroyed by enemy action on 26 August 1940.

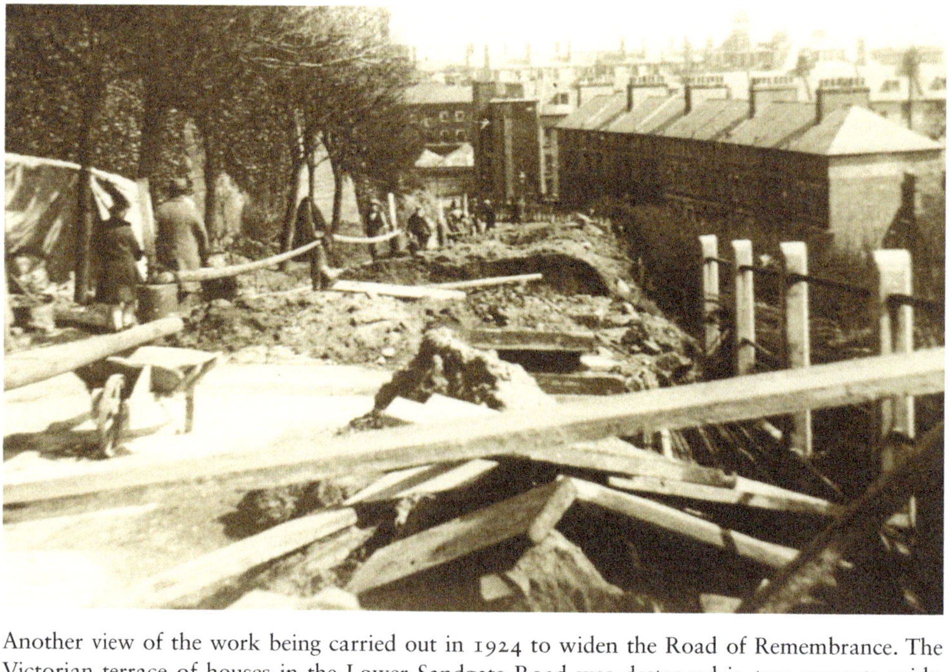

Another view of the work being carried out in 1924 to widen the Road of Remembrance. The Victorian terrace of houses in the Lower Sandgate Road was destroyed in two separate raids. The first, on 26 August 1940, destroyed Nos 16 and 18, while three years later, on 7 September 1943, Nos 2 to 14 were destroyed.

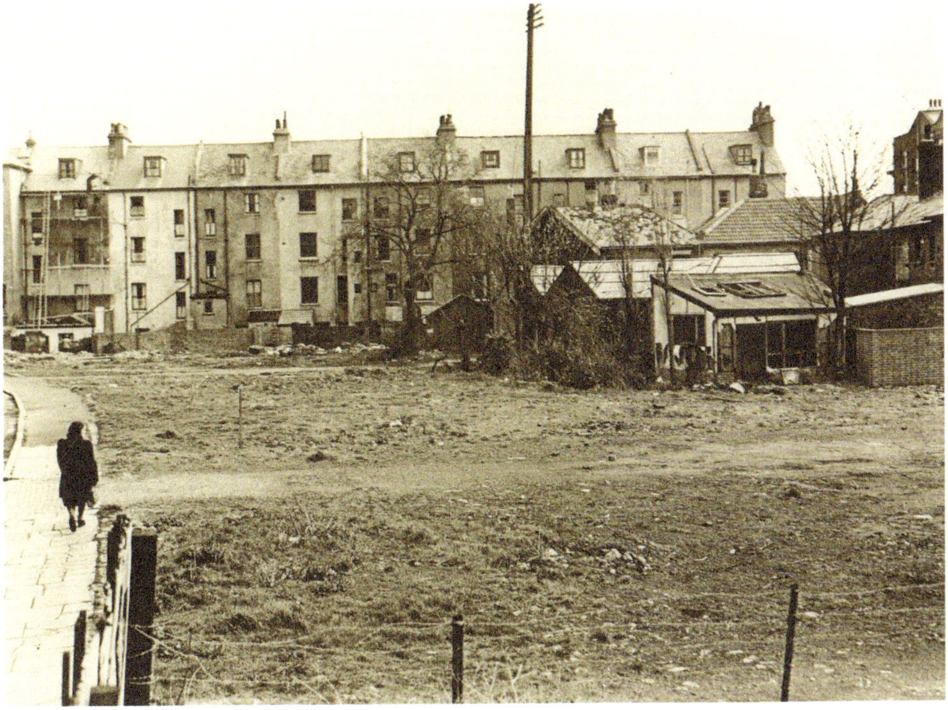

The Lower Sandgate Road, *c.* 1950, looking towards the backs of the houses in Marine Terrace. A Victorian terrace of houses stood along the road where the lady is walking (see bottom photograph on page 84 for details).

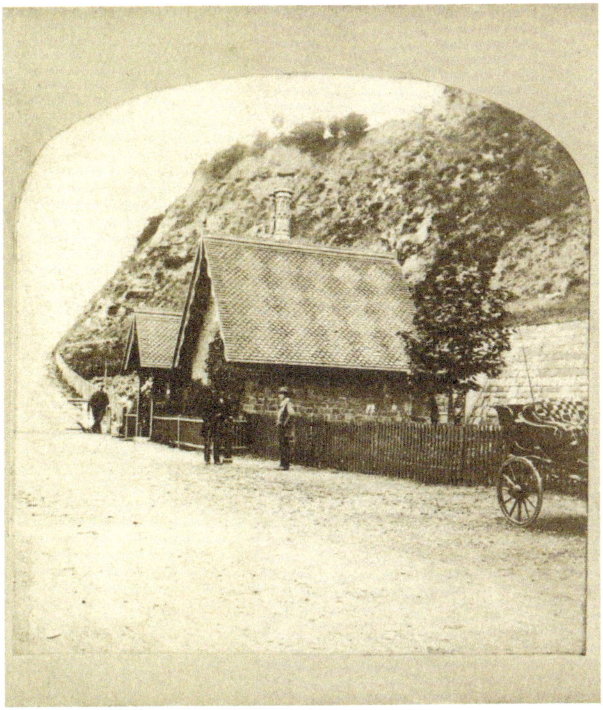

This photograph shows Swiss Cottage at the bottom of the Slope Road. It was built for the turnpike toll, and, after the turnpikes were abolished in 1877, it was occupied by council workers until it was demolished in 1977. It's interesting to note that one can just see the gate!

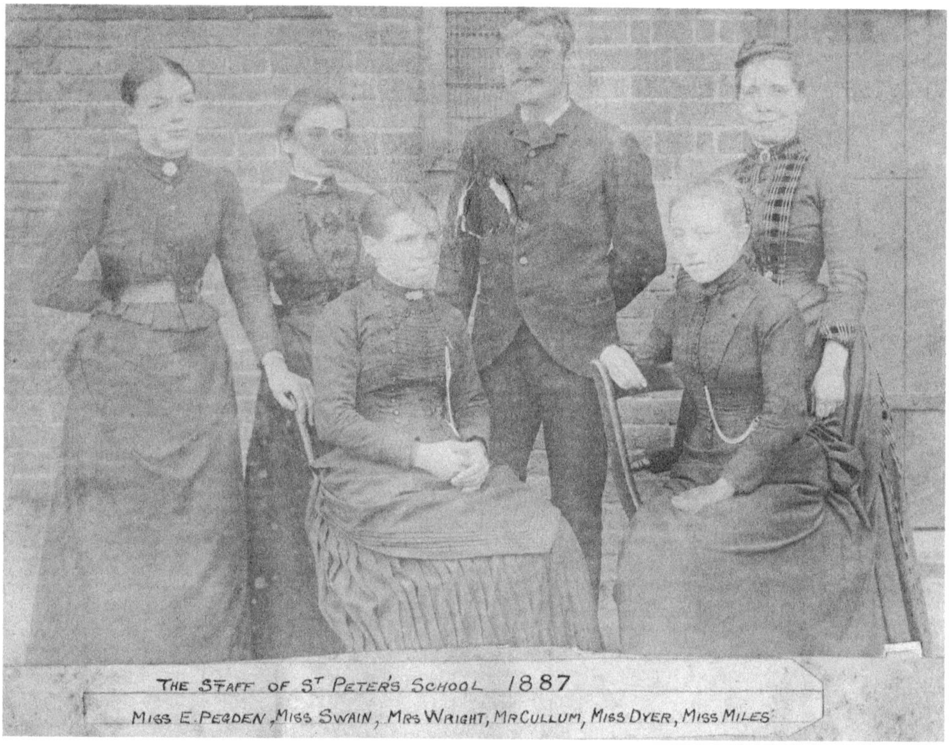


The following photographs of St Peter's School come from an album compiled by The Revd C. J. Ridsdale 1868–1923, founder of schools. The staff in 1887: Miss E. Pegden, Miss Swain, Mrs Wright, Mr Cullum, Miss Dyer and Miss Miles.

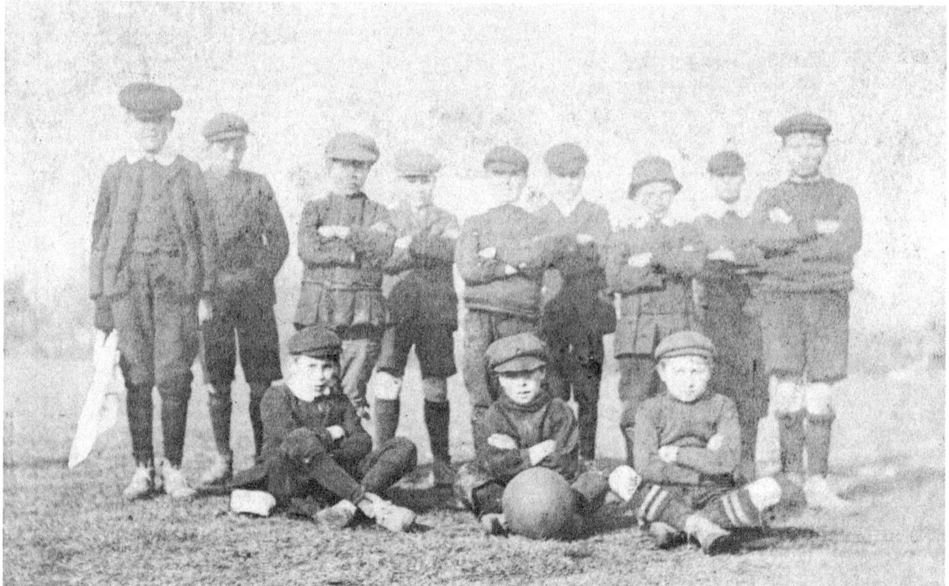

St Peter's School football, team 1911–12. Standing: J. Winter, Curtis, R. Taylor, S. Clark, A. Dawkins, G. Ellen, J. Vallintine, H. Cook, E, Hart. Sitting: H. Marshall, H. Milton and R. Banks.

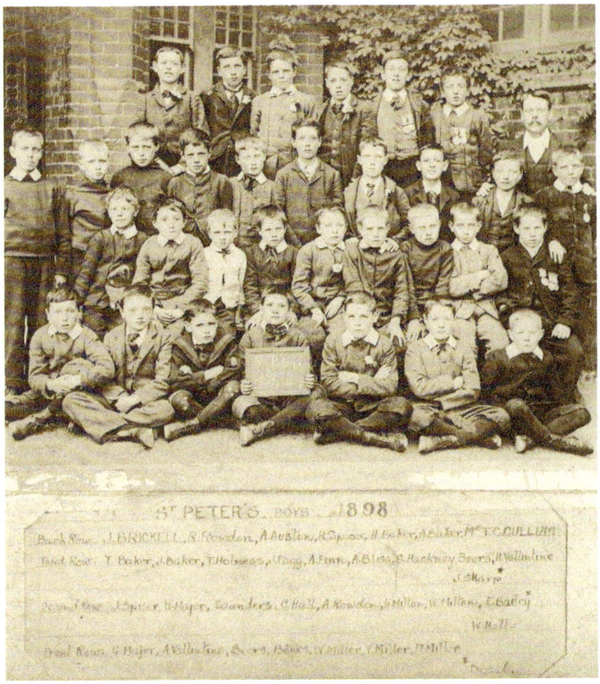


St Peter's Boy's, 1898. Back row: J. Brickell, R. Rowden, A. Austin, R. Spicer, H. Baker, A. Baker and Mr C. T. Cullum. Third row: T. Baker, J. Baker, T. Holness, J. Fagg, A. Finn, A. Bliss, S. Hackney, Beers, H. Vallintine and J. Sharp. Second row: J. Spicer, W. Major, Saunders, C. Hall, A. Rowden, H. Milton, W. Milton, E. Bailey and W. Hall. Front row: G. Major, A. Vallintine, Beers, Beers, W. Miller, V. Miller and R. Miller.

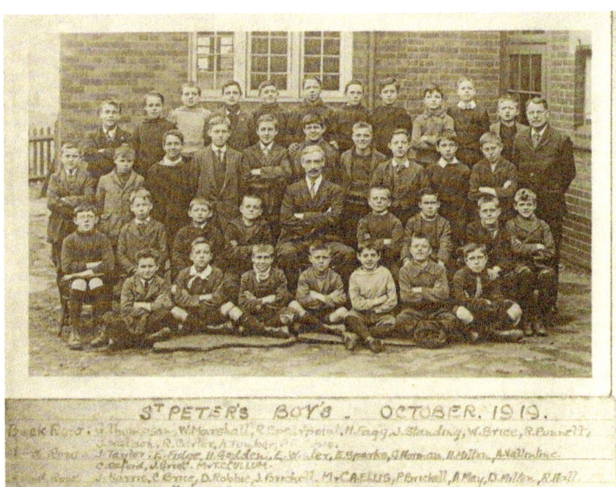


St Peter's Boy's, October 1919. Back row: G. Thompson, W. Marshall, R. Spearpoint, H. Fagg, J. Standing: W. Brice, R. Punnett, J. Watson, R. Carter, A. Tumber and P. Featherbe.

Third row: J. Taylor, E. Fidge, H. Godden, E. Winter, E. Starks, G. Norman, H. Milton, A. Vallintine, C. Oxford, J. Grist and Mr T. C. Cullum. Second row: J. Harris, C. Brice, D. Robbie, J. Brickell, Mr C. A. Ellis, P. Brickell May, D. Milton and R. Hall Front row: A. Hogben, A. Vallintine, E. Godden, F. Milton, S. Spearpoint, W. Hall and J Norman.

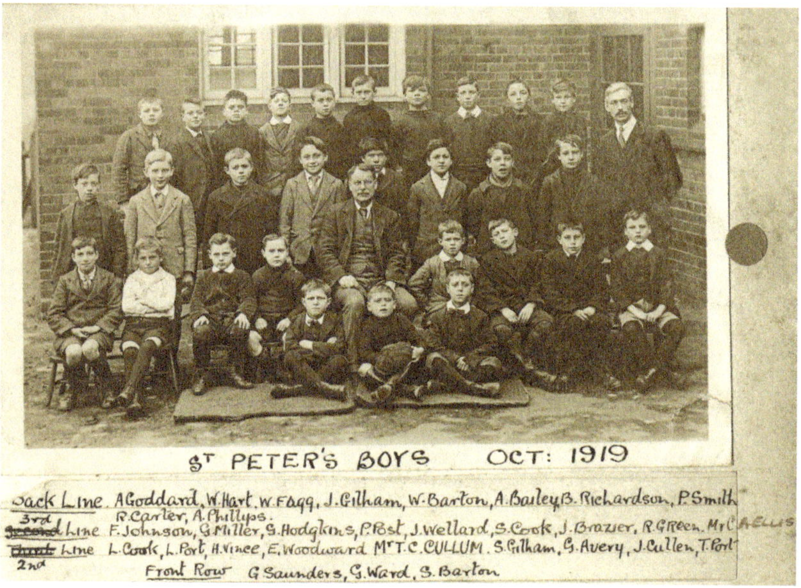


St Peter's School, October 1919. Back row: A. Goddard, W. Hart, W. Fagg, J. Gilham, W. Barton, A. Bailey, B. Richardson, P. Smith, R. Carter and A. Phillips. Third row: F. Johnson, G. Miller, G. Hodgkins, P. Post, J. Wellard, S. Cook, J. Brazier, R. Green and Mr C. A. Ellis. Second row: L. Cook, L. Port, H. Vince, E. Woodward, Mr T. C. Cullum, S Gilham, G. Avery, G. Cullen and T. Port. Front row: G. Saunders, G. Ward and S. Barton.

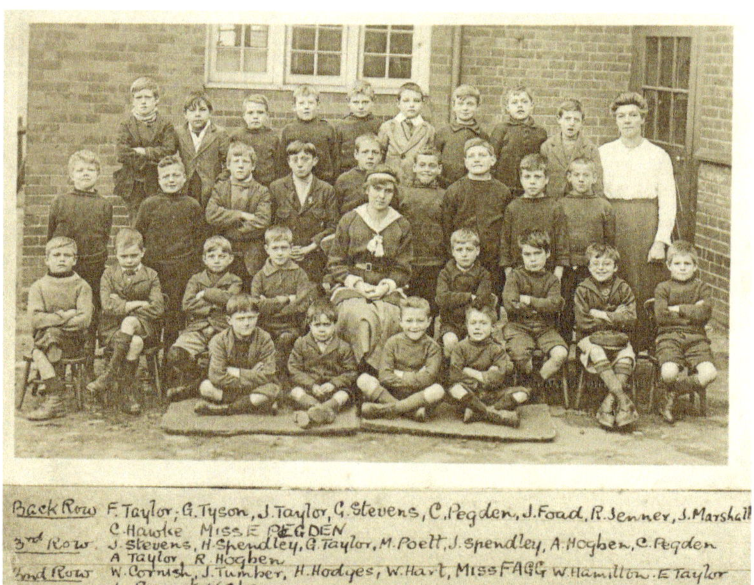


Back row: F. Taylor, G. Tyson, J. Taylor, G. Stevens, C. Pegden, J. Foad, R. Jenner, J. Marshall, C. Hawke and Miss E. Pegden. Third row: J. Stevens, H. Spendley, G. Taylor, M. Poett, J. Spendley, A. Hogben, R. Pegden, A. Taylor and R. Hogben. Second row: W. Cornish, J. Tumber, H. Hodges, W. Hart, Miss Fagg, W. Hamilton, E. Taylor, L. Punnet and W. Sharp Front row: W. Carey, R. Tyson, A. Cornish and J. Punnet. Front row: W. Cary, R. Tyson, A. Cornish and J. Punnet.

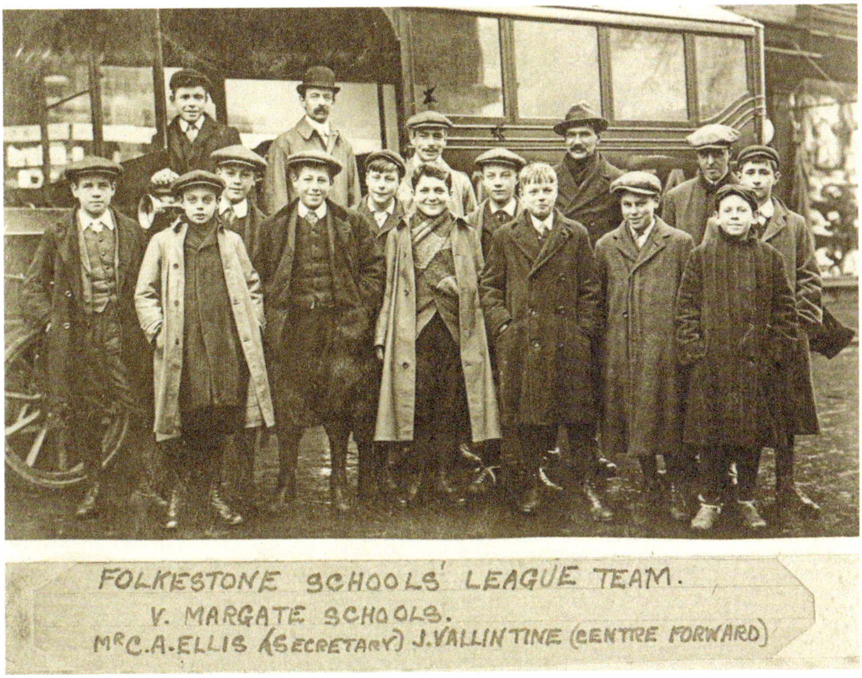


Folkestone School's League Team Verses Margate Schools: Mr C. A. Ellis (Secretary), J. Vallintine (centre forward).

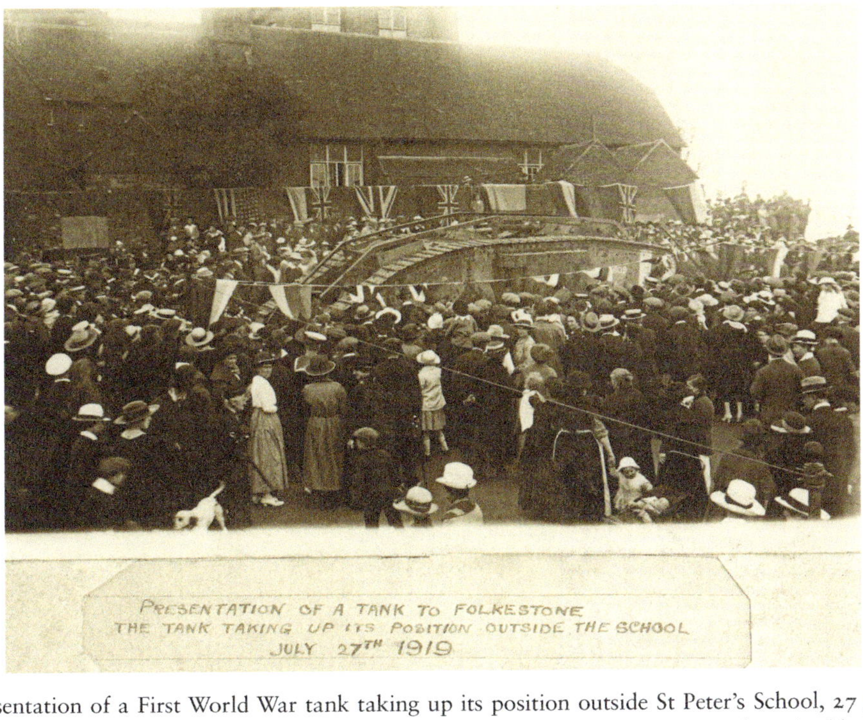


Presentation of a First World War tank taking up its position outside St Peter's School, 27 July 1919. It was presented to the town by Major-General Sir E. D. Swinton KCB, and received by MP Sir Philip Sassoon and Sir Stephen Penfold, Mayor of Folkestone.

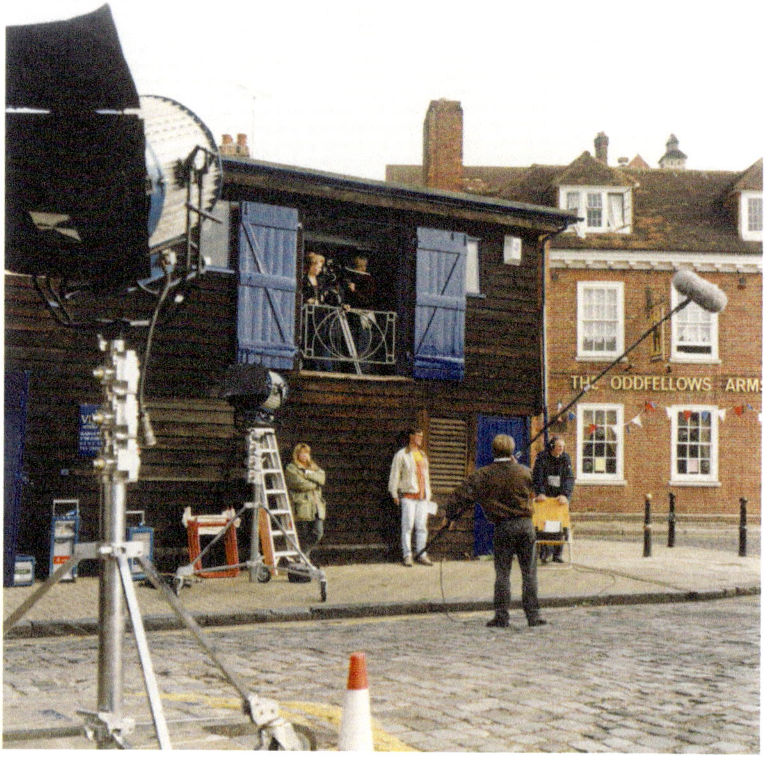


BBC TV filming *Moon & Sun* in what was Arthur Goddard's fish wholesalers' store, The Stade, 25 September 1991.

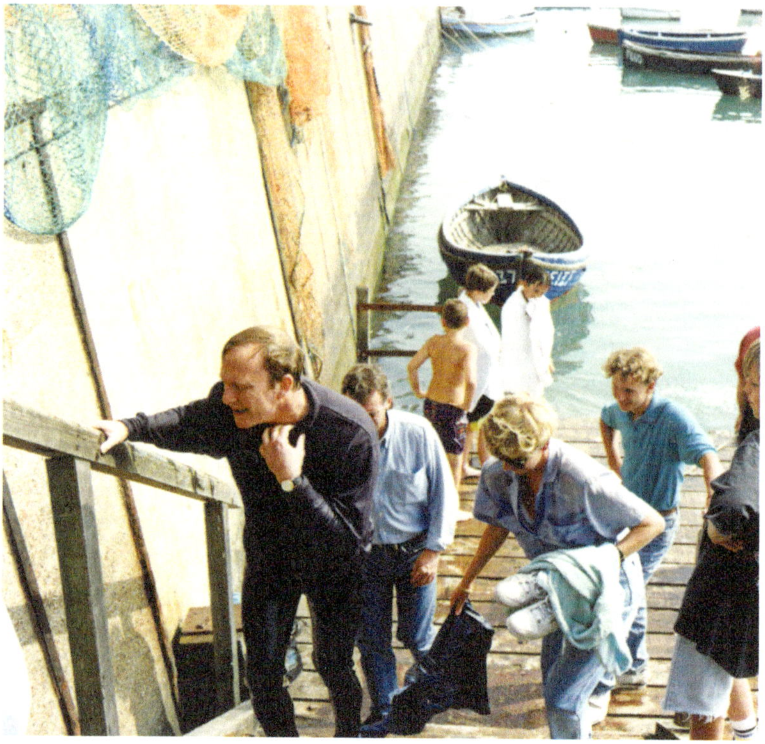

BBC TV filming *Moon & Sun* featuring Dennis Waterman as Thomas Gynn on the fish market steps, 25 September 1991.

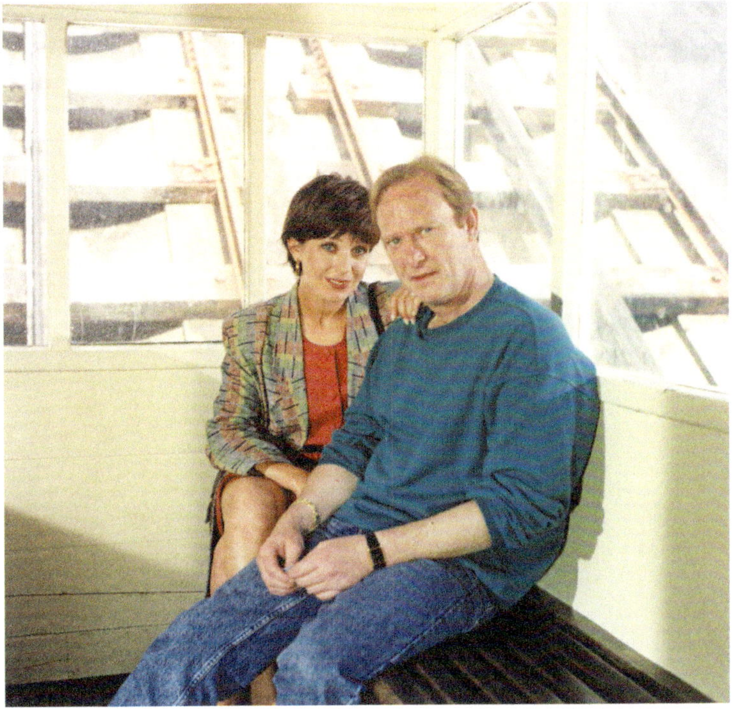

Yorkshire TV filming *Stay Lucky* featuring Dennis Waterman as Thomas Gynn and Jan Fancies as Sally Hardcastle seen here in the Leas Cliff Carriage, 28 August 1991.

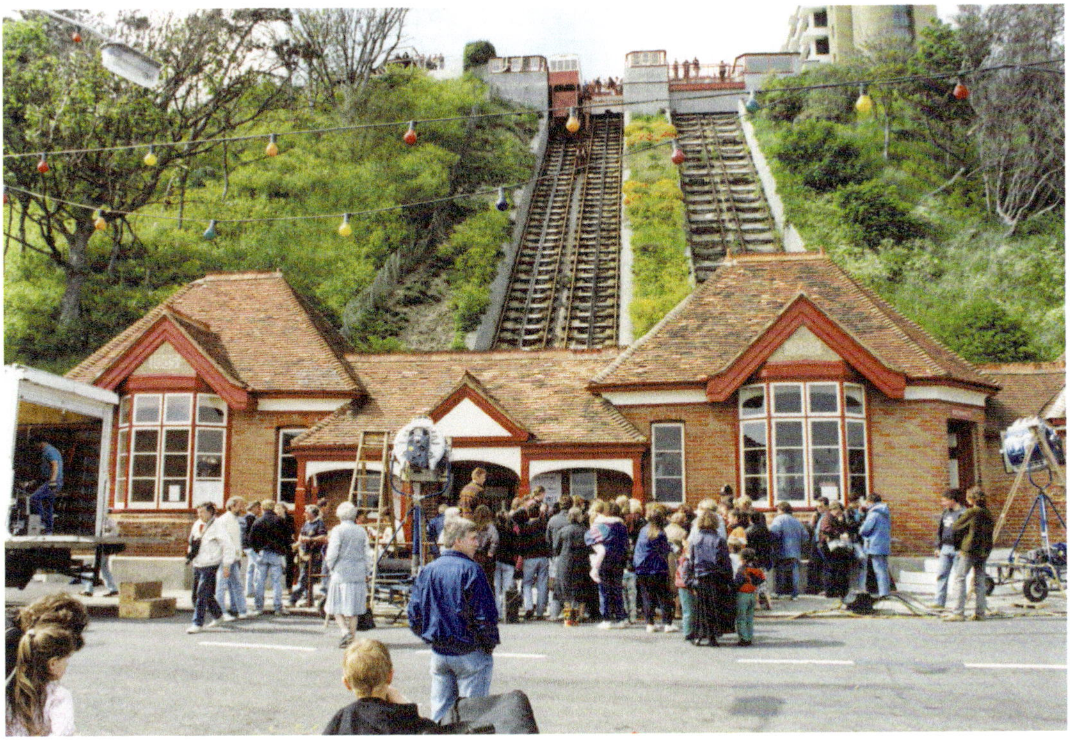

Yorkshire TV filming *Darling Buds of May*, 31 May 1991, in which David Jason, Pam Ferris, Catherine Zeta-Jones, Philip Franks, Anna Massey and Philip Watson all appeared.

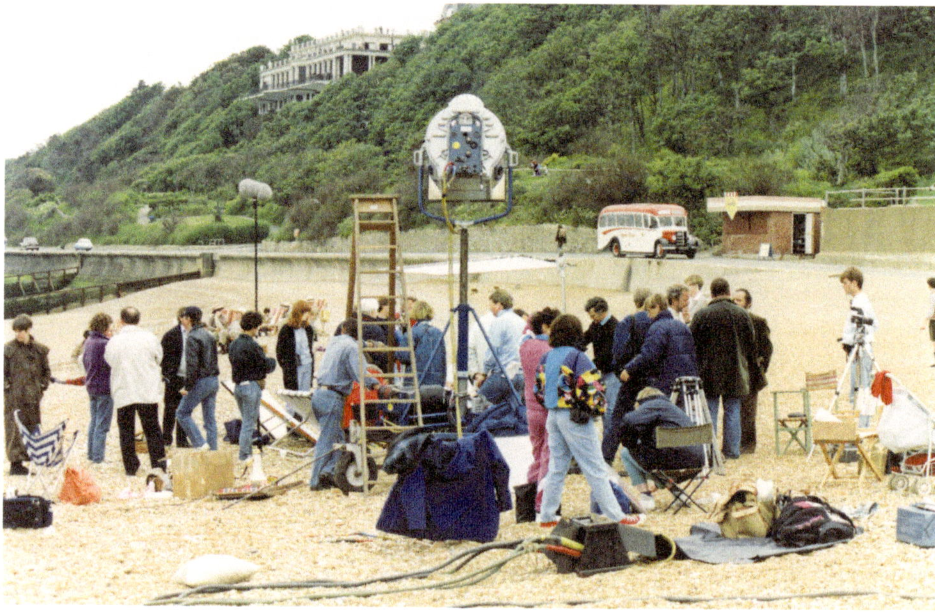

Yorkshire TV filming *Darling Buds of May*, 31 May 1991, staring Catherine Zeta-Jones as Mariette, David Jason as Pop Larkin, Pam Ferris as Ma Larkin and Philip Frances as Charley, the husband of Mariette.

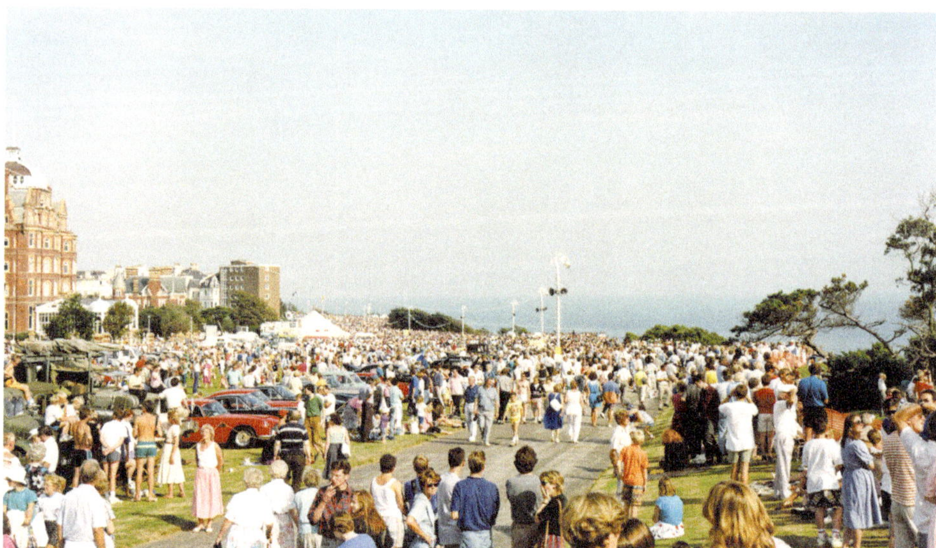

The Leas 200 feet above the English Channel is one of the most unique venues for Airshows. The first major Airshow held here was the 50th Anniversary of the Battle of Britain, 7–15 September 1991. This photograph shows an estimated crowd of 100,000 people on The Leas. Sadly the last Shepway Council organised Airshow was in 2003; however, the Queen's Diamond Jubilee (2012) saw air displays return with the Jubilee Airshow, organised by Town Centre Management, after which an attempt to revive this show annually didn't take place due to lack of funds. However, in 2014 there was a two-day event dubbed 'FlyFolkestone', which sadly was the last event.

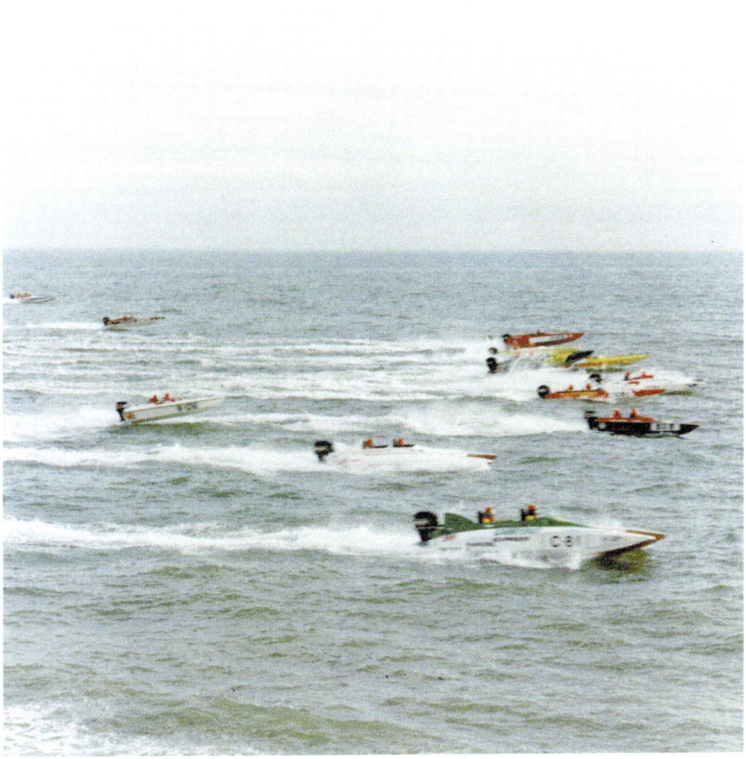

Another event for the Shepway Festival was the International Offshore Powerboat Championship, which started on 10 September 1991.

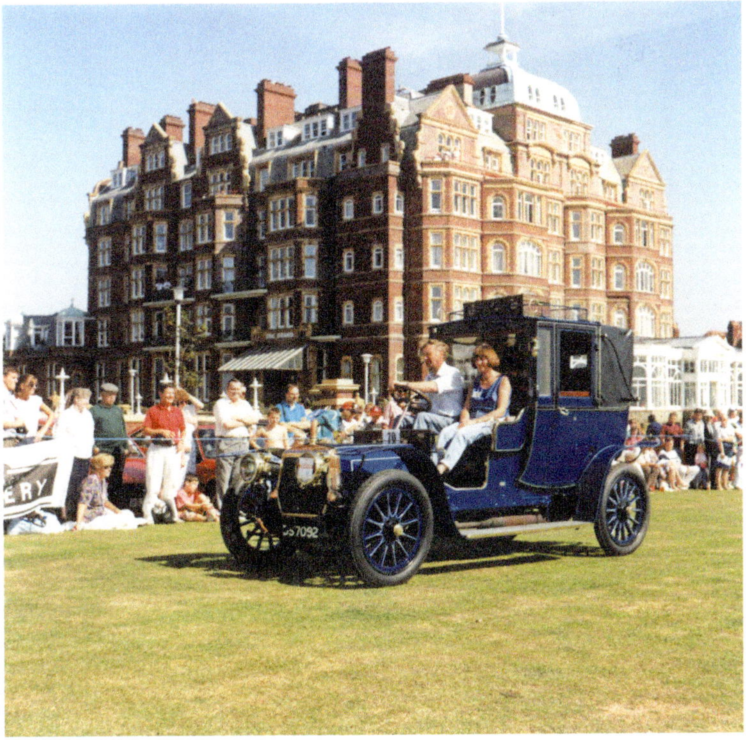

The 1991 Shepway Festival, 7–15 September, featured: paddle steamer cruises, steam rail trips, omnibus bonanza, military vehicle parade, race day, car rallies, steam and farming fayre, full concert programme, and exhibitions and displays.

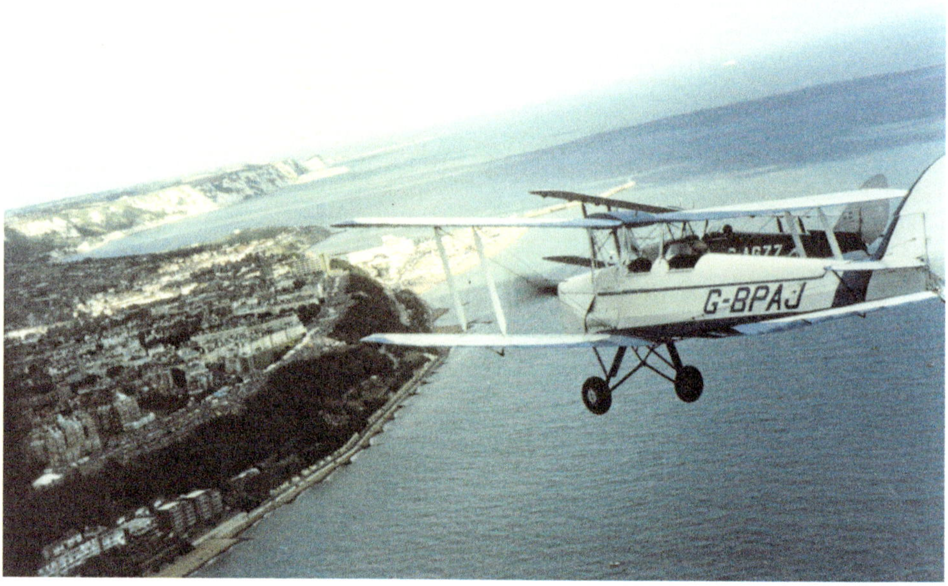


Shepway Festival 1993; this photograph was taken by one of the Tiger Moths.

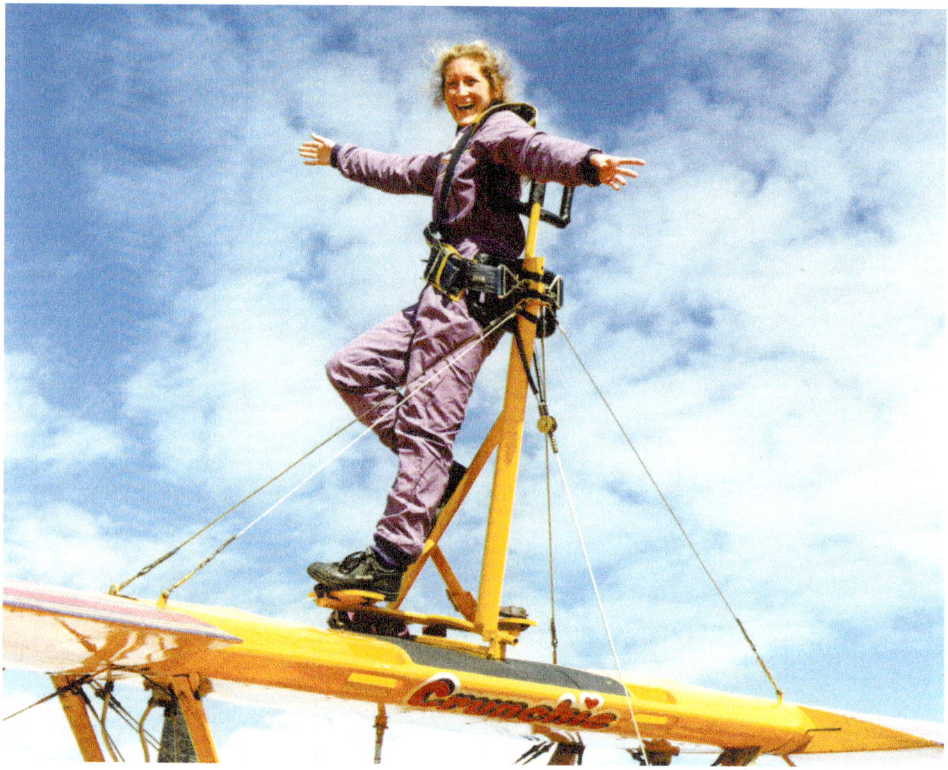


Sarah Kidd – winner of Crunchie Wing walking – leaving Lydd Airport for the Shepway Airshow, 26 August 1993.

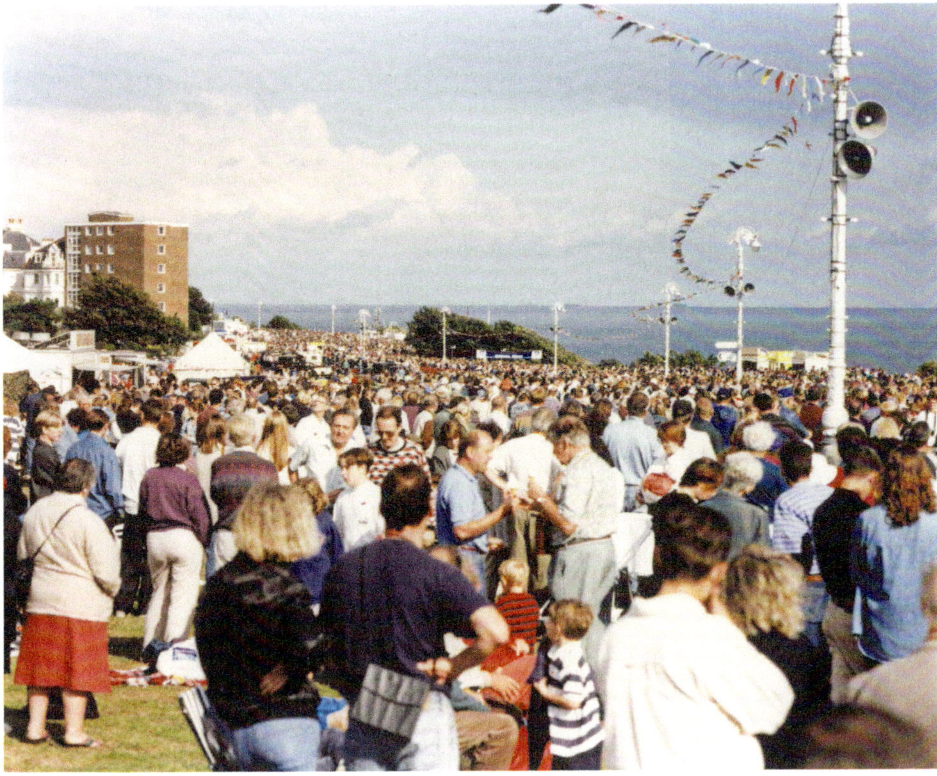

Shepway Festival 1–3 September 1995: On Friday 1 there was a varied programme of street entertainment. On Saturday 2, Pageant of Motoring, fireworks and a dazzling display of music. Sunday 3, Airshow, a solo RAF and varied vintage jets formation, aerobatics and Second World War fighters and bombers.

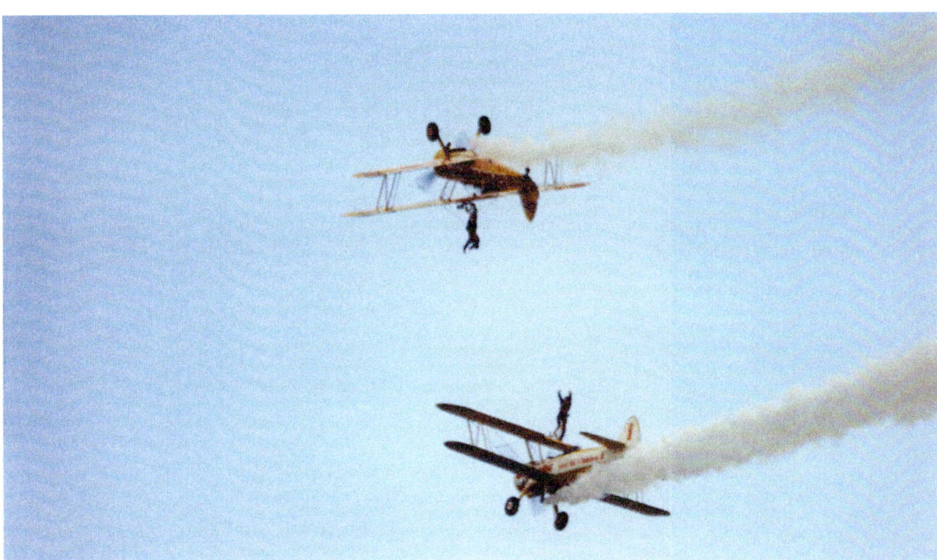

Shepway Festival, Sunday 3 September 1995 – a daring display of Wing walking.

# Acknowledgements

I would like to thank the following people for allowing me to use their images: Nik & Trick Services Photographiques (Richard Taylor) No. 63 The Old High Street, Folkestone; Peter Hooper; John Gale; Jack Gill; Peter Austen; Steve Popple; Mrs M. Baker (née Spearpoint); Vince Williams; Eamonn Rooney; David Anslow; John McLaren; David Featherbe; Mary Sharp; Margaret Stone; Fred Palmer; Richard Bridgeland; Jill Heathorn (née Thompson); Mrs S. Butcher; Ann O'Brian (née Castree); Barbara Hughes; Mr Norman Smith; Rebecca Frier; Jessica Kilburn; Patrick Marrin for information about the Hennell family; and Frank Bond for proofreading. Some of these people are members of the Folkestone & District Local History Society. I offer my sincere apologies to anybody who I have missed.